THE GOTHAM LIBRARY
OF THE NEW YORK UNIVERSITY PRESS

The Gotham Library is a series of original works and critical studies, published in paperback primarily for student use. The Gotham hardcover edition is primarily for use by libraries and the general reader. Devoted to significant works and major authors and to literary topics of enduring importance, Gotham Library texts offer the best in literature and criticism.

Comparative and Foreign Language Literature:
Robert J. Clements, Editor
Comparative and English Language Literature:
James W. Tuttleton, Editor

Neither White Nor Black

The Mulatto Character
in American Fiction

Judith R. Berzon

New York · New York University Press · 1978

Copyright ©1978 by New York University

Library of Congress Cataloging in Publication Data

Berzon, Judith R. 1945-
  Neither white nor black.

  (The Gotham library)
  Bibliography: p.

1. American fiction—History and criticism.
2. Mulattoes in literature. I. Title.
PS374.M84B47   813'.03   77-94392
ISBN 0-8147-0996-6
ISBN 0-8147-0997-4 pbk.

Manufactured in the United States of America

ACKNOWLEDGEMENTS

Quotations from *Pudd'nhead Wilson and Those Extraordinary Twins* by Mark Twain by permission of Macmillan, Inc.

Quotations from Ernest J. Gaines, *The Autobiography of Miss Jane Pittman*, copyright © 1971 by Ernest J. Gaines. Reprinted by permission of The Dial Press.

Quotations from James Weldon Johnson, *The Autobiography of an Ex-Colored Man*, copyright © 1927 by Alfred A. Knopf, Inc., and renewed 1955 by Carl Van Vechten. Reprinted by permission of Alfred A. Knopf, Inc.

Grateful acknowledgement is made to Random House, Inc. and Pantheon Books, a Division of Random House, Inc. for permission to quote from the copyrighted works of Sinclair Lewis, William Faulkner, Robert Penn Warren, and Eugene D. Genovese.

Quotations from Dorothy West, *The Living is Easy,* copyright © 1947 by Dorothy West. Reprinted by permission of Bertha Klausner International Literary Agency, Inc.

Specified excerpts from pages 2, 79-80, 118, 125, 162, 164, 232, 254-55, 277-78 in *The Black Image In The White Mind* by George M. Fredrikson, Copyright © 1971 by George M. Fredrikson, reprinted by permission of Harper & Row Publishers, Inc.

Quotations from Winthrop Jordan, *White Over Black: American Attitudes Toward the Negro,* 1550-1812, Copyright © 1968 by the University of North Carolina Press, published for the Institute of Early American History and Culture, Williamsburg, Virginia. By permission of the publisher.

Contents

Part I

1. The Mulatto: An Introduction   3

2. Racist Ideologies and the Mulatto   18

3. Mulatto Fiction: Myths, Stereotypes, and Reality   52

    Historical Review   53

    Archetypal Themes in Mulatto Fiction   81

    Faulkner and the Mulatto Character: *Intruder in the Dust*, "The Fire and the Hearth," and *Absalom, Absalom!*   87

4. The Tragic Mulatto   99

Part II

5. The Crisis Experience   119

6. The Novel of Passing; or Black No More   140

7. The Mulatto as Black Bourgeois   162

8. The Mulatto as Race Leader   190

9. The Mulatto as Existential Man   218

Postscript: Recent Mulatto Fiction   238

Selected Bibliography   255

Index   272

Part I

1.

The Mulatto: An Introduction

In the United States, "racist ideology" provides one system by which the individual can order and unify his perception of society. Racism can be a very comforting belief system to the "elect," since such status is determined by factors which are, by definition, irrevocable: [1] skin color and other physiological attributes. As H. Rap Brown has pointed out, color and physical characteristics—particularly hair color and texture and width of nose and lips—have no meaning in and of themselves. But black people...

> are born into a world that has given color meaning and color becomes the single most determining factor of your existence. Color determines where you live, how you live, and, under certain circumstances, if you will live. Color determines your friends, your education, your mother's and father's jobs, where you play, and more importantly, what you think of yourself.
>
> In and of itself, color has no meaning. But the white world has given it meaning—political, social, economic, historical, physiological and philosphical. Once color has been given

meaning, an order is thereby established. If you are born Black in america, you are the last of that order. As kids we learned the formula for the structure of american society:

> If you're white,
> You're all right.
> If you're brown,
> Stick around,
> But if you're black,
> Get back, get back.[2]

Brown's statement provides an excellent description of both racist ideology and the caste system. To be black, to be a member of the nonelect, is to be despised by white America, and perhaps by oneself as well. His statement contains another significant truth about the caste system and color in this country: while there are only two castes,[3] historically there have been distinctions made between lighter- and darker-skinned members of the oppressed caste. While to many members of the upper caste, it matters not whether a nonwhite is a very light brown or deep black in color, it is also true that lighter-skinned blacks have sometimes received preferential treatment by whites. Furthermore, there is historical and sociological evidence of intracaste color distinctions within the lower caste. Mixed-blood individuals have been both hated and envied by their full-blooded black brothers and sisters. Because of this fact, the mulatto's position in American culture has appeared, to many social scientists and novelists, to be more ambiguous than that of the full-blooded black. The mixed blood, caught between two cultures, has had to exist in an indeterminate area between the boundaries of the American caste system. The widespread preoccupation by black writers with the question of identity, both individual and collective, is given special significance in the case of the mixed-blood individual.

White Americans are not exempt from this search for identity. In fact, whites are virtually addicted to the quest for self-knowledge and for rootedness within a society that has worshiped mobility, change, growth, and "progress." But whatever folly is committed, whatever failures are suffered during the continuing process of self-definition, at least white Americans are working within a cultural matrix that is their own. They are white people living in a white society. The images of American culture reflect a white aesthetic.[4] Even before the discovery of the New World, the diametrically opposed concepts of whiteness and blackness defined an all-encompassing philosophical dualism of "purity and filthiness, virginity and sin, virtue and baseness, beauty and ugliness, beneficence and evil, God and the devil." [5] White was always considered right.

As Carolyn F. Gerald has remarked in her excellent essay, "The Black Writer and His Role," African-Americans are black people living in a white world. This basic fact of life in America has enormously important consequences for black people. "Image," as Gerald defines it, means "self-concept," and whoever is in control of our image has the power to shape our reality. As Gerald explains: "When we consider that the black man sees white cultural and racial images projected upon the whole extent of his universe, we cannot help but realize that a very great deal of the time the black man sees a zero image of himself." [6] How, then, is the self-concept of the mixed-blood individual effected by this black-white mythology, and what roles has he played in American culture? These are important questions. Because of his position in American society, the mulatto is a significant figure in the contact of two cultures. And, according to Everett V. Stonequist's influential work on mixed bloods entitled *The Marginal Man: A Study in Personality and Culture Conflict* (1937), "It is in his [the mulatto's] mind that the cultures come together, conflict, and eventually work out some kind of mutual adjustment and interpenetration." [7]

The identity crisis of *all* African-Americans, as defined by W. E. B. Du Bois in *The Souls of Black Folk* (1903), concerns the merging of two cultures within the soul of every black American. But his classic statement is inadequate by itself in capturing the complexity of the thoughts and actions of the mulatto. Du Bois wrote of the "twoness" of the black American, who, he argued, has two identities—one as a Negro, the other as an American. He has "two souls, two thoughts, two unreconciled strivings, two warring ideals in one dark body. . . . The history of the American Negro is the history of this strife,—this longing to merge his double self into a better and truer self. In this merging he wishes neither of the other selves to be lost. He would not Africanize America. . . . He would not bleach his Negro soul in a flood of white Americanism. . . . He simply wishes to make it possible for a man to be both a Negro and an American." [8]

But not all Negroes have wanted to acknowledge the African heritage Du Bois embraced. There have been both full-blooded and mixed-blooded blacks who have rejected their African roots—with one significant difference between these groups: light skin color and Caucasian features have allowed some mulattoes to live out their rejection of black culture. The most extreme form of this denial is "passing for white," wherein the mulatto abandons all affiliation with the black community. A second form of rejection has been membership in elitist black bourgeois communities (which is not to say that all members of the black middle class reject their blackness), many of whose members are light skinned. In certain places—New Orleans, Charleston, Atlanta, Washington, D.C., and Philadelphia, among others—black middle- and upper-class communities have emphasized their rejection of the black proletariat and have embraced white middle-class values in which physical appearance, (white) ancestry, money, status, and conspicuous consumption play major roles. Membership within these elitist communities has provided the means for making the American dream work—to some extent—for an oppressed racial minority.

The American dream has exerted a powerful magnetism for many black Americans, and some black writers have reflected this magnetism in their works. Writing of these black artists, Addison Gayle, Jr., states: "They were, in the main, anxious to become Americans, to share in the fruits of the country's economic system and to surrender their history and culture to a universal melting pot. They were men of another era who believed in the American dream more fervently than their white contemporaries." [9] And John Oliver Killens, in his essay, "The Black Writer Vis-à-vis His Country," echoes Langston Hughes when he asserts that ". . . the Negro remembers better than anybody else the American dream, deferred and forgotten by most Americans. He remembers, because he lives constantly the dream's negation, yet lives for the day when the dream will become a reality." [10]

Later in his essay, Killens restates the "American dilemma" Gunnar Myrdal identified in his major study of the American

Negro—the conflict between the fact of racial prejudice and our proclaimed egalitarianism. Killens says that "The Negro, in his black presence, is the barometer of this nation's Constitution, and all its democratic traditions yet unrealized. Still deferred." [11] In "Beating That Boy," Ralph Ellison calls America "a nation of ethical schizophrenics": "Believing truly in democracy on one side of their minds, they act on the other in violation of its most sacred principles; holding that all men are created equal, they treat thirteen million Americans as though they were not." [12]

But elsewhere, Ellison recognizes the shortcomings of Myrdal's analysis of black-white interaction in America, arguing that it will not be enough for white Americans to begin to act upon their faith in what Myrdal calls the "American Creed." Ellison understands that black Americans must define *themselves* and bring about justice for *themselves*. And the successful completion of these goals can only be brought about if African-Americans have a pride in their cultural patterns. Myrdal, Ellison explains in his review of *An American Dilemma*, "sees Negro culture and personality simply as the product of a 'social pathology.' Thus he assumes that 'it is to the advantage of American Negroes as individuals and as a group to become assimilated into American culture, to acquire the traits held in esteem by the dominant white Americans.' " [13]

How different Myrdal's ideas are from those recent social scientists who, like Eugene Genovese, argue that "the slaves, as an objective social class, laid the foundations for a separate black national culture while enormously enriching American culture as a whole." [14] Similarly, the intellectual and political distance between, say, Booker T. Washington's *Up from Slavery* and Alex Haley's *Roots* is great (even considering Haley's acceptance of America as an idea). Even wider is the gulf between those black writers who have embraced the American dream and white American values and those black artists who seek to discover a "black aesthetic." According to Addison Gayle, Jr., one of the major theoreticians of this movement, "The Black Aesthetic . . . is a corrective—a means of helping black people out of the polluted mainstream of Americanism." [15] While the espousal of black ethnocentrism is not new (one can find expressions of this attitude by blacks throughout the nineteenth century), the 1970s is the first period in American intellectual history during which the leading

white social scientists have tried to understand black cultural
autonomy.

American fiction about the mulatto has reflected the individual
author's interpretation of the issues outlined above, the historical
period which formed these interpretations, and the conscious and
unconscious biases and beliefs of the author. If we are to bring
intelligence and insight to this literature, it is imperative that we
try to understand the dynamics that lie behind its creation. This
work identifies patterns and themes in mulatto fiction and, in
addition, seeks to distinguish cultural myths from historical and
sociological realities. While literature is neither history nor sociol
ogy, the creators of literature utilize both in their work. Hence, 1
have attempted an interdisciplinary study of mulatto fiction: this is
the only way in which we can have some sense of the validity of
their presentation, over and above the value of their work as art.

Who are the mulattoes of fact and fiction? The term "mulatto"
refers literally to one whose biological parents are drawn from both
the Caucasian caste and the Negro caste. Both parents are full
bloods, and the offspring of such a union is therefore half white
and half black. However, the term is rarely used with such
precision, either in the fiction or in the literature about the real
mixed-blood person or his fictional · counterpart. The term
"mulatto" as I will use it in this study refers to all mixed bloods—
quadroons, octoroons, and indistinguishable mixtures. But the key
elements in distinguishing the mulatto from the full-blooded black
are sociological and psychological rather than biological. The
mulatto is defined in this study in terms of his position within
American culture; that is, he or she is an individual who reaps
certain advantages and disadvantages in his interaction with both
blacks and whites, advantages and disadvantages which are a
direct result of his mixed racial heritage. The self-concept of the
mixed-blood character and the perceptions others have of him,
then, are the crucial elements in my decision as to which fictional
characters to analyze in this study—that plus the character's
centrality in the novel. Almost always, the characters I have chosen
to examine have been physically indistinguishable, or almost so,
from the Caucasian group; but it is the psychological and
sociological results of this physical fact that have made him the

object of so much interest to American novelists, both black and white.

Historically, the mixed-blood individual was usually the product of miscegenation between black women and white men. The term for these individuals—"mulatto"—was borrowed from the Spanish (and is derived from the Latin *mulus* meaning mule) and used by the English from about 1600 onward. According to Winthrop Jordan, the term was probably first used in Virginia records in 1666.[16] The inclusion of the term and the way it is used are important because the laws dealing with Negro slaves "add 'and mulattoes,' presumably to make clear that mixed blood did not confer exemption from slavery." [17] How mulattoes were to be treated is, according to Jordan, "profoundly revelatory." Jordan defines the questions: "Were they to be free or slave, acknowledged or denied, white or black?" And he explains further: "The questions arose, of course, in the cultural matrix of purpose, accomplishment, self-conception, and social circumstances of settlement in the New World. The social-identification of children requires self-identification in the fathers." [18]

The answers to these questions can be understood only in terms of the functioning of the two-caste system in the South and the reasons behind the development of this system. Genovese observes that "The two-caste system in the Old South drove the mulattoes into the arms of the blacks, no matter how hard some tried to build a make-believe third world for themselves." [19] Throughout the South, as a general rule, whites made little distinction between blacks and mulattoes, thus relegating the mulatto to the lower caste. There were only two exceptions to the way in which the caste system operated, and relatively few mulattoes were involved. New Orleans, Charleston, Mobile, and certain other cities did have some semblance of a three-caste system in which the mulattoes constituted a separate caste of the haughty bourgeoisie; and mulattoes constituted a third caste on some of the "great plantations."

Some obvious differences between a two- and three-caste system can be clarified easily enough. In both Santo Domingo and Jamaica, mulattoes constituted a separate caste in a three-caste system. According to Genovese, they were usually free and were often skilled tradesmen, overseers, or even wealthy slaveholding planters. It was regarded as improper to work mulattoes in the fields, a distinction that was not made in the United States.[20] The political and economic outlook of the mulattoes clearly reflected their caste status: "Their class interests bound them to the whites, and their political efforts were devoted to attempts to win white acceptance as partners in the business of exploiting the slaves." [21] Winthrop Jordan, drawing upon the work of Edward Long, describes the Jamaican practice of "publicly transforming Negroes into white men":

> Beginning in the 1730's the Jamaican legislature passed numerous private acts conferring upon the colored offspring and sometimes the colored mistress of such and such a planter the rights and privileges of white persons, especially the right to inherit the planter's estate. . . . And Edward Long . . . noted that those beyond the third generation were "called English, and consider themselves as free from all taint of the Negroe race" and then went on to declare that all mulattoes ought to be regarded more highly than the blacks, "above whom (in point of due policy) they ought to hold some degree of distinction." [22]

Genovese accounts for the development of the three-caste system of the West Indies in terms of demographic and economic considerations: "In the Caribbean whites constituted a small minority of the population and had to build up an intermediary colored class of managers, tradesmen, and small proprietors. In the South, whites constituted the majority and had no such problem." [23] Jordan emphasizes the relationship between the status of mulattoes and the differing patterns of miscegenation within the two- and three-caste systems:

> Mulattoes in the West Indies were products of accepted practice, something they assuredly were not in the continental colonies. . . . If he [the white male southerner] could not restrain his sexual nature, he could at least reject its fruits and thus solace himself that he had done no harm. Perhaps he sensed as well that continued racial intermixture would

eventually undermine the logic of the racial slavery upon which his society was based. For the separation of slaves from free men depended on a class demarcation of the races, and the presence of mulattoes blurred this essential distinction. Accordingly he made every effort to nullify the effects of racial intermixture. By classifying the mulatto as a Negro he was in effect denying that intermixture had occurred at all.[24]

But the existence of the mulatto could not really be denied. By 1860, 13 to 20 percent of the African-American population had white ancestry.[25] In addition to the visibility of racially mixed blacks within the slave population, the free Negro segment was a continuing reminder of the existence of the mulatto. Much of the free Negro population came from the mulatto children of planters who were educated and manumitted by their fathers.[26] Most free Negroes could read and write,[27] and many were craftsmen. Sometimes free Negroes were themselves slaveholders; this was particularly true in Louisiana and South Carolina.[28] The social position of the free Negro was problematic; as Jordan so aptly remarks: "The association of slavery with race had transformed a free black man into a walking contradiction in terms, a social anomaly, a third party in a system built for two." [29] The fact that so many free Negroes were light skinned as well only served to make the distinctions between lower and upper castes even less distinct.

These data are very important to a study of mulatto fiction because it is often the free Negro population that appears in the literature set in the antebellum period; and it is often the "haughty but tiny mulatto bourgeoisie of New Orleans and Charleston and the small class of slaves attached as house servants to the town houses of the great white planters" [30] which appear in the fiction dealing with the postbellum South. Exclusive southern rural mulatto communities are treated fictionally as well (elitist mulattoes in the North—in Philadelphia, New York, and Boston—also make frequent appearances).

There are two major points to keep in mind here: these exclusive mulatto groups did exist in reality, and the intracaste distinctions used in the fiction (based upon color and physical characteristics, family background, education, manners, and occupation) are reflective of historical fact. However, the fictional presentation can be misleading because we are often given the impression that mulattoes always constituted a separate group as distinct from full-blooded blacks. In fact, as Genovese reports, while it is true that "most of those emancipated originated in miscegenation, most issue from miscegenation did not gain their freedom, for a large majority of mulatto children born to slaveholders lived their lives as slaves, often with no special consideration or privileges." [31] Furthermore, Genovese observes that "the numerous free Negro and urban slaves who worked at similar skilled and unskilled jobs apparently displayed little of the caste feeling that allegedly divided the Negro population of the cities." [32]

Another recurring theme in mulatto fiction concerns the distinction between "house slaves" and "field slaves," house slaves usually being depicted as privileged mulattoes. Once again, Genovese draws upon dozens of historical documents and concludes:

> However much the quadroon and mulatto servants, stiffly parading in full dress, dominated the Big House of the legend, they did not dominate the Big House of reality. A preference for light-skinned slaves to work in the house existed in Charleston, New Orleans, and some other cities, but even there it was far from general. As often as not, southern slaveholders of the British Caribbean, enjoyed being served by blacks—the blacker the better—as well as by light-skinned Negroes. . . . Mulattoes came to be preferred for house work roughly to the extent that they had acquired certain cultural advantages that made them more presentable to upper-class white society. Typically, the great plantations and town houses employed servants of every shade, and no caste lines grew up except in a few places like New Orleans and Charleston, where the Caribbean three-caste tradition had never wholly disappeared. . . . The legend of the house-slave elite grew up primarily in the cities, where town-house slaves and the more economically secure free Negroes combined in a special way.[33]

I can only speculate on the causes of the somewhat misleading fictional treatment of the mulatto bourgeoisie of the cities and the house servants of the plantation. One obvious cause is ignorance. Because there were some great plantations where mulatto house slaves refused to marry darker-skinned field slaves, this situation was assumed to be more widespread than it was in actuality.[34] Another factor might have been the conscious decision by black and white abolitionist writers to present light-skinned blacks as heroes and heroines in order to capitalize upon racist ideology: how can we enslave one who is in part "one of us" by virtue of his or her white blood—and may in addition be educated and talented? Sometimes, the depiction of the mulatto as elite member of a (spurious) caste could be a reflection of the author's unconscious reflection of racist ideology. For a good many of the white writers whose works we will examine, the all-but-white, usually female and beautiful, often tormented character is titillating and effectively meets the specifications for successful melodrama. For more serious white and black writers, there is the challenge of exploring the psychological and sociological dimensions of mulatto characters who seek to create a third caste in what is essentially a two-caste system. For some black writers, these particular mulatto characters are utilized to attack the aping of white bourgeois values and to praise the values and life-style of the black "folk."

The common denominator that links these depictions of the mulatto is the concept of "marginality": the mulatto is defined in terms of his marginal position within the culture. It should be noted that the concept of marginality can be viewed as a denial of a viable black cultural tradition; it may also assume greater intracaste color prejudice than actually exists. In fact, because of the preoccupation with marginality evidenced by authors of mulatto fiction, contemporary critics understandably designate much of this fiction racist. I agree that a racist perspective is present in much mulatto fiction; nevertheless, it is precisely this concept of marginality that provides the key to an understanding of mulatto fiction; it is an organizing principle in this study. As the majority of nineteenth- and twentieth-century black and white authors view him or her, the mulatto touches both castes and feels the pull of the white culture's mythology differently from the full-blooded black. Yet he or she knows, with other African-Americans, the pain of exclusion from the American dream. In this study, then, the "mulatto character" is defined as a marginal figure who, in the words of Everett Stonequist, is "poised in psychological uncertainty between two social worlds, reflecting in his soul the discords and harmonies, repulsions and attractions of these worlds." [35]

Some real-life mulattoes have lived out the various phases of marginality and responses to that condition. Thus, while the mulatto (both in fact and in fiction) has sometimes directed his hatred toward full-blooded blacks, many of whom have been lower-class members, he has not always escaped from hatred directed toward himself. While he wants very much to be defined in terms of a white middle-class image, he is still excluded from the white group. Furthermore, his prejudice toward other blacks often produces feelings of guilt.

For the mixed-blood individual who wants to be part of the lower caste, there are other problems. The mulatto has reason to fear nonacceptance by blacks because of his or her white skin. Many darker-skinned Negroes have felt resentment toward, and envy of, those with lighter-colored skin and Caucasian features. Many full-blooded blacks have also strongly disliked mulattoes for their "dicky" ways, that is, for the pretentious airs they exhibit. Thus, some mixed-blood individuals may never succeed in establishing a complete identity with the black group. Like one such man interviewed by Abraham Kardiner and Lionel Ovesey, he may "perpetually feel an outsider, a bystander instead of an active participant." [36] While I have devoted a chapter to those fictional mulattoes who solve the identity issue by becoming leaders of their race (a completely different response from those I have been describing), theirs is a response to marginality that is far less common than "passing," adopting a white middle-class image and value system, or succumbing to despair.

The mulatto has captured the imagination of American novelists writing during every period of our literature. The mulatto has been the central character in the works of some of America's most influential white writers. Mark Twain and William Faulkner, Robert Penn Warren and Gertrude Stein, Sinclair Lewis and Willa Cather have all been interested in the mulatto. The mixed-blood character has been used in the novel of propaganda by abolitionist authors like Harriet Beecher Stowe and Richard Hildreth and by a Negrophobe like Thomas Dixon. *Clotelle: or The President's Daughter* (1853) by William Wells Brown, the first American novel by a black author, contains a mulatto character. Some American novelists, both black and white, have depicted the mulatto in such a way as to express the belief that it is possible in America both to be black and to enjoy the benefits of a white middle-class life-style. The early Negro novelist Charles Chesnutt was one such author; Jessie Fauset, an author of the Harlem Renaissance, was another. Other novelists have recorded the frustration that leads light-skinned blacks to flee from their race and to "pass" as white—the only means by which these characters (though often *not* their creators) believe that they can transcend the confines of the American caste system. James Weldon Johnson's *Autobiography of an Ex-Coloured Man* (1912), Nella Larsen's *Passing* (1929) and *Quicksand* (1928), Walter White's *Flight* (1926), and Claude McKay's "Near-White" (1932) are just a few of the works by African-American writers that reflect this theme.

These issues, among others, are explored in this study, which is divided into two parts. Part I provides an introduction in which the historical, sociological, and scientific backgrounds of the fiction are discussed. It also contains an overview of the novels, including a discussion of the most prevalent stereotypes of the mulatto. Part II defines and illustrates the "crisis experience" and analyzes some of the specific modes of adjustment to this experience. The Postscript consists of an examination of three novels of the 1970s written by important black authors: *The Autobiography of Miss Jane Pittman* (1971) by Ernest J. Gaines; *The Cotillion or One Good Bull Is Half the Herd* (1971) by John Oliver Killens; and *The Junior Bachelor Society* (1976) by John A. Williams.

Generalizations about some of the major areas discussed throughout will conclude the study. These include the individual's search for an identity and for a satisfying role in American culture. In addition, speculations are posed about the future of the mulatto in fact and fiction—particularly as he or she attempts to cope with the issues of color, assimilation, black cultural nationalism, and the continuing injustices of the American social system.

NOTES

1. Ruth Benedict, *Race, Science and Politics,* rev. ed. (New York: Viking Press, 1945), p. 4, 98–99.
2. H. Rap Brown, *Die, Nigger, Die!* (New York: Dial Press, 1969), p. 2.
3. This is unlike the three-caste system, which developed in the West Indies and Latin America, which consists of Caucasians, mixed bloods, and full-blooded nonwhites.
4. Winthrop Jordan explores in detail the concept of blackness in *White Over Black: American Attitudes Toward the Negro, 1550–1812* (Chapel Hill: University of North Carolina Press, 1968). Jordan tells us that "Long before they found that some men were black, Englishmen found in the idea of blackness a way of expressing some of their most ingrained values. No other color except white conveyed so much emotional impact" (p. 7). The writers whose essays appear in Addison Gayle, Jr.'s, collection, *The Black Aesthetic* (New York: Doubleday & Company, 1972), are attempting to define a "black aesthetic," which they see as a corrective to the white aesthetic that is promulgated by the dominant caste. In terms of this study, it should be noted that while I recognize the work done by Gayle, Hoyt Fuller, Carolyn Gerald, and other talented black critics, theirs is a perspective not usually maintained by earlier African-American writers. These earlier writers, some of whose works . are relevant to this study, were anxious to be accepted and created their art within the framework of the white aesthetic.
5. Jordan, *White Over Black,* p. 7.
6. In Gayle, *The Black Aesthetic,* p. 352.
7. Everett V. Stonequist, *The Marginal Man: A Study in Personality and Culture Conflict* (1937; rpt. New York: Russell & Russell, 1961), p. 221.
8. W. E. B. Du Bois, *The Souls of Black Folks: Essays and Sketches,* 2d ed. (Chicago: A. C. McClurg & Company, 1903), pp. 3–4.
9. Gayle, *The Black Aesthetic,* pp. xvii–viii.
10. In Ibid., p. 357.
11. Ibid., p. 372.
12. Ralph Ellison, *Shadow and Act* (New York: Random House, 1953, 1964), p. 99.
13. Ibid, p. 316. According to Oscar Handlin ("A Book That Changed American Life," *New York Times Book Review,* April 21, 1963, section 7, p. 1, the book was highly praised when it was first published, challenged only by the Communists, who attacked its gradualism, and the racists, who attacked "the underlying assumption that equality was the American norm" (p. 1). Now many critics reject the book for the same reasons that Ellison presents: Myrdal unconsciously reflected a politically and culturally based white aesthetic. However, the book can be useful for us because it reflects the

powerful magnetism of the American dream that Gayle, Killens, and others analyze vis-à-vis earlier black writing.

14. Eugene Genovese, *Roll, Jordan Roll: The World the Slaves Made* (New York: Pantheon Books, 1974), p. xv. According to George M. Frederickson, in "The Gutman Report," *New York Review of Books,* vol. 23, no. 15, September 30, 1976, even influential revisionist historians like Genovese and Fogel and Engerman *(Time on the Cross)* give white planters too much credit for the world the slaves made: "Slaves made a life for themselves not so much by reacting to particular modes of white domination as by adapting to highly diverse conditions of servitude in certain uniform ways that were truly their own" (p. 20). In Frederickson's view, Herbert Gutman's *The Black Family in Slavery and Freedom, 1750–1925* corrects this view.
15. Jordan, *White Over Black,* p. xxii.
16. Ibid., p. 168. In many of the later "scientific" discussions of the mulatto, the sterility of the hybrid animal provided "proof" of mulatto sterility.
17. Ibid., p. 167.
18. Ibid.
19. Genovese, *Roll, Jordan, Roll,* p. 431.
20. Jordan, *White Over Black,* p. 174.
21. Genovese, *Roll, Jordan, Roll,* p. 341.
22. Edward Long, *Jamaica,* II, 332–35, in Jordan, p. 178.
23. Genovese, *Roll, Jordan, Roll,* p. 431.
24. Jordan, *White Over Black,* pp. 175, 178.
25. Genovese, *Roll, Jordan, Roll,* p. 414.
26. Ibid., pp. 415–16.
27. Genovese bases his claim upon Carter G. Woodson's and Franklin Frazier's work, pp. 402–3.
28. Ibid., p. 408.
29. Jordan, *White Over Black,* p. 134.
30. Genovese, *Roll, Jordan, Roll,* p. 409.
31. Ibid., p. 416.
32. Ibid., p. 409.
33. Ibid., p. 328
34. Genovese is instructive once more: "According to one of the main tenets of the legend of status division, house servants disdained to marry field hands. Blacks as well as whites testify.... Yet, apart from the status-bound great plantations—apart, that is, from a small elite—house servants regularly married field hands with no suggestion of loss of caste. The three-quarters of all slaves who lived on units of fifty or less slaves could hardly afford such pretensions ..." (p. 338).
35. Stonequist, *The Marginal Man,* p. 8. Obviously, not all real mulattoes experience the same kinds or range of problems endured by fictional mulattoes.
36. Abraham Kardiner and Lionel Ovesey, *The Mark of Oppression: A Psychological Study of the American Negro* (Cleveland: World Publishing Company, 1951), pp. 191–96.

2.

Racist Ideologies and the Mulatto

Both racism and the caste system (the antebellum manifestation of which was the slave system) have had long histories in our country. Yet both would seem to be in diametric opposition to the American dream of freedom and equality for all. It is possible, however, according to Kenneth Clark, to see racism and the caste system as "not contradictory but compatible elements of American history and social psychology." [1] Racism, as Gunnar Myrdal observes, "is nearly the only way out for a people so moralistically equalitarian, if it is not prepared to live up to its faith. A nation less fervently committed to democracy could, probably, live happily in a caste system with a somewhat less intensive belief in the biological inferiority of the subordinate group. [Thus] . . . race prejudice is, in this sense, a function of equalitarianism." [2] Sociologist Pierre L. van den Berghe formulated the term "*Herrenvolk* democracy" to explain the reconciliation of racist and democratic ideologies in America. A "*Herrenvolk* democracy" is a society which operates democratically for the master race but tyrannically for the subordinate groups.[3]

In order to maintain a *Herrenvolk* democracy, the elect and nonelect groups must be readily distinguishable, and the rationale for the system of distinctions should be reasonably convincing. This is not to say that an invariable rationale must be promulgated. In fact, any functional ideology must be flexible—able to incorporate or overcome any opposition or competing ideology. Indeed, racist ideology evolved gradually and reflected the need for an intellectual justification of the slave system and the social, political, and economic developments which characterized the postbellum caste arrangements.

In order to understand the social and intellectual milieu of the nineteenth- and twentieth-century authors of mulatto fiction, we must have some sense of the history of these developments. Without it, there can be little hope of evaluating intelligently certain fundamental concerns reflected in the fictional accounts of American race relations. And because of (1) a widespread fear of miscegenation; (2) the tenacious view that mulattoes are a "degenerate, sterile and short-lived breed" [4]; (3) the unresolved dilemma of the social and economic roles of the emancipated African-American; and (4) the unease with which Caucasians generally have regarded those who carry the traits of both racial groups—because of the importance of these factors, the formulations and theories advanced by scientists and others about mulattoes have been pivotal aspects of the various types of racist ideology.

As Winthrop Jordan reminds us, the English did not plan to establish the institution of Negro slavery when they settled in America.[5] To this day, we do not have anything like complete answers about the legal status of the slave during the early and middle parts of the seventeenth century (between 1640 and 1660, we know almost nothing of their precise status). This lack of knowledge is unfortunate, since, as Eugene Genovese asserts, "The debate has considerable significance for the interpretation of race relations in American history." [6] Genovese tells us that the earliest blacks may not have had a position in society significantly different from that of the white indentured servants. He even speculates that

> for a brief period a less oppressive pattern of race relations had had a chance to develop in the Upper South; it is doubtful

that any such alternative ever existed in South Carolina, which as a slave society virtually derived from Barbados. In any case, before the turn of the century the issue had been resolved and blacks condemned to the status of slaves for life.

The laws of Virginia and Maryland, as well as those of the colonies to the south, increasingly gave masters the widest possible power over the slaves and also, through prohibition of interracial marriage and the general restriction of slave status to non-whites, codified and simultaneously preached white supremacy. Kenneth Stampp writes: "Thus the master class, for its own purposes, wrote chattel slavery, the caste system, and color prejudice into American custom and law." [7]

Increasingly, the sacraments of marriage and baptism were denied to blacks; one by one legal and social rights were denied until finally the status of the Negro in American society was not that of a full human being. According to Genovese, there were, however, two factors in southern society that tended to modify the conditions described above. The first was the "hegemonic function of law." Genovese claims that "the law cannot be viewed as something passive and reflective, but must be viewed as an active, partially autonomous force, which mediated among the several classes and compelled the rulers to bend to the demands of the ruled." [8] The second factor that modified the legal system was paternalism: if the local custom had it that slaves might have garden plots of their own, "then woe to the master or overseer who summarily withdrew the 'privilege.' " [9] Genovese is not arguing, of course, that the hegemonic function of law and/or paternalism so modified the slave system that slaves were not denied full human rights.

Although we do not know the details of the process by which blacks came to be treated so differently from whites, we can identify certain beliefs and attitudes in Europeans that encouraged the development of a racist ideology. According to Winthrop Jordan, the two most important attributes of the African that account for his enslavement were his heathenism and his color. In the seventeenth century, the religious difference between blacks and whites seems to have been more significant to whites than the color difference. Jordan explains that the term "Christian" "seems to have conveyed the idea and feeling of *we* as against *they:* to be Christian was to be civilized rather than barbarous, English rather than African, white rather than black." [10] However, as Jordan is quick to point out, heathenism alone could not have led to slavery, since conversion could have corrected that difference. For Jordan the answer lies in the concepts of white and black in the English mind, concepts that predated the actual physical introduction of the English to black people. Before the sixteenth century the meaning of "black" included, "Deeply stained with dirt, foul. . . . Having dark or deadly purposes, malignant; pertaining to or involving death, deadly; banely, disastrous; sinister. . . . Foul, iniquitous, atrocious, horrible, wicked." [11]

Thus, the development of a caste system was aided by color differences and negative connotations. David Brion Davis's study of slavery in Western culture reveals that although slaves in most ancient societies did not belong to a different race from their masters, the slaves were marked "with visible symbols of their lowly status. No doubt the original purposes of such labeling were identification and prevention of escape." Whatever the original intent of such labeling, the fact is that "From the earliest times such skin markings became indelible signs of a servile status, and suggested a deformity of character which deserved contempt. . . . In later centuries men would come to regard darkness of skin as a brand which God or nature impressed upon an inferior people." [12] Finally, "other qualities—the utter strangeness of his language, gestures, eating habits, and so on—certainly must have contributed to the colonists' sense that [the African] was very different, perhaps disturbingly so." [13]

As philosophical radicalism and rationalistic optimism developed in the eighteenth century, scientists and intellectuals generally began to adhere to the position that Negroes and other nonwhite races had the potential intelligence and virtue of the white race. Locke's concept of the mind as a tabula rasa, with its emphasis on the importance of environment in the formation of human character, was solidly within the mainstream of eighteenth-century thought. One aspect of eighteenth-century environmentalism that related directly to the race issue was the belief that "differences in pigmentation were a comparatively short-range result of climate and other environmental factors." [14] But this idea, according to George Fredrickson, had begun to erode by 1810.[15]

Thomas Jefferson's *Notes on Virginia* (1786) is probably the best summary expression of eighteenth-century Enlightenment perceptions of the Negro. His central dilemma, according to Jordan, was that "he hated slavery but thought Negroes inferior to white men." [16]

Jefferson argued that the Negro is ugly and lacks the blushes which lend to the "expression of every passion" in the white race. The Negro's expression, moreover, is one of "eternal monotony"; his emotions are covered by an "immovable veil." The Negro has "a very strong and disagreeable odor," as opposed to the white race. He also praised the "flowing hair" and "more elegant symmetry of form" of white people. But, for Jefferson, the most obvious proofs of the Negro's inferiority were his mental and moral characteristics. Because Jefferson was aware "that the environmentalist argument could serve (and actually had) to make a case for Negro equality, . . . he went to great lengths to prove that the Negro's lack of talent did not stem from their condition." [17] The Negro, Jefferson argued, is "much inferior" in reason, and "in imagination [he is] dull, tasteless, and anomalous." He is "more ardent after [his] female" but cannot genuinely experience love, which is a "higher" emotion. His griefs "are transient." And Jefferson will not even allow the Negro the purported musical ability which was to become a familiar aspect of the stereotype. The Negro may have some musical ability, Jefferson wrote, but he probably could not learn a complicated melody. The black man is "at least as brave, and more adventuresome than the whites," but he quickly adds that this bravery "may proceed from a want of forethought." [18] In summary, Jefferson concluded in *Notes on Virginia*, "It is not their [blacks'] condition, then, but nature, which has produced the distinction." [19]

Although Jefferson clearly states his belief in the Negro's innate inferiority, he enganges in verbal sleight-of-hand in order to avoid the full implications of his position. He says that he is not certain whether "further observation" will substantiate his belief in black inferiority; he also warns that "caution must be exercised where our conclusions would degrade a whole race of men from the rank in the scale of beings which their Creator may perhaps have given them." [20] Jefferson's *Notes on Virginia* is an important work because it is an index of the intellectual milieu of late-eighteenth-century America. But, more importantly, Jefferson's ideas on race represent a classic example of the contradiction inherent in American democratic ideology. As Jean Fagan Yellin has asserted, "His *Notes* . . . embodies both an assertion of human liberty, and a classic statement of the racism which has prevented its realization in America." [21]

While a belief in black inferiority was a commonly held assumption before the end of the first third of the nineteenth century, according to George M. Fredrickson, it was not until the 1830s and 1840s that a thoroughgoing racist ideology developed: "For its full growth intellectual and ideological racism required a body of 'scientific' and cultural thought which would give credence to the notion that blacks were, for unalterable reasons of race, morally and intellectually inferior to whites, and, more importantly, it required a historical context which would make such ideology seem necessary for the effective defense of Negro slavery or other forms of white supremacy." [22]

During the course of the nineteenth century, race dogma played a central role in defining the American intellectual milieu. Scientific race theories exerted tremendous influence over nineteenth-century social scientists, as societies came to be studied in terms of racial theories. Heredity was considered to outweigh by far the influence of environment in the formation of human character. And heredity meant mostly race to many social theorists. According to Thomas Gossett, the nineteenth century "was obsessed with the idea that it was race which explained the character of peoples. The notion that traits of temperament and intelligence are inborn in races and only superficially changed by environment or education was enough to blind the dominant whites. . . . Many social theorists of the period interpreted almost any human phenomenon which was not readily explicable to racial characteristics." [23]

The dominant forms of racist ideology, from the 1830s onward, all had certain basic propositions in common: to wit, that blacks differed from and were inferior—in intelligence and/or temperament—to whites; that this inferiority was permanent or subject to change only by a very slow process of evolution; that because of these differences, "miscegenation—especially in the form of intermarriage—should be discouraged (to put it as mildly as possible) because the crossing of such diverse types leads either to a short-lived and unprolific breed or to a type that, even if permanent, is inferior to the whites in those innate qualities giving Caucasian civilization its progressive and creative characteristics." [24] From the above, it was deduced that racial prejudice is a natural white response, and that a biracial equalitarian society is impossible, or possible only in the distant future.

Many nineteenth-century issues debated within the scientific community were directly or indirectly connected with racist ideology. There was the debate over the origin of the species. The polygenist school, which argued for the separate-species concept, was led by Dr. Samuel George Morton (*Crania Americana,* 1839), who argued in support of the notion of a multiple origin of species. The pivotal factor in support of this concept was the sterility of the "hybrid," that is, the mulatto. Some said that Negroes and whites could interbreed successfully but that their offspring would be barren, just as the mule is barren. Others made a claim for lessened fertility.

John Bachman, a minister and naturalist, was the principal scientific proponent of the monogenic theory of the origin of the races. In *The Doctrine of the Unity of the Human Race Examined on the Principles of Science* (1850), he attacked Morton and others who upheld the notion of separate species and of the relative infertility of hybrids. There can be only absolute sterility or the concept has no meaning, he asserted. Furthermore, even if relative sterility could be proved, this would not necessarily mean that Negroes and whites belonged to separate species. Finally, he dismissed the theory that there is a "natural repugnance" between races.

Scientific theorizing about race mixture was closely related to the issues involved in the monogenic-polygenic debate. Many scientists asserted that race mixture between widely different peoples would lead to "disharmonies"—to physical, mental, and emotional deformaties. The belief in hybrid degeneration (i.e., the idea that the offspring of race mixture inherit none of the good qualities of either of the parental stocks and thus are likely to die off in several generations) was a commonly held belief. Even those who did not accept the theory of racial disharmonies objected to miscegenation on the ground that races differ in innate intelligence and that the offspring of such unions would have lower intelligence than full-blooded whites.

Of all of the scientists in the mid-nineteenth century who argued for the polygenic origin of species, it was Dr. Josiah C. Nott of Mobile, Alabama, who "was the most fervent of the scientific apologists for the American system of racial subordination." According to George Fredrickson, Nott's writings "would seem to belong at least as much to the history of proslavery and racist propaganda as to the history of science. The fact that Nott was recognized as a leading scientist was perhaps more indicative of the racial preconceptions of his audience than of the quality of his research and theoretical formulations." [25] Fredrickson goes on to explain that Nott's "research" actually consisted of his observations of his own Negro patients (Nott was a physician). He strenuously defended the concept of hybrid degeneration. It should be made clear that despite the differences between the monogenic and polygenic theories, the dissimilarities have to do only with the question of the *origin* of the Caucasian and Negro races. Proponents of both regarded Negroes as an inferior race. For Bachman and Professor J. L. Cabell of the University of Virginia, leading proponents of the monogenic theory, Negro inferiority was the result of environmental factors; however, they argued that this inferiority was *not* reversible by present or future changes in the environment.[26]

Such pseudo-scientific theorizing found its way into the literature. In Claude McKay's story "Near-White," one character explains to her daughter: "You know what they say about us light-colored, what they *write* about us. That we're degenerate, that we're criminal—and their biggest bare-faced lie, that we can't propagate our own stock. They hate us even more than they do the blacks. For they're never sure about us, they can't place us." [27] The hybrid-degeneration theory appears in novels by Negrophobes like Thomas Dixon (*The Clansman* [1905] and *The Leopard's Spots* [1903]) and Robert Lee Durham's *The Call of the South* (1908), which will be discussed in detail later on in this chapter. On the other hand, the black turn-of-the century novelist Sutton Griggs used his novels to argue *against* such racist theorizing. Nevertheless, many of these theories continued to crop up again and again, even though particular forms of racist ideology may differ. In antislavery circles during the antebellum period there existed an ideology which Fredrickson has isolated and called "romantic racialism." Adherents of this philosophy viewed the Negro as a child and saw his docility as a Christian virtue and as a corrective to Anglo-Saxon aggressiveness. This view of the Negro did not impress Dr. Samuel Gridley Howe, a physician, philanthropist, reformer, and member of the three-man American Freedmen's Inquiry Commission appointed by Abraham Lincoln in 1863. He saw "mulatto-ism" as one of the chief evils of a slave system he was striving to abolish. He had corresponded with the great biologist, Louis Agassiz, who had advanced the racial-degeneration theory and thus saw the lighter-skinned African-Americans dying out and the darker-skinned blacks clustering in the South. In Howe's 1864 report to Lincoln, he stated that mulattoism had already impaired "the purity of the national blood taken as a whole." [28] As George M. Fredrickson remarks, "like so many other whites who stood with him against slavery, he was unable to visualize a permanent future for Negroes in America. His ideal America was all white; he was quite willing to see the Negroes diminish and even disappear." [29]

Two romantic racialists who were extremists even within their own camp "openly defended intermarriage as a way of taking the rough edges off the overly aggressive Anglo-Saxons." [30] Both Moncure Daniel Conway, an abolitionist of southern origin, and Gilbert Haven, Methodist bishop of Massachusetts, openly advocated amalgamation and praised the mulatto as a superior human type. Other abolitionists, Mrs. Stowe among them, presented mulattoes as superior types (although it would seem that their superiority derived from the Anglo-Saxon fathers). Nevertheless, advocating intermarriage was decidedly atypical.

Charles Darwin's work was of course related to the issues under discussion. In *On the Origin of Species,* he reviewed the arguments of the monogenic and polygenic schools of thought and explained why he adhered to the monogenic position. Although an acceptance of Darwinism undermined certain theories for many racist ideologies, it did not foreclose the possibility that blacks had evolved into "a variety of the *genus homo* which stood as far below the whites in capacities necessary for survival and progress as any adherent of the American School [of racist ideology] could have wished." [31] Darwin discussed heredity as the means by which traits were passed from one generation to the next. Like the other scientists of his day, he devoted considerable attention to the areas of plant hybridization and sterility (in *On the Origin of Species*) and to the question of sterility in mulattoes, which he says is scientifically invalid *(The Descent of Man)*. In *The Descent of Man*, Darwin discussed the "principle of reversion," which he defined as the principle "by which long-lost dormant structures are called back into existence." [32] The pseudo-scientific concept of "atavism" is a perversion of this principle. Like so much of Darwin's thought, this concept was appropriated and distorted by theorists in other disciplines and by the public in general.

Social Darwinism itself was a perversion of Darwinian thought. Darwinism, in the words of George Fredrickson,

> provided the basis for a necessary reformulation of the set of racist concepts originally developed in the middle of the nineteenth century as a rationale for slavery. The "ethnological" defenders of servitude had of course anticipated "reversion to savagery" and ultimate black extinction as the fruit of emancipation but had lacked a world view that would make such developments part of nature's plan for continuing biological progress. [Thus] . . . if the blacks were a degenerating race with no future, the problem ceased to be one of how to prepare them for citizenship or even how to make them more productive and useful members of the community. . . . By appealing to a simplistic Darwinian or hereditarian formula, white Americans could make their crimes against humanity appear as contributions to the inevitable unfolding of biological destiny. [33]

During the late nineteenth and early twentieth centuries, increasing currency was given not only to Social Darwinism but also to eugenics, which purported to prove that geniuses came from superior human stock and that feeblemindedness, criminality, and pauperism were strongly influenced by hereditary factors. [34] Jim Crowism at home and imperialism abroad also tended to promote the acceptance of racist ideology (which in turn helped to promote the acceptance of the foregoing ideas, attitudes, and institutions).

Books like Frederick L. Hoffman's *Race Traits and Tendencies of the American Negro* (1896), William B. Smith's *The Color Line: A Brief in Behalf of the Unborn* (1905), and Robert W. Shufeldt's *The Negro, A Menace to American Civilization* (1907), all of which proclaimed the inherent inferiority of the Negro and were expressions of current racist ideology, enjoyed wide and receptive audiences.

During the 1890s, militant racism was at its peak. The idea of the Negro as a "beast" who could "revert to type" at any moment, wreaking havoc upon white civilization, gained ascendancy at this time. Some racists enlisted supernatural endorsement for their cause. Such justification was carried to its ultimate absurdity in a book entitled *The Negro a Beast,* published in 1900 by the American Book and Bible House. The author, Charles Carroll, was so anxious to prove to his readers that the Negro is "simply a beast without a soul" that he included pictures of God in order to prove that only white people were made in the image of God.[35]

Carroll also had something to say about the mulatto. Mulattoes, he asserted, do not have the "right to live," for it was the mulattoes who were the rapists and criminals. There was some support for this idea, according to Fredrickson, who gives the example of a southern woman, Mrs. L. H. Harris, who in 1899 wrote to the editor of the *Independent* that

> the "negro brute" who attacked some Southern women and struck fear and terror in the hearts of all others was "nearly always a mulatto with enough white blood in him to replace native humility and cowardice with Caucasian audacity." This monster "had the savage nature and murderous instincts of the wild beast and the cunning and lust of a fiend." [Fredrickson explains:] attributing the worst outrages to the mulatto was clearly one way of reconciling the traditional stereotype of black docility with the image of bold and violent offenders against the color line which was central to the new propaganda.[36]

Dismissing these nightmare racist fantasies, let us consider the "behavior" of mulattoes, about which much has been written. It seems to have occurred to very few natural and social scientists of the period that the "apparently irrational, moody, 'temperamental' conduct of racial hybrids" (if such behavior even existed) was not the result of biology but of their marginal social status. As Everett Stonequist points out, "racially pure cultural hybrids" often exhibit the same kind of "disharmonious" behavior. What has frequently been viewed "in terms of 'racial disharmony,' 'the clash of blood,' 'unstable genetic constitution,' and the like should be seen as the result of the mulatto's ambivalence toward his identification with one group or the other." [37] While the sociological explanation seems natural and "comfortable" to us, its logic was not consistent with the racist ideologies of the nineteenth and early twentieth centuries. If the Negro appeared inferior, his inferiority was caused by unchangeable racial characteristics. If the mulatto appeared to be restless and dissatisfied with his position in society, it was due to his biology, to his "impure blood." Although by the early twentieth century many scientists were aware that the observed characteritics under discussion were not heritable qualities, but rather were socially determined, this fallacious concept was still an entrenched, popularly held superstition. "Race" and "blood" were used as synonyms.[38]

Franz Boas, more than any other thinker of his time, turned the scientific community away from its emphasis on biology toward "social process as an explanation for cultural differences." But even with this shift of opinion, "the increasing emphasis on the latter did not necessarily imply a rejection of the former." [39] There were, and still are, political and social reasons for the tenacity of racist ideology. As Gunnar Myrdal has demonstrated, specific beliefs about Negroes "seem to have specific rationalization purposes." Some beliefs are designed to justify vocational segregation: the argument as to the Negro's innate intellectual inferiority, his unreliablity, and his laziness is used for this purpose. Social intercourse and miscegenation have been discouraged through myths about the "hircine odor" of Negroes and stories of the animality of the male Negro. The belief in the moral laxity of black women, on the other hand, was a means of assuaging the guilt of white men who had forced themselves upon these supposedly loose women. The stereotype of the Negro as childish, immature, and servile has been used to justify the denial of full civil rights.[40]

In his 1947 novel, *Kingsblood Royal*, Sinclair Lewis attacks both the dehumanization of the Negro in America and its justification. When the protagonist of Lewis's novel, Neil Kingsblood, discovers that he has a fraction of "Negro blood" flowing through his veins, he tries desperately to balance all of the stereotypical associations of "Negro" with the newly discovered knowledge of his own "mixed blood." To be a Negro, Neil has been taught, is to be bestial, animalistic in every way. It is to know that your children and their children's children will be forever cursed. How close this is to the primitive concept of "unclean," as Myrdal notes. Nothing—neither education nor intelligence, neither diligence nor honesty—can alter one's "blood":

> ... Negroes are not human beings but a cross between the monkey and the *colonel.* This is proven by their invariably having skulls so thick that, as experiments at the University of Louisiana have conclusively shown, cocoanuts, sledgehammers and very large rocks may be dropped upon their heads without their noticing anything except that they have been kissed by butterflies. This is called Science.
>
> (But what it really all comes down to is, would you want your daughter to marry a nigger?). . . .
>
> All Negro males have such wondrous sexual powers that they unholily fascinate all white women and all Negro males are such uncouth monsters that no white woman whatsoever could possibly be attracted by one. This is called Biology.
>
> All mixed breeds are bad. [The] ... mulatto invariably lacks both the honor and creativeness of the whites, and the patience and merriment of the blacks. So, the reason why so many mulattoes display talent and high morality is because they have so much white blood, and the reason why so many extremely dark Negroes show just as much talent and morality is because it simply ain't so. This is called Ethnology, Eugenics, or Winston Churchill.[41]

Measurement of the shape and size of the skull of races played a significant role in the nineteenth-century scientific battle over the race issue: Negroes, the racist myth goes, are less intelligent because of their smaller brain size. Like so many of the theories relating to this issue, the controversy over the significance of skull size and shape found its way into popular fiction. In the novels of Cooper, Negroes generally have very limited intelligence. "One has a skull so thick that he is almost immune to Indian tomahawk attacks." [42] In T. S. Stribling's 1922 novel, *Birthright,* one of the white characters says that a "nigger baby has no fontanelles. It has a window toward heaven; the nigger brain can never expand and absorb the universe. . . . It's congenital." [43] Stribling is one of the white authors of the early twentieth century who wanted to break away from the dehumanized depiction of the Negro in American fiction (his works were heralded by many, along with Faulkner's, as revolutionary in their treatment of the Negro). [44] Yet his novel is filled with racist sentiments, and it is not always clear how we are to interpret his statements. He does try to point to the importance of environment in the formation of some of the Negro characteristics which white society has defined as less than socially acceptable. But he often falls back into stereotypical thinking—employing the concept of atavism in describing certain behavior traits of his mulatto hero, Peter Siner, and heroine, Cissie Dildine. Atavism is the notion that the mixed blood who has attained a veneer of white civilization can, at any time, "revert" to the savage, primitivistic behavior of the jungle from which his ancestors came and to which he is inextricably tied. This view of course assumes that all tribal behavior was "primitivistic" in the first place. Of Cissie, for example, Stribling says: she is "flexuous and passionate, kindly and loving, childish and naively wise. . . . For all her precise English, she was untamed, perhaps untamable." [45]

Racist ideologies, particularly ideas relating to the biological differentiation of the races, characterize much of the literature of the early twentieth century. Because the writers of the naturalistic novel usually emphasized the role of determinism in men's lives, they often explored character through an examination of the ways in which we are the victims of our biological heritage and our environment. Since racist ideologies were so prevalent during this period, they were often invoked to explain character motivation and destiny. Jack London was one such novelist (especially in *The Call of the Wild*); Frank Norris was another.

Norris had been taught by Joseph Le Conte, geologist and

popularizer of Darwin, Lamarck, and Lombrosso, that "the brute insticts which remain in civilized man are a necessary part of his equipment for the social struggle, which parallels the earlier tooth-and-claw struggle of primitive man." Le Conte regarded the "lower" insticts of man as his "sensual cravings" and the "higher," the "use of reason and conscience; . . . he invited the drawing of parallels in the social structure." He also popularized Lombroso and taught "that the criminal type forms a separate subspecies characterized by atavism, and a swift degeneration to racial type may come about if his nervous system is disturbed." [46] The white blood–black blood dichotomy, with its connotations of higher versus lower instincts, is an example of the application of these pseudo-scientific ideas to racial issues. In "The Wife of Chino," an early story by Frank Norris, a white man becomes involved with a married half-breed woman, who urges her husband's murder. Norris writes: "All the baseness of her tribe, all the degraded savagery of a degenerate race, all the capabilities for wrong, for sordid treachery, that lay dormant in her, leaped to life at this unguarded moment." [47] In *The Octopus,* Norris applies the concept of atavism to his Caucasian farmers: "For upwards of an hour the gang ate. It was no longer a supper. It was a veritable barbecue, a crude and primitive feasting, barbaric, Homeric. . . . Presley would have abhorred [this scene]—this feeding of the people, this gorging of the human animal, eager for its meat." [48] In *Vandover and the Brute,* Norris portrayed an upper-class man whose sensual cravings destroy him. "As an accompaniment to Vandover's descent, Norris conceived of him as the victim of lycanthropy, so that at his lowest moments he would strip naked and gambol about his room on all fours, howling like a wolf." [49]

A 1908 novel by the white racist Robert Lee Durham, entitled *The Call of the South,* is an excellent example of how racist ideology was reflected in the literature of the day. The protagonist of Durham's novel is Hayward Graham, a Harvard-educated all-but-white man who is described in terms typical of the white hero of the time. He is handsome, proud, brave, and of noble bearing. He secretly woos and wins the heart of Helen Phillips, the daughter of the president of the United States. He tells her of his battle adventures, and, like Othello, he wins his Desdemona. They marry secretly, but their relationship remains platonic. Hayward idolizes

Helen, and for a long time he accepts the peculiar nature of their relationship. Finally, however, he can wait no longer to consummate their love: in Durham's atavistic scheme of things, the blood of Graham's grandfather, a half-savage slave named Guinea Gumbo, inevitably asserts itself. Durham prepares us for Hayward's return to savagery through a passage in which he propounds his theory of racial atavism: "An occasional isolated negro may have broken the shackles of ignorance, measurably and admirably brought under control the half-savage passions of his nature, acquired palpable elegances of person and manner, and taken on largely the indefinable graces of culture: yet beneath all this creditable but thin veneer of civilization there slumbers in his blood the primitive passions and propensities of his immediate ancestors, which are transmitted to him as latent forces of evil to burst out of his children and grandchildren in answer to the call of the wild." [50]

Hayward Graham is clearly one of these occasional, isolated Negroes. Although Durham's treatment of his protagonist at first seems sympathetic, it soon becomes evident that he has created Graham only to fictionalize his racist message. Thus, Graham attacks Helen during a "raging" storm that, in true melodramatic fashion, is paralleled to the storm raging inside Hayward. During a flash of lightning Helen sees her husband's "distorted" face. "With a shriek of terror she wildly tries to push him from her: but the demon of the blood of Guinea Gumbo is pitiless, and against the fury of it, as of the storm, she fights and cries—in vain." [51]

Elsewhere, Durham uses his spokesman in the novel to warn of the dangers of "amalgamation." This speech epitomizes the lengths to which Negrophobe novelists would go in fighting for "racial purity":

When the blood of your daughter of your son is mixed with that of one of this race, however *risen*, redolent of newly applied polish or bewrapped with a fresh culture, how shall sickly sentimentalities solace your shame if in the blood of your mulatto grandchild the vigorous red jungle corpuscles of some savage ancestor shall overmatch your more gentle endowment, and under your name and in a face and form perhaps where a world may see your very image in darker hue there shall be distorted primitive appetites, propensities, passions fit only to endow an Ashanti warrior or grace the orgies of an African bacchanalia? [52]

Durham's white liberal politician, who has preached racial equality and had blacks to dinner, suffers as his punishment his daughter's marriage to a black man. He is horrified, but it is too late. His death blow (literally) comes as a result of his visit to his grandson. The child represents a "recession below the father's type!—this resurgence of the negro blood, with its 'vile unknown ancestral impulses!' " The baby "was the colour that was of Ethiopia" and has features to match. The prophecy made earlier in the novel is fulfilled: the child is a "caricature" of the president's daughter, "a horrible travesty" of her features, not in combination with Hayward's but with those of . . . Guinea Gumbo! [53] And Helen is punished too. She ends up in an insane asylum, violently clawing at herself as she shrieks, "The poison of your blood [Hayward's] is in my veins and will not come out! It is polluted, forever polluted! . . . Kill me—*save* me! My blood is *unclean,* and he did it! My baby was black, black!—and its negro blood is in my veins!" [54]

Most of the novelists of the nineteenth and early twentieth centuries who dealt with the mulatto character relied almost exclusively on the heredity-race formula to interpret character. Even abolitionist and Negro novelists often utilized this formula. There are, however, some exceptions—authors who accepted the importance of environment in the shaping of human personality. Harriet Beecher Stowe provides an example of "the exception that proves the rule" in her antislavery novel, *Dred: A Tale of the Dismal Swamp.*

Mrs. Stowe utilizes two half brothers, Harry and Tom Gordon, in order to showcase her ideas about the training of human beings. Harry is the all-but-white, highly intelligent son of Colonel Gordon. He is trapped because he has "all the family blood and the family pride," [55] yet he is unable to transcend the stultifying restrictions of the caste system. Harry has been educated, has traveled in Europe as his father's valet, and manages his father's plantation. His training and responsibilities insure his development into a man of uncommon abilities. The history of Tom

Gordon, however, is quite different. Because Tom has had "an apprenticeship in tyranny," [56] the talents he might have developed do not have an opportunity to emerge. His entire history is described at some length—his exploitation of foolish, doting parents; his cruel treatment of his brother; his terrorizing of one tutor after another; his wild, hedonistic debauchery at college and at home. These are the details of Tom's development; they are used by Mrs. Stowe to illustrate the enormous importance of nurture in shaping the individual. Although she does not ignore the relevance of hereditary factors, she states unequivocally that training will determine the direction in which an individual's talents will develop. Thus, Tom's quick intelligence becomes cunning. He uses his cleverness to manipulate all who come into his sphere of influence; he employs his boldness and daring in gambling and horse racing:

> Nature had endowed him with no mean share of talent, and with that perilous quickness of nervous organization, which, like fire, is a good servant, but a bad master. Out of these elements, with due training, might have been formed an efficient and eloquent public man; but, brought up from childhood among servants to whom his infant will was law, indulged during the period of infantile beauty and grace in the full expression of every whim, growing into boyhood among slaves with but the average amount of plantation morality, his passions developed at a fearfully early time of life; and before his father thought of seizing the reins of authority, they had gone out of his hands forever.
> . . . As often happens in such cases of utter ruin, Tom Gordon was a much worse character for all the elements of good which he possessed.[57]

William Pickens, a little-known black author, wrote a story in 1922, "The Vengeance of the Gods," in which he upheld the importance of environment in playing "the major influence on the destinies of men." [58] He tells the story of two children: William is destined to be the heir to his family's plantation; Jimmie is intended to lead the usual life of the black "debt-slave"—the sharecroppers who have been exploited by the white land owners in the postbellum South. But Jimmie and William are half-brothers and are virtually indistinguishable. When the babies are switched by Jimmie's grandmother, no one—not even the mothers of the two children—can tell. For, while "environment is not omnipotent, . . . it is so almost all-powerful that it deserves the major consideration in the making of a man on earth." [59] Pickens ascribes definite motives to the switch made by "Aunt" Katy: fear and revenge. Fear of what her white employer would do to her because of a minor injury that William sustained while in Katy's care. Revenge for the treatment both she and her daughter had received at the lustful hands of the Elliotts. By attributing these motives to Katy, Pickens neatly establishes racism as the cause of Jimmie's (né William's) subsequent hanging. This is the "vengeance of the gods."

The major portion of Pickens's story deals with the childhood and youth of the twins, wherein he "documents" the effects of environment. While Jimmie and William were indistinguishable as babies, they had become set apart from each other by the time they were a few years old: "Clothing and the care of their bodies clearly distinguished them. Besides, each had now a personality which could never be confounded with the other. William was generally well-dressed, well-shod, pampered and aristocratic. Essie's 'little nigger Jim' was clad in homemade things or cast-offs, and had a temper to fight and a disposition to carry away the playthings of the little autocrat." [60]

Pickens's story is very poorly written. It is, in fact, not really fiction at all, but rather an essay clothed in some fictional devices. Nonetheless, it illustrates one of the overriding concerns of the day, and how one black author dealt with the nature-nurture issue. The story is so close to Twain's *Pudd'nhead Wilson* in some of its details that one wonders whether Pickens was thinking of Twain's novel when he wrote his story. But the switched-child theme is, of course, common in literature: Twain himself used the device more than once in his career. Like Pickens, he was concerned with the nature-nurture issue and explored the topic over and over again. Twain's interest in this issue was intertwined with his ongoing speculation about man's nature; the sources of an individual's identity; the kinds of societies he creates which, in turn, create him; the distinctions between appearance and reality, both on an individual and on a societal level; and, finally, the kind of American society that our people have created and sustained.

In *The Prince and the Pauper*, Twain illustrates the principle of "election" and "damnation" that was to play a central role in *A Connecticut Yankee in King Arthur's Court* and in *Pudd'nhead Wilson*. In each novel, Twain illustrates the means by which society determines—even before a person is born—just who he is: through distinctions of class and caste and, then, through education (broadly defined). Liberation from these societally imposed straitjackets is rarely possible. However, if the barrier to be crossed is one of class, as it is in Tom Canty's case, we see that highly unusual circumstances may result in a bettering of the individual's condition and in increased freedom to exercise his potential. The caste barrier, however, is impossible to destroy, given the nature of the society that Twain depicts in *Pudd'nhead Wilson*. Thus, in spite of Roxy's apparent triumph over the racist system of slavery—a system which declares one human being elect and his brother damned—it is the system that ultimately devastates Roxy, Thomas à Becket Driscoll, and Valet de Chambre. Although Chambers is only one-thirty-second Negro, he is black according to the arbitrary definitions of caste that reign unchallenged—except, perhaps, by Roxy—in Dawson's Landing.

In *The Prince and the Pauper*, the paired characters—Edward Tudor, the Prince of Wales, and Tom Canty, pauper boy—are born on the same day and in the same country, but they might as well have been born on different planets. While all England rejoices over the birth of the first child, there was no one to notice Tom Canty's entrance into the world "except among the family of paupers he had just come to trouble with his presence." [61] While Prince Edward is destined to rule, Tom Canty is just as clearly destined to endure a dehumanized existence of oppressive poverty. Twain employs the identical device in *Pudd'nhead Wilson:* Thomas a Becket Driscoll and Valet de Chambre are born on the same day. Thomas, however, is not only white but is born into the "F.F.V."— the "First Families of Virginia." Valet de Chambre is born into a predestined role of subjugation.

However, the switch of the paired characters occurs at significantly different points in the two novels. By the time Tom Canty and Prince Edward switch places, each has had his identity well established. Changing clothes affects the manner in which *others* treat the two boys. Since Tom Canty appears to be Prince Edward—by virtue of his physical charcteristics, his dress, and his manner (which he had acquired through acting out his fantasies of being a prince)—he is assumed to be the prince in reality. But neither he nor Prince Edward is in any doubt about the real identity of each. When they try to explain that they are not what they seem, no one will believe them. Why should they? All the cues by which identity is determined suggest that the boy who appears to be a prince is a prince; the apparent beggar is a beggar boy indeed.

But clothes alone "do not make the man." Had Tom Canty not had the air of a prince it is unlikely, even with the similarity in appearance to Prince Edward, that Tom would have been taken for him. There is a very funny chapter in *A Connecticut Yankee in King Arthur's Court* in which Hank drills King Arthur on the art of behaving like a commoner. They are traveling around the realm dressed as commoners. The king certainly looks the part. However, he cannot walk, talk, or think like the peasant he is dressed to be. As Hank Morgan says, "He looked as humble as the leaning tower of Pisa." And later, when Hank tries to teach King Arthur how to behave like a poor man, he explains: "Your soldierly stride, your lordly port—these will not do. You stand too straight, your looks are too high, too confident. . . . You must imitate the trademarks of poverty, misery, oppression, insult, and the other several and common inhumanities that sap the manliness out of a man and make him a loyal and proper and approved subject and a satisfaction to his masters, or the very infants will know you for better than your disguise." [62]

Neither Tom Driscoll nor Chambers had to be reeducated to their false roles, for they were switched in the cradle. Therefore, the training that each received was that appropriate to the station into which he had been thrust by Roxy. Twain would have agreed with Pickens's contention that environment is the primary causative factor in the individual's development. It is true that in one of Twain's early works, *The Innocents Abroad,* he does seem to have written within the framework of racist ideology, at least to some degree. He often speaks in sweeping generalizations about whole races and groups of people and clearly assigns major importance to heredity as well as to environment. But in his later works, Twain exhibits no such uncertainty: "Training—training is everything; training is all there is *to* a person. We speak of nature; it is folly; there is no such thing as nature; what we call by that misleading name is merely heredity and training. We have no thoughts of our own, no opinions of our own; they are transmitted to us, trained into us." [63] And in Twain's Socratic dialogue entitled *What is Man?* (which was not published until after his death, but upon which he worked for several years at the end of his life), he reiterated his ideas on training, the importance of environment, the fallacy of free will, and the existence of a virtually absolute determinism: "Personally you did not create even the smallest microscopic fragment of the materials out of which your opinion is made; and personally you cannot claim even the slender merit of *putting the borrowed materials together.* That was done automatically— by your mental machinery, in strict accordance with the law of that machinery's construction. And you not only did not make that machinery yourself, but you *have not even any command over it.*" [64] And, finally, in *The Mysterious Stranger,* Satan tells Theodor that human life is determined absolutely by circumstances and environ- ment. He compares a man's life to the child's game in which a row of bricks is stood on end and the first brick is pushed, which then knocks over the second, and so on: "A child's first act knocks over the initial, and the rest will follow inexorably. [A man's] . . . first act determines the second and all that follow after." [65]

Twain's belief in the power of training was directly related to his enormous concern about the society in which he lived and the world at large. Everywhere Twain looked, "sivilization" seemed characterized by violence, deceit, hypocrisy, cruelty, vanity, and the inhumanity of men toward men. Racist ideology and apathy toward social reform were interrelated: social engineering could be of little use in the creation of a better world if men were biologically determined. For Twain, as for many others who have adhered to behaviorist principles, human values and behavior were subject to modification and improvement through social engineer- ing. Throughout his career, Twain applied this intellectual frame- work to his examination of the small towns of the South; the religious beliefs of his day; the social pretensions and crass materialism of American life; the relationship between ethnocentric and racist ideology and war and imperialism, missionary and economic; and the system of slavery that debased and dehumanized both master and slave.

The "image of slavery," Robert Rowlette remarks, "holds a special meaning for Twain ..., for slavery is an appropriate metaphor for his philosophy of determinism, with its idea of environmental conditioning that he calls training." [66] Dawson's Landing, the scene of *Pudd'nhead Wilson,* is a slaveholding town that is "sleepy and comfortable—and contented." [67] It is a society in which the First Families of Virginia are virtually omnipotent, one in which a white master can casually threaten his slaves with being "sold down the river"—sold to a life of brutality and almost certain death. And, like members of any closed society, the citizens of Dawson's Landing are not even aware that their attitudes and behavior are inhumane. When Percy Northumberland Driscoll decides *not* to sell his slaves down river, he feels only satisfaction over his own generosity but is utterly blind to his essential inhumanity. Twain is brutally scornful of Percy for his blindness: "[Percy] was privately well pleased with his magnanimity; and that night he set the incident down in his diary, so that his son might read it in after years, and be thereby moved to deeds of gentleness and humanity himself." [68] This is the same kind of reasoning that allowed Huck to tell Mrs. Phelps, an otherwise kind and good woman, that no one was killed—just a nigger; and for her to answer, "Well, it's lucky; because sometimes people do get hurt." [69] In *A Connecticut Yankee,* Twain explains how seemingly intelligent, decent people can be brought up "to believe anything": "Inherited ideas are a curious thing, and interesting to observe and examine. I [Hank Morgan] had mine, the king and his people had theirs. In both cases they flowed in ruts worn deep by time and habit, and the man who should have proposed to divert them by reason and argument would have had a long contract on his hands." [70]

In Dawson's Landing, the F.F.V. rule with a code——the values of which are based upon white supremacy, racist ideology and the slave system—which insures blindness to the condition of black people, to the injustices of the economic, political and social system, as well as to the sexual abuse of black women that lay hidden beneath the placid surface of Dawson's Landing. Thus,

Tom Driscoll (né Chambers) "is the nightmare plaguing the moral sleep of Dawson's Landing. [He] stands always in the foreground as the figure embodying the long history of miscegenation in the background. . . . [And, as the forces of evil often are, he] is invisible to his victims." [71]

In Dawson's Landing, everyone is taught that white is right; white is beautiful; white is all powerful—and the best of the whites are the members of the F.F.V. Conversely, to be black is to be inferior, ugly both physically and spiritually, and enslaved. The blacks carry with them, thanks to their training, as abiding a sense of their own lack of worth as the whites have of their own superiority. As many commentators on *Pudd'nhead Wilson* have remarked, Twain is clearly showing the corruption of *all* those who live under the slave system—the blacks by virtue of their dehumanization by oppression, the whites by means of their cruelty, which leads to the "blunting [of] sensibilities and fostering [of] an unwarranted pride of'place." [72] Never does Twain ascribe this situation to anything but the values and institutions of the society. Whites do not have power because of some mysterious Aryan magic in their blood; blacks are corrupted only by their enslavement and by their acceptance of their inferiority. They are not tainted, less-than-human, apelike creatures.

Training has done a good enough job of corrupting blacks and whites, Twain would say, without any aid from biology. Roxy is a highly intelligent all-but-white woman of great dignity. Yet even she is awed by the F.F.V. and is very proud that one of their important members is the father of her illegitimate mixed-blood son. She tells Tom: "Dey ain't another nigger in dis town dat's as highbawn as you is. [She goes on] . . . En jes you hold yo' head up as high as you want to—you has de right, en dat I kin swah." [73] Roxy also accepts the attitudes toward color that prevail in her culture. The darker one is, the further removed he is from white standards of beauty and acceptance by whites and blacks alike. When Roxy meets a dark-skinned slave, she says, "I got somep'n better to do den sociat'n' wid niggers as black as you is." [74]

Roxy assumes—for this is what she has been taught—that "white is right." As she contemplates switching the babies because she wants to protect her son from the possibility of ever being sold down river, she is uncertain of the rightness of her act. However, when she remembers that the preacher told of an earlier switch, she thinks that her own "ain't no sin, 'ca'se white folks done it. *Dey* done it—yes, *dey* done it; en not on'y jus common whites folks nuther, but de biggest quality dey is in de whole bilin.' Oh, I's *so* glad I 'member 'bout dat!" [75]

When Pudd'nhead Wilson tells Roxy that one baby is just as handsome as the other, she answers: "Bless yo' soul, Misto Wilson, it's po'ful nice o' you to say dat, 'ca'se one of 'em ain't on'y a nigger." [76] And when Roxy hears that Tom would not uphold the code of the F.F.V. and duel with Count Luigi, she says: "It's de nigger in you, dat's what it is. Thirty-one part o' you is white en on'y one part nigger, en dat po' little part is yo' soul." [77] After Tom finds out that he is in reality a Negro and a slave, he immediately perceives himself as inferior. He cringes when he hears "Chambers" call him "Young Marster"; he can barely shake the hands of friends, sit down to eat with his aunt and uncle, or allow his aunt's endearments toward him. In addition, "Tom" interprets his behavior in terms of racial atavistic theories. When he cannot shake a friend's hand, he does not think that this inability is caused by his recent discovery of his "black blood." He attributes his failure rather to "the nigger in him asserting its humility. . . . He found the 'nigger' in him involuntarily giving the road. . . . The 'nigger' in him went shrinking and skulking here and there and yonder." [78] Hank Morgan's comment on Sandy's attitude provides an apt analysis of Roxy's and "Tom's" distorted perceptions: "Here she was, as sane a person as the kingdom could produce, and yet, from my point of view she was acting like a crazy woman. My land, the power of training! Of influence! Of education! It can bring a body up to believe anything. I had to put myself in Sandy's place to realize that she was not a lunatic. Yes, and put her in mine, to demonstrate how easy it is to seem a lunatic to a person who has not been taught as you have been taught." [79]

Certainly a good example of the power of training over rationality can be seen in Roxy's behavior toward the newly switched babies. The night she switches the babies, she immediately begins to practice the correct behavior and attitudes toward each child: "As she progressed with her practice, she was surprised to see how steadily and surely the awe which had kept her tongue reverent and her manner humble toward her young master was transferring itself to her speech and manner toward the usurper, and how similarly handy she was becoming in transferring her motherly curtness of speech and peremptoriness of manner to the unlucky heir of the ancient house of Driscoll." [80] Furthermore, as time passes, Roxy becomes "the dupe of her own deception": "the mock reverence became real reverence, the mock obsequiousness real obsequiousness, the mock homage real homage; the little counterfeit rift of separation between imitation-slave and imitation-master widened and widened, and became an abyss." [81]

Those who contend that Twain builds *Pudd'nhead Wilson* around his attack on the slave system and the institutions and social conditioning that perpetuate that system, rather than around the heredity-environment issue per se, are correct. *Pudd'nhead Wilson* is not a simplistic thesis novel designed to illustrate that a Negro raised as a white will be superior in every way. His book is directed to southern white readers in an attempt to wake them from their ignorant contentment and to see the effects of slavery on themselves as well as on their slaves. Thus the indulgence baby Tom received and the submission of those around him to this young tyrant are held up by Twain as the essential causes of his debasement. This indulgence led to Tom's cruelty toward and lack of regard for others; his manipulation of his guardians, schoolmates, and the townspeople; his lack of desire or ability to stay away from the gambling tables; and his egocentrism and hedonism in general. Twain's purpose is to show that his education in exploitation and oppression began in babyhood:

> Tom got all the petting, Chambers got none. Tom got all the delicacies, Chambers got mush and milk, and clabber without sugar. In consequence Tom was a sickly child and Chambers wasn't.
>   ... In babyhood Tom cuffed and banged and scratched Chambers unrebuked, and Chambers early learned that between meekly bearing it and resenting it, the advantage all lay with the former policy. [Chambers] ... was strong beyond his years, and a good fighter, strong because he was coarsely fed and hard worked about the house, and a good fighter

because Tom furnished him plenty of practice—on white boys whom he hated and was afraid of. . . .[82]

All throughout the novel, "Tom" is thoroughly despicable. Henry Nash Smith is correct when he says that Tom "exhibits the worst traits ascribed to both races in this fictive world—the laxity of morals and cowardice of the Negro, together with the hatred of the master that is putatively expressed in his murder of Judge Driscoll; the indolence and affectation of white aristocrats . . . [and] cruelty toward slaves." [83] But why did Twain heap all of these negative traits upon the fake Tom Driscoll? The fact that Tom's "sweet tooth" was indulged could have led to poor health, but would it not have been far more likely for the false Negro boy to have been in poor health for lack of adequate meat, milk, vegetables, and so on? More important, why did Tom not learn to revere the code of the F.F.V.? Surely if Twain wanted to show the effects of bad training on the southern whites who lived under the slave system, he should have made Tom a loyal proponent of the code by which he was raised. His uncle and guardian, Judge Driscoll, his own father, members of his class, all lived by the code. And the other whites and blacks too at least accept it. In fact it seems that only Tom does not adhere to the unwritten laws of his society.

Two related problems reassert themselves: Tom's utter immorality, his complete lack of compassion or even of decency; and Chambers's strength, skill, bravery, kindness, and generosity. (Upon his restoration as heir, he gives Roxy, the author of his twenty-three-year-long degradation, a pension of $35 per month.) The crucial question here is: If Twain wanted to come down clearly on the side of training in the controversy surrounding the importance of nature versus nurture, why did he present "Tom" in such a negative light and "Chambers" in such a positive light?

We can find a partial explanation for the difference in their behavior in *What Is Man?* In that essay, Twain argues that man is controlled by the training which is brought to bear upon his inherited characteristics. But while Twain's major emphasis is on the power of training, he makes clear that temperament cannot be ignored. It is "the disposition you were born with. *You can't eradicate your disposition nor any rag of it*—you can only put a pressure on it and keep it down and quiet." [84] So temperament may provide a partial explanation of Tom's "evil" and Chambers's "goodness." At one point in the novel, Tom torments Chambers partly, Twain says, "out of native viciousness, and partly because he hated him for his superiority of physique and pluck, and for his manifold cleverness." [85] This remark certainly places heavy emphasis upon Tom's temperament, and in fact his "native viciousness" helps to explain why only he, of all the white characters in the novel, seems to exhibit cruelty toward his slaves.

We can find further explanation for Tom's utterly debased character when we examine Twain's considerations of theme as opposed to clarity of character development.[86] According to Robert Rowlette, Tom "is made as diabolical as he is so that Roxy will be motivated to reveal his identity" [87] and finally overcome the force of her mother love. It is, in fact, partly this mother love that is responsible for Tom's development. Roxy has excessively indulged her son. For example, "she ... permits him to maul Chambers, unrebuked, thus unconsciously encouraging him to regard the slaves, including herself, as below the brutes." [88]

Even with this further clarification, Tom's melodramatic villainy is disturbing (and has always been problematic to the critics of *Pudd'nhead Wilson*). The fact is that Tom "is a victim of Twain's literary card-stacking which amounts nearly to character assassination. A stereotype of depravity, he comes to embody the worst features of a corrupting system. For thematic as well as dramatic reasons, his viciousness is instantly established and thereafter used to emphasize his callousness towards Roxy and his hatred of Chambers, in whose tattered shoes he is fated to stand." [89] Perhaps it is because Twain believed that dramatic considerations were paramount that he deleted a passage in which he ascribed Tom's kicking of Chambers to training rather than to native disposition: "At this distance of time it seems incredible that such a performance as the above would have furnished to a stranger no sure indication of Tom's character—for the reason that such conduct was not confined to young men of such harsh nature. Humane young men were quite capable of it, good-hearted young fellows who would protect with their brave lives a dog that was being treated so. Slavery was to blame, not innate nature. It placed the slave below the brute, without the white man's realizing it." [90] Even in this passage, it should be noted, Twain makes reference to

Tom's temperament—his "harsh nature." Twain does not want us to forget Tom's villainy even though in this passage he wants to emphasize the power of training.

The Morgan manuscript of *Pudd'nhead Wilson* [91] indicates various kinds of confusion and inconsistencies between one passage and the next. It seems unlikely that we will ever know absolutely why Twain deleted the passage quoted above or deleted another passage in the working versions of the novel in which Twain has Tom consider his motivation in refusing the duel. In the second passage, we are told that "what was high came from either blood, & was the monopoly of neither color; but that which was base was the *white* blood in him debased by the brutalizing effects of a long-drawn heredity of slave-owning, with the habit of abuse which the possession of irresponsible power always created & perpetuates, by a law of human nature." [92]

Even though Twain deleted these two passages, it seems to me that their presence in the working version of his manuscript is significant and is an accurate reflection of his belief in the importance of nurture over nature. Furthermore, the various passages *not* deleted from the novel that indicate Twain's belief in the power of training as well as the expression of this belief throughout most of his work (especially all of his later works) reveal clearly Twain's emphasis on the importance of the effects of training as opposed to the hereditarian emphasis of racist ideology. The society depicted in *Pudd'nhead Wilson* is an inhumane, corrupt society, and it trains its rulers and its enslaved to be less-than-complete human beings. In such a society, "the master is a slave, . . . [and] both master and slave are degraded." [93] Such a society is obviously unhealthy and is ripe for the murder of its "living symbol of law and order, . . . [a] murder [that] suggests the anarchy which white society has by its own action released upon itself." [94]

In *What Is Man?* Twain observes that it is not a single environmental factor that influences a man to commit a dishonest act, but a slow wearing away at what might once have been a completely honest character. This principle is certainly illuminated in *Pudd'nhead Wilson,* wherein the training of the two boys has taken away their humanity. At the end of the novel, the real heir finds himself rich and free "but in a most embarrassing situation. He could neither read nor write, and his speech was the basest dialect of the Negro quarter. His gait, his attitudes, his gestures, his bearing, his laugh—all were vulgar and uncouth; his manners were the manners of a slave. Money and fine clothes could not mend these defects or cover them up; they only made them the more glaring and the more pathetic. The poor fellow could not endure the terrors of the white man's parlor, and felt at home and at peace nowhere but in the kitchen." [95]

In a society that has imposed the arbitrary distinctions of Negro and white, master and slave—in a society that has made brothers enemies (at some level of Mark Twain's mind, Tom and Chambers *are* half brothers)—in such a society there will be no certainty of *anyone's* identity: of slave or master, Negro or white, guilty or innocent, hunter or hunted, true or false leader.[96] Twain's use of the mulatto character to dramatize these truths is particularly appropriate. For it is the mulatto character who is *both* Negro and white; it is he who has the blood of both the oppressor and the oppressed; he who can be either master or slave. It is an accident of biology in the case of every human being as to whether he is king or slave. But in the case of the mulatto, fate seems to be capricious. In Twain's novel, we see how the master of one day becomes the slave of the next. It is not just "fate," of course, that Twain attacks as he explores the mulatto character, but the institutions and values of the society within which individual and collective fate are determined.

Throughout the novel, the threat of being "sold down the river" reverberates. And with superb irony, this is precisely what happens to "Tom." For, like the queen's child in the tale Roxy recalled to justify her own action, retribution is paid to the would-be ruler. The doom that was foreshadowed early in the novel is brought to fruition. There is no happy ending for anyone in Dawson's Landing: the Judge is killed; Tom is sold down river; Chambers will remain a marginal man forever; and Roxy is a broken woman. Since the institution of slavery has not been destroyed at the end of *Pudd'nhead Wilson,* Twain does not give us hope. As John Freimarck has said, "There is no happy ending in a novel that is uniquely American, at once working the dream of democratic possibilities and examining the institutions which destroyed it." [97] To quote

Pudd'nhead Wilson's Diary, *"October 12, the Discovery.* It was wonderful to find America, but it would have been more wonderful to miss it." [98]

NOTES

1. Kenneth Clark, *Prejudice and Your Child,* 2d ed. enl. (Boston: Beacon Press, 1963), p.8.
2. Gunnar Myrdal, *An American Dilemma: The Negro Problem and Modern Democracy* (New York: Harper & Brothers, 1944), p. 89.
3. Pierre L. van den Berghe, from *Race and Racism: A Comparative Perspective* (New York, 1967), pp. 17–18 in George M. Fredrickson, *The Black Image in the White Mind: The Debate on Afro-American Character and Destiny, 1817–1914* (New York, Evanston, San Francisco, London: Harper & Row, 1971), p. 61.
4. Louis Agassiz, "Agassiz to Howe, August 9 and 10, 1863, in Elizabeth Cary Agassiz, *Louis Agassiz: His Life and Correspondence* (Boston and New York, 1890), pp. 592–93, 595, 596–601, as quoted in George M. Fredrickson, *The Black Image in the White Mind,* p. 162.
5. Winthrop Jordan, *White Over Black: American Attitudes Toward the Negro, 1550–1812* (Chapel Hill: University of North Carolina Press, 1968), p. 44.
6. Eugene Genovese, *Roll, Jordan, Roll: The World the Slaves Made* (New York: Pantheon Books, 1974), p. 31.
7. Ibid.
8. Ibid., p. 26.
9. Ibid., p. 30.
10. Jordan, *White Over Black,* p. 94.
11. *Oxford English Dictionary* in Jordan, *White Over Black,* p. 7.
12. David Brian Davis, *The Problem of Slavery in Western Culture* (Ithaca, N.Y.: Cornell University Press, 1966), p. 49.
13. Jordan, *White Over Black,* p. 97.
14. George M. Fredrickson, *The Black Image in the White Mind: The Debate on Afro-American Character and Destiny, 1817–1914* (New York, Evanston, San Francisco, London: Harper & Row, 1971), p. 2.
15. Ibid.
16. Jordan, *White Over Black,* p. 429.
17. Ibid., p. 438.
18. Summary of Jefferson's ideas from *The Writings of Thomas Jefferson* (Washington, 1903), II, 194–96, in Thomas Gossett, *Race: The History of an Idea in America* (Dallas, Tex.: Southern Methodist University Press, 1963), p. 42.
19. The one important attribute that Jefferson ascribed to both Caucasians and Negroes is the "moral sense," which, he argued, all human beings possess— even those inferior in reason and moral propriety. It is "the Jeffersonian

analogue of the Christian axiom that the Negro possessed a soul" (Jordan, *White Over Black,* pp. 439–40).

20. Jordan, *White Over Black,* p. 438.
21. Jean Fagan Yellin, *The Intricate Knot: Black Figures in American Literature, 1776–1863* (New York: New York University Press, 1972), p. 11.
22. Fredrickson, *The Black Image in the White Mind,* p. 2.
23. Gossett, *Race: The History of an Idea in America,* pp. 144, 244. 152.
24. Fredrickson, *The Black Image in the White Mind,* p. 321. This entire list is a paraphrase of Fredrickson, pp. 321–22.
25. Ibid., pp. 79–80.
26. Ibid., p. 83.
27. Claude McKay, in *Gingertown* (Freeport, N.Y.: Books for Libraries Press, 1972; rpt. Harper & Brothers Edition, 1932), p. 96.
28. Fredrickson, *The Black Image in the White Mind,* p. 162. My discussion of romantic racialism is drawn from Fredrickson's work, pp. 102–64.
29. Ibid., p. 164.
30. Ibid., p. 125.
31. Ibid., p. 232.
32. Charles Darwin, *The Descent of Man, and Selection in Relation to Sex,* vol. I (New York: D. Appleton and Company, 1871), p. 119.
33. Fredrickson, *The Black Image in the White Mind,* pp. 254–55.
34. Gossett, *Race: The History of an Idea in America,* p. 155.
35. As reported by E. Franklin Frazier, *Black Bourgeoisie* (New York: The Free Press, 1969), pp. 143–44.
36. Fredrickson, *The Black Image in the White Mind,* pp. 277–78.
37. Everett V. Stonequist, *The Marginal Man: A Study in Personality and Culture Conflict* (1937; rpt. New York: Russell & Russell, 1961), pp. 147–48.
38. Ashley Montagu, *Man's Most Dangerous Myth: The Fallacy of Race,* 4th ed. (Cleveland: World Publishing Company, 1964), p. 182.
39. The above discussion is based directly or indirectly on Gossett, *Race: The History of an Idea in America,* pp. 373, 409, 414, 416.
40. Myrdal, *An American Dilemma,* pp. 106–8.
41. Sinclair Lewis, *Kingsblood Royal* (New York: Random House, 1947), pp. 66–67, 194, 196.
42. Gossett, *Race: The History of an Idea in America,* p. 198.
43. T. S. Stribling, *Birthright* (New York: The Century Company, 1922), p. 81.
44. In "His Own Country," Paul Kester states that "Mr. Stribling's book broke ground for a white author in giving us a Negro hero and heroine. There is an obvious attempt to see objectively. But the formula of the Nineties-atavistic-race-heredity still survives." In *Black Expression,* ed. Addison Gayle, Jr. (New York: Weybright & Talley, 1969), pp. 173–74. See also Wilton E. Eckley, "The Novels of T. S. Stribling: A Socio-Literary Study," diss., Western Reserve University, 1965.
45. Stribling, *Birthright,* p. 264.
46. Larzer Ziff, *The American 1890s: Life and Times of a Lost Generation* (New York: Viking Press, 1966), pp. 256–57.

47. Frank Norris, *Works* (Garden City, N.Y., 1928), IV, 201–2 in Ibid., p. 259.

48. Norris, *The Octopus: A Story of California* (New York: Doubleday, Page & Company, 1904), p. 97.

49. Ziff, *The American 1890s*, p. 264.

50. Robert Lee Durham, *The Call of the South* (Boston: L. C. Page & Company, 1908), pp. 31, 119–20.

51. Ibid., p. 290. Other novelists also invoke the specter of atavism in order to frighten their white readers. The famous Negrophobe of the Reconstruction era, Thomas Dixon (whose 1905 novel *The Clansman: An Historical Romance of the Ku Klux Klan* was the basis for D. W. Griffith's classic film, *Birth of a Nation*) freely used the concept of atavism in his novels. The best example is his Silas Lynch, an important mulatto character in *The Clansman*. While he is civilized, polished, and charming on the exterior, inside, his savage blood boils: "his dark yellowish eyes beneath his heavy brows glowed with the brightness of the African jungle. It was impossible to look at his superb face . . . and watch his eyes gleam beneath the projecting forehead, without seeing pictures of the primeval forest" ([New York: Doubleday, Page & Company, 1905], pp. 92–93).

52. Ibid., p. 186.

53. Ibid., pp. 383–85.

54. Ibid., p. 439.

55. Harriet Beecher Stowe, *Dred: A Tale of the Dismal Swamp* in *The Writings of Harriet Beecher Stowe*, 16 vols. (Boston: Houghton Mifflin & Company, 1906), III, 76–77.

56. Richard Hildreth, *The Slave: or Memoirs of Archy Moore* (1836; rpt. Upper River, N.J.: Gregg Press, 1968), p. 8. Hildreth also uses half brothers much like Harry and Tom Gordon.

57. *Dred*, III, p. 46, 48.

58. *The Vengeance of the Gods and Three Other Stories of Real American Color Line Life* (Philadelphia: A. M. E. Book Concern, 1922), p. 11.

59. Ibid., p. 35.

60. Ibid., pp. 37–38.

61. Twain, *The Prince and the Pauper: A Tale for Young People of All Ages,* Harper and Brothers Edition (New York: P. F. Collier & Sons Company, 1921).

62. Twain, *A Connecticut Yankee in King Arthur's Court,* Harper & Brothers Edition (New York: P. F. Collier & Sons Company, 1917), pp. 265, 274–75.

63. Ibid., p. 114.

64. Twain, *What Is Man? and Other Essays* (New York and London: Harper & Brothers, 1917), p. 5.

65. William M. Gibson, ed., *The Chronicle of Young Satan in Mark Twain's Mysterious Stranger Manuscripts* (Berkeley and Los Angeles: University of California Press, 1969), p. 115.

66. Robert Rowlette, Mark Twain's Pudd'nhead Wilson: The Development and Design (Bowling Green, Ohio: Bowling Green University Popular Press, 1971), p. ix.

67. Twain, *Pudd'nhead Wilson and Those Extraordinary Twins,* Harper & Brothers edition (New York: P. F. Collier & Sons Company, 1922), p. 3.

68. Ibid., p. 17.
69. Twain, *The Adventures of Huckleberry Finn*, Harper & Brothers Edition (New York: P. F. Collier & Sons Company, 1912), pp. 306-7.
70. Twain, *A Connecticut Yankee*, p. 63. It is clear from a reading of Twain's works that while he explores "two possibilities for resisting the pressures of training: reason, which would expose the false assumptions underlying coercive social institutions; and switched-identity, which would teach the oppressor mercy by making him the victim of his own attitudes" (Rowlette, p. x), he has little faith in the reasoning and ability of the "damned human race." Thus, Twain turned again and again to the theme of switched identity.
71. James Melville Cox, *Mark Twain: The Fate of Humor* (Princeton, N.J.: Princeton University Press, 1966), pp. 228-29.
72. Henry Nash Smith, *Mark Twain: The Development of a Writer* (Cambridge, Mass.: Harvard University Press, 1962), pp. 73-74.
73. Twain, *Pudd'nhead Wilson*, p. 75.
74. Ibid., p. 10.
75. Ibid., p. 23.
76. Ibid., p. 13.
77. Ibid., p. 123.
78. Ibid., p. 97.
79. Twain, *Connecticut Yankee*, p. 177.
80. Twain, *Pudd'nhead Wilson*, p. 23.
81. Ibid., p. 29.
82. Ibid., p. 28.
83. Smith, *Mark Twain: The Development of a Writer*, pp. 179-80.
84. Twain, *What Is Man?*, pp. 52-53.
85. Twain, *Pudd'nhead Wilson*, p. 31.
86. Rowlette, *Twain's Pudd'nhead Wilson*, p. 96.
87. Ibid., p. 97.
88. Ibid.
89. Ibid.
90. Smith, *Mark Twain: The Development of a Writer*, pp. 179-80.
91. The Morgan manuscript, which contains Twain's working version of the novel, has been edited by Daniel Morley McKeithan in *The Morgan Manuscript of Mark Twain's Pudd'nhead Wilson* (Cambridge, Mass., 1961).
92. Twain, *Twain's Pudd'nhead Wilson*, pp. 137-38.
93. Ibid., p. 216.
94. Cox, *Mark Twain*, pp. 232-33.
95. *Pudd'nhead Wilson*, p. 203.
96. Robert Regan, *Unpromising Heroes: Mark Twain and His Characters* (Berkeley and Los Angeles: University of California Press, 1966), p. 216.
97. John Freimarck, "*Pudd'nhead Wilson*: A Tale of Blood and Brotherhood," *University Review*, 33-34 (October 1967-June 1968), 303.
98. Twain, *Pudd'nhead Wilson*, p. 201.

3.

Mulatto Fiction:
Myths, Stereotypes, and Reality

One motif is repeated again and again in the literature on the mulatto experience: the tragic dichotomy between the promise of the American dream and the grim reality of life in America for the marginal member of the lower caste. Richard Wright has said that "The History of the Negro in America is the history of America written in vivid bloody terms; it is the history of Western Man writ small." [1] But the mulatto, even more than the full-blooded Negro, is "America's metaphor." Many of the offspring of interracial unions suffered rejection by their white fathers and white siblings, and sometimes by their "own group" as well. While the mulatto may advance more rapidly in the areas of education, employment opportunity, and social standing, he often suffers greater psychological oppression because of his uncertain affiliation with either group and the envy with which many members of the lower caste regard him.

Many authors, both black and white, have regarded the mulatto as a particularly apt figure to symbolize the failure of the American myth of egalitarianism. It is essentially racist, of course, to regard the sufferings of lighter-skinned members of the lower caste as somehow greater than those of darker-skinned Negroes. In numerous works by abolitionist authors, in many novels of passing, and in many works that utilize the tragic mulatto theme, white authors have relied upon a greater sense of identification of their audience with the mulatto. Because these mixed-blood characters are so often beautiful or handsome, intelligent and courageous, the caste distinctions assume a tentativeness that these authors do not project when depicting the full-blooded black proletariat. Many of the early black novelists used the mulatto character in order to emphasize his superiority, to show white America that some blacks could succeed within the framework established by the dominant white majority, and to attack American society for not recognizing the worth of some members of the non-Caucasian group.

On many different levels, then, the mulatto character has had a significant role in American fiction, especially in southern fiction. Nancy Tischler says that the mulatto character "is indispensable to a literature that reflects the area, its taboos and myths, its fears and lusts, its shame and its burdens. The mulatto is the only-too-obvious badge of white abuse of the Negro, of the hidden anguish of the system of slavery, of the continuing hypocrisy in racial attitudes. He is a familiar mystery to the Southerner, the bar sinister of his family, his servant and his brother, a man of his own race whose whole life is alien and enigmatic to the white man." [2]

Historical Review

1760-1845

According to Alain Locke, the period from 1760 to 1820 was marked by the development of the "noble savage" figure—the full-blooded African, the "noble captive." In the period between 1820 and 1845, Locke tells us, "the mulatto house servant concubine and her children" are ignored. [3] Locke does not deal with the first American novel in which a mulatto character is significant: James Fenimore Cooper's *The Last of the Mohicans* (1826). As Leslie Fiedler has pointed out, Cora Munro—the dark-haired passionate woman who is the child of a Negro slave and a British officer—and fair-haired, sexless Alice Munro—her half sister—are "pure essences."

"The passionate brunette and the sinless blonde, make once and for all the pattern of female Dark and Light that is to become the standard form in which American writers project their ambivalence toward women." [4] How much greater is this dichotomy when the sinless, sexless Alice is a pure Caucasian and the passionate, instinctual Cora "is corrupted woman, stained even before birth with the blackness of the primitive and passional." [5] Cooper does not permit Cora to be joined with the two Indians who destroy each other; he will not allow miscegenation. Her death is Cooper's admission of American society's inability to provide a meaningful position for Cora and those like her.

1845-1865

During the antebellum period, the mulatto character played a central role in the American novel. Almost all of the novels of this period which feature mulattoes are antislavery tracts. Penelope Bullock effectively summarizes the mulatto character that emerges in the American novel between 1845 and 1865. This figure is, first of all, the all-but-white son (or occasionally a daughter) of a southern white gentleman and a slave, often a mixed blood herself. He is extremely intelligent, sensitive, proud, upright, and respectable. All of these qualities, especially his intellectual abilities, are seen as coming from the father. Yet the mixed blood's life is fraught with tragedy and bitterness because his culture has defined him as a Negro and a slave. But the "indomitable spirit of his father rises up within him, and he rebels. If he is successful in escaping to freedom, he becomes a prosperous, happy, and reputable citizen, an asset to the community, whether he be in Canada, Liberia, or Mississippi. But even if his revolt against slavery proves to be a failure, he meets his tragic death nobly and defiantly." [6]

The antislavery novel was openly propagandistic, and the Negro characters—both mulatto and full-blooded—clearly reflected "the distortions of moralistic controversy"; the Negro was made into "a wax-figure of the market place." [7] The purpose of these novels was to arouse pity for the oppressed slave: floggings, the separation of families, the cruelty of ruthless traders, the squalor and misery of the slave huts that contrasted so sharply from the gaiety and luxury of the "big house" were all stock elements of this genre.[8] The Negro characters of abolitionist literature yearned for freedom and had the courage to try to attain it. And in all of this, the mulatto was extremely important. The antislavery writer "was deeply concerned with miscegenation and its consequences, because he wanted to make his white reader keenly aware of the fact that his own was enslaved, relegated to the level of a chattel, and treated no differently from an inferior Negro. If for no other reason than to free white aristocratic blood, emancipation must be proclaimed." [9] To this end, the mulatto character was the superior character already described. Moreover, these characters were *always* the children of southern aristocratic fathers. In spite of the racism inherent in the attitudes of some abolitionist authors, it should be pointed out that these same authors often portrayed full-blooded blacks as being noble and independent of spirit.

The mixed-blood characters in these novels fit the stereotype outlined by Bullock. The reader was to be dazzled by their beauty, virtue, and intelligence. In *Uncle Tom's Cabin,* George Harris—one of the central characters in the novel—is a mixed blood whose father was a southern aristocrat and whose mother was a beautiful slave. Mrs. Stowe says that "From one of the proudest families in Kentucky he had inherited a set of fine European features, and a high, indomitable spirit. . . . [His] gracefulness of movement and gentlemanly manners had always been perfectly natural to him." [10] When George is hired out by his master to work in a bagging factory, he invents a machine for cleaning hemp, which Mrs. Stowe calls a feat of "mechanical genius." He is extremely bitter about his situation, but his fury over his enslavement makes him all the more attractive to the antislavery author. At one point, just after he has expressed a good deal of self-pity, his "manliness" reasserts itself and he angrily levels an attack touching on the very basis of the slave system. When his wife Eliza reminds him to forbear the harshness of his master, he answers: "My master! and who made him my master? That's what I think of—what right has he to me? I'm a man as much as he is." Had Mrs. Stowe stopped here, we might have said that George spoke for all back people. But in fact he emphasized his abilities and attainments as accounting for equality with his master. Thus George continues: "I know more about business than he does; I am a better manager than he is; I can read better than he can; I can write a better hand,—and I've learned it all myself, and no thanks to him,—I've learned it in spite of him; and now what right does he have to make a dray-horse of me?" [11] George says that he *will* be free: "I'll be free, or I'll die!" [12] George even denies that he has a country, for what country is his when the laws are used only to deny such as he his freedom. "Haven't I heard your Fourth-of-July speeches? Don't you tell us all, once a year, that governments derive their just power from the consent of the governed? Can't a fellow *think*, that hears such things?" [13] And in his greatest despair George even asks, "Is there a God to trust 'n?" [14]

However, Harriet Beecher Stowe was a member of the romantic racialists, to use George M. Fredrickson's terms, who saw blacks as an embodiment of Christian martyrdom. Mrs. Stowe praises the Africans for "their gentleness, their lowly docility of heart, . . . their childlike simplicity of affection, and felicity of forgiveness." [15] Mrs. Stowe's mulatto characters, however, are presented quite differently. Jean Fagan Yellin explains that "This Christian transvaluation enables Mrs. Stowe to include the racist stereotypes of plantation fiction in her antislavery novel. Her color scheme is rigid. Black people are inevitably subservient; mulattoes, who do not exist in plantation fiction, combine the sensitivity of their black mothers with the strength of their white fathers." [16]

Both Yellin and Fredrickson point out that contemporary observers argued about whether Stowe's work was racist.

> Since the restive and rebellious mulattoes who appear in romantic racialist novels like *Uncle Tom's Cabin* and *Maum Guinea* [another popular antislavery novel, written in 1861 by Metta V. Victor] are treated sympathetically, their characterization brings to the fore a serious question about the totality of the commitment, on the part of the white authors, to the submissive virtues attributed to the full-blooded Negro. When he reviewed *Uncle Tom's Cabin* in the *Liberator* in 1852, William Lloyd Garrison, himself a dedicated believer in "Christian non-resistance" for all races, raised the possibility that "Mrs. Stowe might have a double standard." "We are curious to know," he asked, "whether Mrs. Stowe is a believer in the

duty of non-resistance for the white man, under all possible outrage and peril as well as for the black man." [17]

Abolitionist novels are filled with characters like George Harris. His wife, Eliza, a beautiful light-skinned woman of grace and refinement, does not hesitate for a moment when her child is about to be sold. She flies instantly for Canada with the child: she, too, will be free or die. Harry Gordon, a mixed-blood character who plays a major role in *Dred*, is similar to George Harris. Again, Mrs. Stowe emphasizes the injustice of withholding legal rights from a man of education, honor, and breeding.

All of the novels reviewed thus far deal with mulatto characters continuously aware of their status. But several antislavery novels deal with mulatto characters who discover their "Negro blood" only after they become adults. Van Burean Denslow's *Owned and Disowned (1857)*, Mary Pike's *Caste (1856)*, and H. L. Hosmer's *Adela, the Ocotroon* (1860) are three such novels. Like other female mulatto characters of the period, Adela's fate is decided by marriage to a white man and a return to the dominant caste. The type of the noble full-blooded Negro appears in *Adela, the Octoroon, Uncle Tom's Cabin, Dred, The Slave,* and *Clotelle* (1853) by William Wells Brown—the first Negro novel in American literature.

Brown, a celebrated black abolitionist, derived the main narrative of his novel from Lydia Maria Child's sentimental antislavery tale "The Quadroons." [18] Many of Brown's writings included the figure of the beautiful white slave girl. But part of the narrative was based on the actual history of a beautiful light-skinned slave woman named Ellen Craft and her dark-skinned husband William. Ellen had passed disguised as a young white gentleman; William had played the part of her slave. The daring escape of this couple captured the imagination of the many who heard the Crafts' lecture on antislavery or read their *Running a Thousand Miles for Freedom.* [19] According to Jean Fagan Yellin, Brown changed Maria Child's pathetic story so as to model Clotelle in part on Ellen Craft:

When Clotel is a cast off by her weak lover and sold by his jealous wife, instead of dying of a broken heart like Mrs. Child's rejected heroine, she disguises herself as Ellen Craft had, and escapes North with another slave masquerading as her black servant.[20]

When Clotelle returns to Virginia in an attempt to find her daughter, she is seized as a fugitive. She escapes once again but is trapped by slave catchers and jumps to her death in order to avoid capture.

Clotelle offers both sermons about and depictions of the condition of the Negro slave, features common to all abolitionist novels. But Brown's work offers a unique element in a novel of this genre. *Clotelle* depicts the first legal union of a "black" woman and a white man in American literature. She marries twice, once to a white man, the second time to her long-lost black lover.

There is one other significant antislavery work that must be mentioned here because it provides a striking contrast to the work of many of the white abolitionist novelists: Martin Robinson Delaney's 1859 fragment, *Blake; or the Huts of America.* Addison Gayle, Jr., states that this novel, which was rediscovered in 1970 in the incomplete files of the *Weekly Anglo-African,*[21] is the most important novel by a black before Sutton Griggs's *Imperium in Imperio* because it provides a counterimage and attack on both Uncle Tom [22] and mulattoes. Gayle calls the protagonist, Henry Holland, the "first black revolutionary character in black fiction." [23] Holland (also known as Henrico Blacus) is a courageous, determined, pure-blooded Negro who not only denounces the master-father of his mulatto wife for having sold her but organizes a massive slave insurrection and finds and manumits his wife. In sharp contrast to Blacus is Harriet Beecher Stowe's black rebel, Dred. Modeled on Nat Turner, he is supposed to be Denmark Vesey's son. Viewed as a kind of madman, he wanders the swamps wrapped in visions. "To Harriet Beecher Stowe," George Fredrickson asserts, "a black rebel was clearly a warped and deviant personality, forced by unnatural pressures to depart from the racial type of the 'natural' Negro; under more favorable circumstances, Dred might have been an Uncle Tom." [24]

1865-1908

Stereotypes of the mulatto established in the abolitionist period changed drastically during the era of Reconstruction and, later,

the era of Jim Crowism. Abolitionist writers had elevated the
Negro, and especially the mixed-blood character, to the role of
heroic victim who would be free or die. Postbellum literature had
its own stereotypes, both positive and negative.

In the novels of the Negrophobes—writers like Thomas Dixon,
Robert Lee Durham, and (sometimes) Thomas Nelson Page—the
mixed blood combines the worst traits of both races. The "brute
Negro" who lusts after white women is examplified in Moses, the
mulatto trick doctor of Page's 1900 novel, *Red Rock: A Chronicle of
Reconstruction.* He is compared with a "hyena," a "reptile," and a
"wild beast." Page's description of Moses is significant because in it
we can see the irrational landscape of the nightmare. Alain Locke
is partially correct in asserting that much of this kind of literature
is really an expression of the unconscious fears, wishes, and taboos
of the white man.[25] But the Negrophobe authors were consciously
propagandistic, and the expression of their unconscious attitudes is
perhaps even more important than their intentional purposes in
understanding their stereotypical visions of the mixed blood (and
of the Negro in general). Through their literature, they tapped the
complex (often unconscious) reactions to race on the part of their
white readers. Certainly, black authors reacted angrily to the
"brute" Negro, "tigress," and mixed-blood stereotypes drawn by
these authors. Moses is a "grotesque figure":

> His chin stuck so far forward that the lower teeth were outside
> of the upper, or at least, the lower jaw was; for the teeth
> looked as though they had been ground down, and his gums,
> as he grinned, showed as blue on the edges as if he had
> painted them. His nose was so short and the upper part of his
> face receded so much that the nostrils were unusually wide,
> and gave an appearance of a black circle in his yellow
> countenance . . . [on his face] were certain lines which looked
> as if they had been tattooed. Immediately under these were a
> pair of little furtive eyes which looked in quite different
> directions, and yet almost seemed as if they were both focused
> on the same object. Large brass earrings were in his ears, and
> about his throat was a necklace of blue and white beads.

Page carries the mythology to its most frightening conclusion (to whites) when Moses claims, "I'm just as good as any white man, and I'm goin' to show 'em so. I'm goin' to marry a white 'ooman and meck white folks wait on me." [26]

Many black novelists chose to answer the Negrophobes not by emphasizing the pathos or tragedy of being Negro, as many Caucasian authors had done, but by defending the cause of the freedman. Novelists like Sutton Griggs, in *The Hindered Hand: or, The Reign of the Repressionist* (1905), *Imperium in Imperio: A Study of the Negro Race Problem* (1899), and *Pointing the Way* (1908); Frances E. W. Harper in *Iola Leroy* (1892); G. Langhorne Pryor in *Neither Bond Nor Free* (1902); Pauline Hopkins in *Contending Forces: A Romance Illustrative of Negro Life North and South* (1900); and Albion Tourgée, the white author, in *Pactolus Prime* (1890) made this truly the "Age of Discussion" in the novel of Negro life.[27] These authors argued the merits of the differing means of achieving political, social, and economic rights for the Negro. In these novels, the political programs of Booker T. Washington, W. E. B. Du Bois, and various separatist platforms were discussed. The mixed-blood characters in Griggs's novels are almost all political leaders. There are female as well as male race leaders among them. This represents a significant change in the presentation of the female mulatto character. Here she is more aggressive in working for the rights of blacks and is not always confined within traditional female roles. The solutions to the race problem are varied—from settlement in Liberia (the choice of George Harris in *Uncle Tom's Cabin* and Merna Attaway in *Neither Bond nor Free*) to the takeover by force of the state of Texas (the program of one of Griggs's characters).

These novels are continual testimonials to the idea that "black is beautiful" (even if one is almost white), and to the proposition that all Negroes should unite, whatever their color or background. When a white army officer in *Iola Leroy* says that it "is a burning shame to have held such a man as you in slavery" [a very light-skinned, "superior" Negro], the man answers, "I don't think it was any worse to have held me in slavery than the blackest man in the South." [28] All of Mrs. Harper's mixed-blood characters are fervent race leaders and have no prejudice toward darker-skinned Negroes. Various characters express satisfaction that a full-blooded Negro has received public recognition for an achievement. But these matters must be deferred until chapter 8, which deals with the fictional mulatto as race leader and the political arguments expressed in the novels in which this is a major theme.

Robert Bone sees the black authors of the early Negro novel—from *Clotelle, The Garies and Their Friends* (1857) by Frank J. Webb, *Iola Leroy* (1892) by Frances E.W. Harper, *The House Behind the Cedars* (1900) and *The Marrow of Tradition* (1901) by Charles Chesnutt to the novels of the Harlem Renaissance like *There is Confusion* (1924) and *The Chinaberry Tree* (1931) by Jessie Fauset—as part of the "Talented Tenth"—W. E. B. Du Bois's term for the Negro middle class. Whether the subject of these novels is miscegenation, passing, the plight of the tragic mulatto, the virtues of the Negro professional class, or the activities of the mulatto race leader—they all have some essential traits in common. They were written by men and women who had "just arrived" themselves. They took the American dream, with its "success ideology," quite seriously. Their novels are "genteel"; they are marked by a great deal of stilted dialogue and "high-flown" passages of description. Furthermore, virtually all of these literary works are melodramas. This limitation, Bone claims, proved to be an asset: "The early novelist had his own reasons for refusing to venture beyond the plot level of characterization. Caught between anti-Negro stereotypes and his own counter-stereotypes, he was never able to achieve a rounded treatment of his Negro characters. In the end he avoided the problem by seeking refuge in the flat, static characters of conventional melodrama." [29] But the fact that these novelists did not solve the problem of rounded characterization of blacks and mulattoes made the early novel an aesthetic failure: "Most of the early novelists fell between the stools of buffoonery and counterstereotype. Writing for a double audience, they attempted to conciliate both white and colored, by including clown and Apollo in the same novel." [30]

1908-1924: Black-authored Mulatto Fiction

Black novelists between 1908 and 1920 continued to attack the doctrines and mythology of Negrophobes like Dixon and Durham. The Negro novelists answered the white racists with political arguments and with a succession of characters of spotless virtue and outstanding intelligence. The novels of Charles Chesnutt, Oscar Mischeaux, F. Grant Gilmore, Henry F. Downing and others all employ this kind of mixed-blood character. Beulah Johnson found that the black female characters who appear in the Negro novels of this period are beautiful (in Caucasian terms), morally upstanding, prim, and wealthy (or at least comfortable).[31] They are neither passionate, sensual, nor poor—as are so many of the female characters of the novels of the Harlem Renaissance and the later Negro novel. In *Sex and Racism in America,* Calvin Hernton states that the "ideal woman" and the "white woman" somehow are one and the same in the minds of black males. Certainly the mulatto women characters of this period would have been at ease in a Victorian drawing room and are indistinguishable from any of the other "dainty" (white) ladies.

The issues of "passing" and "intermarriage" became important for black novelists during this period. Griggs and Chesnutt, both of whom are discussed at other points in this study, dealt with these topics extensively. The problem of intermarriage is also of central importance in Oscar Mischeaux's two novels, *The Conquest* (1913) and *The Homesteader* (1915). In *Redder Blood* (1915), William M. Ashby "went a step further than Oscar Mischeaux by stressing that no social or legal restrictions are strong enough to keep two lovers apart." [32] In Herman Dreer's 1919 novel, *The Immediate Jewel of His Soul,* intermarriage is approved, and in Joshua Henry Jones's *By Sanction of Law* (1924) intermarriage is unapologetically proposed as a solution to the race problem in this country.[33]

James Weldon Johnson's 1912 *Autobiography of an Ex-Coloured Man* is clearly the most important black-authored novel of this period. Its major theme is passing. The mulatto protagonist must decide whether to pass, in order to benefit from a white middle-class life-style, or to affiliate with the black group, thereby serving his own artistic development and his race. (This novel is discussed in detail in Chapter 6.)

1900-1930: White-authored Mulatto Fiction

White-authored novels during this period fall into several categories. Both black and white novelists were beginning to see new roles for their mulatto (and black) female characters. The old stereotypes, however, were slow to disappear. The white version of the tragic mulatto stereotype—the divided soul of the mixed-blood character who desires a white lover but suffers a "tragic" demise—

was a century old by this time. The Negro version of the unhappy passer or the middle-class mulatto who denies his or her people is essentially a Harlem Renaissance phenomenon. In the white version, the mulatto usually dies; in the black version, he is "summoned back to his people by the spirituals, or their full-throated laughter, or their simple sweet ways." As Sterling Brown points out, both versions are examples of race flattery.[34] The tragic mulatto figure, especially the beautiful, almost-white woman in whom white and black blood do battle, remains a figure of fascination for white authors. Vera Caspary's *The White Girl* (1929), Geoffrey Barnes's *Dark Lustre* (1932), Marie Stanley's *Gulf Stream* (1931), Evans Wall's *The No-Nation Girl* (1929) and *Love Fetish* (1933) contain tragic mulatto characters. (They will be discussed in Chapter 4.) Many of these works have fantastic plots, no characterization, and ridiculous dialogue. The racism of all of the works in this genre is apparent.

In her 1909 novella *Melanctha: Each One as She May,* Gertrude Stein works with a different stereotype—the mulatto as "exotic." However, Melanchtha is not a pure "exotic"; she is sensual and mysterious, but, like the tragic mulatto character, tormented. Also like the tragic mulatto character, Melanctha dies young. Stein describes her as being "pale yellow and mysterious and a little pleasant like her mother, but the real power in Melanctha's nature came through her robust and unpleasant and very unendurable black father." [35] She has an "inborn intense wisdom," [36] which somehow causes her great suffering. Melanctha, never a real character, it seems to me, is an embodiment of what today we would call "soul." She goes with many men; she is restless, yet often quiet and intensely sensuous; she is "mysterious"—an adjective Stein uses over and over; she is languid and yet seems intensely wound up. Her "mystery" seems to arise out of these contradictions. The rhythms of Stein's prose are incantatory; she uses a great deal of repetition in the manner of the oral storyteller. In Melanctha's abandonment to men and to one woman, in her "knowledge of what everybody wanted," in her silent, earthy wisdom, and in her mystery, she reminds us of Toomer's female mulatto characters in *Cane.* However, her need for the lazy, dull, black Rose; her rejection by Jim Richards, a light-skinned gambling man who "had always all his life been understanding"; [37] and her ultimate death by consumption combine traits of the exotic with those of the tragic mulatto. As Stein presents her, Melanctha displays the seemingly irrational, moody conduct that has been viewed as a function of the racial disharmony of the mulatto.

At the end of this period, there appeared a serious work of art by a little-known author, Gilmore Millen's *Sweet Man* (1930). Although it is not always successful, because Millen does not have sufficient control, it is an interesting example of mulatto fiction. The plot concerns John Henry, a light-skinned southern black whose diligent work as a sharecropper comes to an end when he refuses to be exploited and wanders to Memphis and other places. He becomes the "sweet man" of a prostitute; he gets involved with other black women; and finally he is taken as a lover by a white woman. Not only does Millen write well of the sharecropping life and of Beale Street in Memphis, but he also attempts—at times quite successfully—to record John Henry's changing attitude toward whites. His protagonist moves from awe and fear to eventual hatred and contempt. By the end of the novel, he is prepared to return to his light-skinned, educated wife who has remained in the country. However, when he tries to say good-bye to his white lover, she tries to shoot him and is instead accidentally shot herself. When he realizes what has happened, John Henry kills himself rather than wait for death at the hands of the state. The final image of the novel is that of a white woman and a black man, both dead, inextricably imprisoned in the collective psychoses of race and sexism in America. The lost potential of the mulatto black man in America is powerfully realized in this novel.

The Harlem Renaissance

Those who regarded themselves as part of the Harlem Renaissance were intent on proving that "black is beautiful." Most of the major Renaissance authors dealt with the mulatto in one way or another. Jessie Fauset, Walter White, Nella Larsen, Claude McKay, and Rudolph Fisher focused their attention on the black bourgeoisie.[38] Of these authors, only Fauset espoused the virtues of bourgeois gentility, although she, too, did not approve of passing as

could have another child with very little risk of sickle-cell anemia. During the testing, the counselor learns that the wife has the gene but the husband does not- and also realizes that the husband is not the biological father of the child.

6) Should a minor be tested for an untreatable genetic disease?
    If your 16-year-old daughter might have the gene for developing breast cancer, would you want her to know? Only about 5% of the cases of breast cancer are due to inheriting a damaged BRCA1 gene, but 80% of those who inherit the gene develop cancer. There is a probability that the laboratory findings could be false positive or false negative. The results might affect whether she can get health insurance coverage in the future. Who should make the decision about genetic testing?

7) Should a school have special education students genetically tested?
    A New York school board pondered whether special education students should be tested for fragile-X syndrome. Would this affect services provided, as well as the effort made to help these students? Who should make the decision about the testing?

8) Should we legally intervene?
    There are several cases of addicted pregnant women being held in custody to prevent them from drinking and/or using drugs. These drugs would affect the developing child in the womb. Should this happen? Why or why not?

9) Should we require testing?
    Should pregnant women be required to be tested for HIV or other infections? What impact would your decision have on pregnant women? On society?

1) Who are the real parents?

A child is a product of in vitro fertilization. Who are the parents: the anonymous man and woman who donated the sperm and egg, the surrogate mother who carried the pregnancy to term, the surrogate's husband, and the husband and wife who arranged for her birth? In a California case, the husband and wife who arranged for the birth of the child divorced, and the husband claimed that he was not the child's legal father because she was not "a child of the marriage." What do you think the court decided? Why?

2) What should a genetic counselor advise?

A husband and wife are both achondroplastic dwarfs, a genetic condition that affects appearance but not intellect. They want genetic analysis of their fetus, which they intend to abort if it would become a child of normal stature.

3) What should a genetic counselor advise?

A 40-year-old woman chooses to be tested and hears bad news: She as the BRCA1 gene, which gives her about an 80 percent chance of developing breast cancer before age 70, and perhaps ovarian or colon cancer as well. She refuses to believe the evidence and insists that no one tell her family, including her mother, her four sisters, and her three daughters. Several of them probably have the gene and may be in the early stages of cancer without knowing it.

4) What should a genetic counselor advise?

A 30-year-old mother of two daughters (no sons) learns that she is a carrier for hemophilia. She requests pre-implantation analysis, demanding that only male embryos without her hemophilia-carrying X chromosome be implanted. This means that female zygotes, only half of which would even be carriers, would be given no chance to develop.

5) What should a genetic counselor advise?

the means by which to achieve this gentility. Nor did she approve of an excessive concern for respectability. The novels of the other Renaissance authors listed above are unlike the works of the Talented Tenth and Fauset. These "new" novelists attacked the narrow, confining code of the middle-class Negro community, with its excessive concern for color, (white) ancestry, money, and the symbols of status—and its fostering of unspontaneous behavior. Their novels (most of which are covered in detail elsewhere, especially in Chapters 6 and 7) condemn passing and immersion in the bourgeoisie and uphold the virtues of the "Negro folk"—their warmth, vitality, spontaneity, sensuality, and creativity.

One of the most interesting novels of the Renaissance is Rudolph Fisher's *The Walls of Jericho* (1928). In his work, we can see the Renaissance attack on the black bourgeoisie and the positive treatment of "ordinary" blacks described above. But Fisher intended more than this. He wanted to accomplish in fictional form nothing less than the elimination of intracaste prejudice. To unite "dickty" (member of the black bourgeoisie) and "rat" (member of the black folk or proletariat) is his aim, and he achieves it admirably.

Like many authors both before and after him, Fisher was fascinated by the diversity of types found in Harlem. Like Nella Larsen or Ray Stannard Baker, to give just two examples, Fisher describes in detail the "mere matter of complexion." At the conclusion of his list of hues, not one of which is "without its peculiar richness," he avows that "Harlem is superlatively rich in diversity." [39] More important than the mere diversity is what he calls "a complete philosophy of skin color." [40] In order to illustrate this philosophy, Fisher describes in detail the annual costume ball of the General Improvement Association, which he uses as a microcosm for all intracaste relations within black culture. He tells us that everyone was there, from the "rattiest rat to the dicktiest dickty." What is most significant is the pattern of social intercourse that prevails: "Ordinary Negroes and rats below, dickties and fays above. ... Somehow, undeniably, a predominance of darker skins below, and, just as undeniably, of fairer skins above. Between them, stairways to climb. One might have read in that distribution a complete philosophy of skin-color, and from it deduced the past, present, and future of this people. ... Out on the dance floor, everyone, dicky and rat, rubbed joyous elbows, laughing, mingling, forgetting differences. But whenever the music stopped everyone immediately sought his own level." [41]

The particular "dickty" who plays a central role in *The Walls of Jericho* is a wealthy attorney named Fred Merrit. We see him first through the eyes of two comic black characters—Jinx and Bubber—who function as a chorus of "the people." In the opening scene of the novel, they discuss the ethics of Merrit's proposed move to an exclusive white neighborhood. Jinx doesn't believe that "shines" have a right to live in a "fay" neighborhood. Bubber, his buddy and fellow moving man, disagrees with him strongly. Jinx says: " 'Hyeh's a dickty tryin' his damnedest to be fay—like all d' other dickties.' When they git in hot water they all come cryin' to you and me fo' help." Bubber says, "Fays don' see no difference 'tween dickty shines and any other kind of shines. One jig in danger is ev'y jig in danger. They'd lick *them* and come down on *us*. Then we'd have to fight anyhow. What's use o' waitin'?" [42] This early conversation exposes the opposing philosophies—those of intracaste prejudice versus the unity of the oppressed—which Fisher explores throughout *The Walls of Jericho*.

Fisher presents us with ample reason for the bad reputation of the dickties. He shows us a meeting of the Litter Rats Club, the members of which are mostly like J. Pennington Potter, president of the group. He is a self-inflated phony who pretends to care about the black masses but really despises them. At the General Improvement Association's Annual Costume Ball, described above, J. Pennington Potter naturally sits upstairs in a box he shares with the dicktiest of the dickties, and with the few Caucasian "do-gooders" in attendance. Potter has no difficulty getting along with patronizing white racists like Miss Agatha Cramp, who observes how primeval the blacks are as they dance at the ball.

Fred Merrit's attitude toward whites and blacks is diametrically opposed to Potter's. Although he has rosy cheeks, virtually white skin and sandy (although kinky) hair, he identifies wholly with the black group. Fisher tells us that "not the blackest of Negroes could have hated the dominant race more thoroughly." [43] And while he cursed all those responsible for his "mongrel heritage," he made an exception of his mother: "She had always seemed to him a symbol of sexual martyrdom, a bearer of the cross, as he put it, which fair manhood universally placed on dark womanhood's shoulders." [44]

Fred Merrit's racial philosophy is made apparent during a conversation that occurs during the costume ball. Like the other dickties, he sits above the rats and ordinary Negroes. However, there the similarity ends. When Agatha Cramp, who thinks Merrit is white, remarks upon the unspoiled nature of blacks, Merrit answers, "Beautiful savages." Miss Cramp, encouraged by Merrit's response, says "What abandonment—what restraint—." Then Merrit, eyes twinkling, adds: "Almost as bad as a Yale-Harvard football game."[45]

Earlier in the novel Merrit had demonstrated his camaraderie with other blacks, even those clearly outside his class. When Jinx and Bubber move Merrit's possessions to the elite Court Avenue, they are astonished by his cordiality. They are confused by Merrit. After all, they know that dickties cannot be trusted. The problem is that Merrit's behavior does not conform to the stereotype held by Jinx, Bubber and Joshua Jones (also known as "Shine"), the "tranquil young Titan" [46] who is the protagonist of the novel: "What manner of dickty was this? He greeted you like an equal, casually shared his troubles with you, and did not seem to care in the least what the devil you did with his furniture. . . . Shine said to himself, "If this bird wasn't a dickty he'd be o.k. But they never was a dickty worth a damn." [47]

During the course of the novel, however, Shine is proven wrong. Fisher shows us the "coming of age" of Joshua Jones. Through his love for a lovely young woman named Linda, he has become softened, humanized. Thus, even though at one point in the novel Shine believes Merrit to have been Linda's attacker, the "young Titan" does what he could never have done before—he exits and leaves his enemy alone when he sees Merrit crying over a picture of his mother. Joshua Jones has won the "Battle" for which the penultimate section of the book is entitled.

The concluding section of the novel, entitled "Jericho," depicts the victorious unity of the oppressed. Shine, Jinx, and Bubber are all out of work when the elderly owner of the small moving company dies. As Shine and Merrit drink, "rat and dickty, as equals," [48] Merrit suggests that he buy the one-truck moving business and turn it over to Shine to run. He offers Shine 50 percent of the profits with an option to buy.

In a speech that provides a striking illustration of the Harlem Renaissance philosophy of self-help and racial pride, Merrit explained to Shine: "That's what we Negroes need, business class, an economic backbone. What kind of a social structure can anybody have with nothing but the extremes—bootblacks on one end and doctors on the other. Nothing in between." [49] Addison Gayle admirably sums up the import of the novel when he says that "Joshua Jones and Fred Merrit, men separated by color, education, and status, are sharers of the same culture, both outsiders in the American society, forged into unity as a result of historical patterns. ... When Fred Merrit, who is fair enough to pass for white, joins hands with Shine at the end of the novel, diversity remains still; it is, however, diversity with uniformity which enables the group, outsiders all, to unite in the pursuit of self-definition." [50]

Like Fisher, Jean Toomer also examined the issue of black identity in a way that was different from previous explorations. Toomer and other Harlem Renaissance writers took the formerly negative or patronizing appraisals of the Negro as "childlike" and "uncivilized" and viewed these traits and the characters who embodied them in a positive light.[51] In Toomer's classic work, *Cane* (1923), the longest and most compelling piece is "Kabnis," the portrait of a mulatto tormented by the magnetism of the black South yet unable to find his identity within it.

Toomer utilizes the mulatto elsewhere as well. In "Becky," the story of a white woman with two black sons, neither the white nor the black population will acknowledge Becky and her sons as their own, although she receives clandestine help from people of both races. The boys were "sullen and cunning" and no one knew to what race they belonged. "White or colored? No one knew, and least of all themselves." [52] Toomer's narrator says that the boys drifted from job to job, pariahs in their homeland: "We, who had cast out their mother because of them, could we take them in? They answered black and white folks by shooting up two men and leaving town. 'Goddam the white folks; goddam the niggers,' they shouted as they left town." [53]

"Fern" is the haunting story of a beautiful mulatto woman whose mother was black and father was Jewish. By virtue of her mingled blood, Toomer seems to be saying, she embodies the rich beauty and fullness of the South ("like her face, the whole countryside seemed to flow into her eyes" [54]) and the tormented spirituality of the Jews ("If you have heard a Jewish cantor sing, if he has touched you and made your own sorrow seem trivial when compared with his, you will know my feeling when I follow the curves of her profile, like mobile rivers, to their common delta" [55]). She is a compelling figure to the men who seek to possess her and instead find themselves possessed by her mystery. Toomer's figures, as many critics have observed, are mythic.

In "Esther," Toomer contrasted a mulatto girl who "looks like a little white child, starched, frilled," [56] prim and proper, with a powerful, fascinating, black-skinned Negro named King Barlo. Through his religious trances and preaching, King Barlo sways both whites and blacks. When Esther was nine years old, King Barlo shared his most magnificient vision with the townspeople and then disappeared—leaving his image imprinted upon Esther's mind. At sixteen, she begins to experience sexual fantasies that involve giving birth to an ugly black baby, Negroid in feature, who (like King Barlo) is sweet beneath the forbidding exterior. At twenty-two, Esther decides that she loves King Barlo, and at the age of twenty-seven she finally has the opportunity to offer herself to her dreamed-of lover. When she goes to the whorehouse to claim him, one of the women calls the richest colored man's daughter a "dictie nigger." [57] When Barlo understands Esther's purpose, he leers at her, and like the baby of Esther's dream he is a hideous, frightening black man very close indeed to the brute Negro stereotype of the 1890s. Unable to reconcile her sexuality and her defensive repressions, Esther is doomed to lonely spinsterhood.

In "Bona and Paul," Toomer tells the story of a white girl's attraction to a handsome mulatto boy whom she has met at school. Bona is powerfully drawn by Paul's difference, even though he presents himself as neither black nor white. Bona arranges for a date with Paul, and when they enter the fancy restaurant Paul becomes the object of the patrons' stares. People wonder: "What is he, a Spaniard, an Indian, an Italian, a Mexican, a Hindu, or a Japanese?" [58] Paul has a kind of revelation in response to this white attitude: "Suddenly he knew that he was apart from the people around him. Apart from the pain which they had unconsciously caused. Suddenly he knew that people saw, not attractiveness in his dark skin, but difference. Their stares, giving him to himself, filled something long empty within him, and were like green blades sprouting in his consciousness. There was fullness, and strength and peace about it all." [59] But when Paul attempts to explain his vision to the Negro doorman, to tell the black man why it is all right for him to go with Bona, Paul loses the girl. His moment has passed.

The last Renaissance work to be discussed is a work of satire in a class of its own: George S. Schuyler's *Black No More: Being an Account of the Strange and Wonderful Workings of Science in the Land of the Free, A.D. 1933-40* (1931). David Littlejohn is correct in saying that Schuyler writes "without control . . . and dilutes the high potential of his provocative idea." [60] But there is no other novel like it in American literature, and there are so many fine satiric touches that it deserves attention. A Dr. Junius Crookman discovers a way to turn black people into whites, and he opens a Sanitorium called BLACK-NO-MORE. He reasoned that "if there were no Negroes, there could be no Negro problem. . . . Like most men with a vision, a plan, a program, or a remedy, he fondly imagined people to be intelligent enough to accept a good thing when it was offered to them, which was conclusive evidence that he knew little about the human race." [61] All the blacks begin moving out of Harlem once they have had the treatment. Then Crookman reveals that the artificial Caucasians are lighter than the genuine whites. So a society that has been racist for so long swings right into gear, and segregation for pale children is established. "A Dr. Cutten Prod wrote a book proving that all enduring gifts to society come from those races whose skin color was not exceedingly pale." [62] The upper classes begin buying powders named Poudre Nigre, Poudre le Egyptienne, and L'Afrique. "A white face became startingly rare. America was definitely enthusiastically mulatto-minded." [63] Thus ends a novel in which Schuyler manages to attack just about everyone, black and white, and to satirize the various "solutions" to the race problem.

1932-1977: Black- and White-authored Mulatto Fiction

The novels of this period exhibit the influence of both the past and the present, as old patterns continue and new influences are brought to bear. In *Stephen Kent* (1935), by Hallie F. Dickerman, the old formula of racial atavism is utilized. In *Double Muscadine* (1949) by Frances Gaither, two mulatto women vie for the affections of their master in a plot marked by murder, intrigue, and suicide. *Mandingo* (1957) by Kyle Onstott is set in Latin America and comes close to being overt pornography.

Willa Cather's *Sapphira and the Slave Girl* (1940) covers the years between 1856 and 1892. Sapphira, a proud white woman who had been reared as an aristocrat on her father's Virginia plantation, is at odds with both her husband's and daughter's abolitionist views. When Sapphira observes the close relationship between her husband and the lovely mulatto slave Nancy, she will not be convinced that her jealousy has no basis, that the relationship is that of master and slave. (In fact, they share a mutual liking, but no more.) Sapphira's jealousy moves her to encourage her nephew Martin to seduce Nancy. The girl resists, however, and is eventually helped to freedom by Sapphira's own daughter. In Canada, she marries a well-to-do Scotch-Indian man.

While Cather's primary focus is on Sapphira's obsession with her husband's relationship with Nancy and her dissatisfaction with the life her miller husband provides her, the author also expresses her anti-slavery sentiments. Cather's portrayal of Nancy is very appealing: the young mulatto woman is sensitive, proud, brave, and independent. Unfortunately, the novel as a whole is weak, for Cather utilized many stereotypes and stock situations.

Frank Yerby, author of twenty-seven historical novels to date, has successfully employed the conventions of the genre. In *The Foxes of Harrow* (1946), Yerby's first published novel, the setting is New Orleans between 1825 and 1865. Stephen Fox, Yerby's dashing hero, is an outsider who builds the greatest mansion in Louisiana and marries New Orlean's most beautiful Creole belle. Because of his wife's frigidity, however, Stephen seeks comfort in the arms of the beautiful, passionate Desiree—a quadroon girl of sixteen who has been schooled in the art of loving since she was a small child.

Desiree explains to Stephen: " 'We are never young. We cannot afford youth. This wisdom, as you call it, is a thing handed down from mother to daughter for generations. This is what I was born for, monsieur.' " [64]

Yerby's depiction of the quadroons of New Orleans adheres to the usual pattern. He describes the magnificant quadroon balls at the Orleans Ballroom: "On the magnificent dance floor, constructed . . . of three thicknesses of cypress topped by a layer of quarter-sawed oak, the young, and not so young, gentlemen of New Orleans were dancing." [65] Against this backdrop, Stephen meets Desiree and woos her according to the rules of *plaçage:* he builds a beautiful home and secures servants for his mistress and agrees to provide for and educate any children born of the connection. Desiree's brother, Aupre, a cultivated, sensitive young man who has known freedom in France, is humiliated when he finds Stephen with Desiree. Aupre cannot "fight for his sister's honor," and her concubinage makes it intolerable for him to remain in New Orleans. When Stephen asks his mistress why she does not therefore marry one of her own men, Desiree replies: " 'They are not men. You do not permit them to be. When they rise up and attempt manhood, you shoot them down like dogs and exhibit their bodies in Jackson Square—like Brass Coupe, remember. To live at all they have to fawn and bow, and permit you the liberty of their homes and the favors of their daughters. I am a woman, monsieur; I can only love a man—not a thing!' " [66]

We next see Aupre several years later as he returns from France in the company of Stephen Fox's legitimate son, Etienne, and a painter named Paul Dumaine. Neither of these young men knows that Aupre is a mulatto. In France, Aupre had been hailed as one of France's leading playwrights. In fact, Etienne had fought a duel with Aupre because of the playwright's utilization of Stephen Fox as an object of satire. When Etienne is informed that he has fought a duel with a mulatto, he sets three powerful black field hands to inflict a beating upon Aupre. In the process, Aupre is killed. Desiree plans to take vengeance upon Etienne for the murder of her brother by killing him. However, she cannot go through with her plan because the son so reminds her of the father. At the conclusion of the novel, we see Desiree, now a woman of forty-three, wife of the highly cultured black politician, Inch—once boyhood companion and servant of Etienne Fox and now Commissioner of Police of New Orleans. Inch introduces Stephen and Etienne to his "son," the twenty-five year old Cyrus—the golden-haired, fair-skinned son of Stephen Fox and Desiree Hippolyte and half-brother of Etienne—the son Stephen had never known he had.

In *The Vixens* (1947), Yerby's next novel, Desiree makes a very brief appearance as she and her husband, Inch, leave New Orleans for an all-black community. But Desiree cannot share her husband's sense of peace and tranquillity as she prepares to leave her home because she is still a New Orleans quadroon. Inch provides a final characterization of Desiree when he reflects that "his wife's attitude towards the blacks differed only in degree from that of a white woman—not in kind. In her ordained scheme of things, he was the only exception. Inch sighed deeply. He knew the futility of trying to change attitudes that are based upon custom rather than reason. Yet, in a very real sense, he pitied her. By years of study and effort, by a relentless discipline of will, he had freed himself from prejudices of any sort, even against his enemies. But for Desiree it was too late—it had always been too late. . . ." [67]

The subject of sex plays some role in virtually every one of these novels of mulatto life. In *Sex and Racism in America,* Calvin C. Hernton analyzes the extraordinarily complex relationships—real and fantasized, individual and collective—that exist between white men and women, black men and women, white men and black women, and between black men and white women. Again and again in mulatto fiction, sex and racism are connected. Miscegenation (and all of the reactions it has spawned) naturally plays a major role in the fiction of the mixed blood. Indeed, the course of love relationships between "black" women and white men provides the most common plots in mulatto fiction.

Few authors have exploited the subject of sex and racism in mulatto fiction more consciously than Erskine Caldwell. In his 1949 novel, *Place Called Esterville,* he depicts the sexual exploitation of blacks by the white community. Caldwell is a poor writer and certainly does no justice to the complexity of his ideas. It is interesting to note, however, that more than a few critics and students of black literature regard Caldwell as a serious author of Negro-white life. *Place Called Esterville* does illustrate Hernton's contention that "the system of racism and white supremacy in the South has twisted the white man's concept of both Negro sexuality and his own" and that *"Southern white women are not only sexually attracted* by Negroes, but it is they who are the aggressors." [64] The brute Negro stereotype of Reconstruction times (Moses, Silas Lynch) and the suave, often talented, educated male mulatto whose lust or love for a white woman lies beneath a calm, civilized exterior (Hayward Graham) represents one aspect of the black-white sexual mythology. The male protagonist of Caldwell's novel, Ganus Bazemore, is used to illustrate another side of the relation-ship between sex and racism: he is sought after again and again by white women; he is "blackmailed" into sexual relations in spite of the lengths to which he goes to prevent them; and he is eventually killed by an outraged white husband for an act he never committed. Caldwell's novel also illustrates the more familiar degradation of the black woman by the white man. Kathyanne, Ganus's sister, is forced to submit to a white banker, sexually humiliated by a group of white boys, beaten by the patrolman who chases the boys home (because she will not submit sexually to him), and raped by other white men.

Ganus Bazemore is a victim in a more complete sense than most other male mulatto characters. In most novels with mulatto characters, the male mixed-blood characters are brave, honest, intelligent, and rebellious. Such characterization is true of aboli-tionist literature as well as of twentieth-century novels *(Clara, The Store,* and *The Southerner* are three examples). Few male mixed-blood characters are tragic mulattoes in the traditional sense. Clarence Garie *(The Garies and Their Friends)* is one, but he is unusual. John Warwick *(The House Behind the Cedars),* certainly no victim, is aggressive in pursuing his way in the world as a white man. Even Joe Christmas *(Light in August)* and Charles Bon *(Absalom, Absalom!),* both tormented figures, have far greater stature than the lovesick female mulatto characters who kill themselves for love of a white man. There are almost no male suicides, whereas there are quite a few suicides by female mulatto characters. While there are some female characters who are race leaders (Iola Leroy, Charlotte Le Jeune in *Daughter of Strangers* are examples), there are not many such women in mulatto fiction. Except for one female in *The Leopard's Sports,* next to none is a villainess. There are, however, several mulatto villains, both in Negrophobe literature (Silas Lynch, Moses the Trick Doctor) and in black novels *(Neither Bond nor Free, The House Behind the Cedars).* Authors of mulatto fiction, like American authors in general, do not give their female characters very great breadth or depth, or very many options.

An exception to this pattern is Zora Neale Hurston's 1937 novel, *Their Eyes Were Watching God.* Hurston is a black writer about whom there is continuing interest, and for good reason. Her portrayal of Janie Starks, a beautiful mulatto, shows us a woman who, by the force of her own spirit and will, moves into full personhood in spite of the attempts of society to force her into a narrow, confining role.

Janie, who had lived among whites, did not recognize the difference between herself and them until she was six years old. Raised by a grandmother whose goal for her was gentility, Janie felt frustrated and hampered. Janie explains to her friend Phoeby that her grandmother had been born during slavery when blacks did not sit down any time they wanted to. So, "sittin' on de porch lak de white madam looked lak uh mighty fine thing tuh her. Dat's what she wanted for me—don't keer what it cost. . . . Ah done nearly languished tuh death up dere. Ah felt like de world wuz cryin' extry and Ah ain't read de common news yet." [65] In order to fulfill her expectations for her granddaughter, Janie's grandmother marries the girl to an unattractive older man who is quite well-to-do. But Janie yearns for love, and as soon as a likely man presents himself she runs away with him. When Joe Starks becomes mayor of the all-black town to which they move, he puts Janie in a position analogous to that of "sittin' on de porch." He believes that she is pleased to be "Mrs. Mayor," but she does not like the position at all because it separates her from all of the other blacks. They live in a new house that makes the rest of the town look like servants' quarters surrounding the "Big House." In response to what Joe has done for her, Janie feels "coldness and fear. . . . She felt far away from things and lonely." [66]

Janie is a vital woman who finally finds love and companionship with a dark-skinned man named Tea Cake. With Tea Cake she lives a vagabonding life; with him, she "reads the common news." Whereas Joe had never wanted her to play checkers, Tea Cake thinks it natural for her to play. He teaches her to shoot, and she turns out to be a better shot than he. When an acquaintance seeks Janie as a friend because of Janie's coffee-and-cream complexion and her luxurious hair, Janie is uninterested. Hurston satirizes the psychology of a black who gains a sense of superiority because she had thin lips and a slightly pointed nose. "Anyone who looked more white folkish than herself was better than she was in her criteria. . . . She didn't cling to Janie Woods the woman. She paid homage to Janie's Caucasian characteristics as such. And when she was with Janie she had a feeling of transmutation, as if she herself had become whiter and with straighter hair and she hated Tea Cake first for his defilement of divinity and next for his telling mockery of her [Mrs. Turner]." [67]

Janie is very much a Harlem Renaissance figure: she is proud of who she is and lives unselfconsciously among the black folk. During the course of the novel she moves steadily toward self-definition, and she does so by discarding first her grandmother's definitions and then the definitions imposed by her two husbands. Addison Gayle, Jr., justifiably gives high praise to Miss Hurston's creation of Janie and to the novel as a whole when he says:

> Neither sexual object, nor shallow imitation woman of the big house, she [Janie] emerged from the novel as a modern black woman, as strange and alien to American thought as the new men of the literature of McKay and Fisher. *Their Eyes Were Watching God,* a novel of intense power, evidences the strength and promises of African-American culture. Miss Hurston, like Fisher, Toomer, Hughes, and McKay, went to the proletariat to seek values, to create and recreate images and symbols that had been partially obliterated or distorted through years of white nationalist propaganda. Her characters were outsiders in America because they were the inheritors of a culture different from that of others.[68]

The frequency with which novels about the mulatto bourgeoisie are still being written has diminished. *Children of Strangers* (1937), by Lyle Saxon, is a fairly good local-color novel about an exclusive mulatto community in Louisiana. Chester Himes's important 1945 novel *If He Hollers Let Him Go* explores the attractions and repulsions of affiliation with the black bourgeoisie as one way for blacks to endure life in America. *The Living Is Easy* (1948), by Dorothy West, is a trenchant satire on the black bourgeois community in Boston (these three novels will be discussed in Chapter 7). *Stranger and Alone* (1950), by J. Saunders Redding, is a fairly strong novel in which a mulatto man ruthlessly "makes his way to the top" of the educational establishment of his state and thereby achieves the status he obsessively needs. Chester Himes's 1954 novel, *The Third Generation,* is an intensive, although melodramatic, study of color phobia and its effects on one black family. It is instructive to look more closely at this novel, since it incorporates many of the themes of mulatto fiction.

Himes's thesis is clear: the "battle of color [that] waged continuously" [69] between Lillian Taylor and her husband eventually destroyed the entire family. She wanted to rear her children "in the belief that they were, in large part, white; that their best traits came from their white inheritance. He wanted to prepare them for the reality of being black." [70] Lillian Taylor's color prejudice virtually destroys communication and the expression of compassion among family members. She had been "reared in the tradition that Negroes with straight hair and light complexions were superior to dark-complexioned Negroes with kinky hair. . . . This conviction was supported by the fact that light-complexioned skin and straight hair did give Negroes a certain prestige within their race." [71]

She is extremely ambitious for her sons and rests her hopes particularly on Charles, who is a beautiful light-skinned child with a small, straight nose (she pinches it every day to keep it from flattening out) and "good" hair, of which she takes meticulous care.

We are told that Mrs. Taylor's preoccupation with color had yielded several positive results: "At first it had been protective, a shield for her wounded pride. . . . Quite often it had been constructive, enabling her to set her sights higher than most Negroes would have dared. It extended the limitations of her ambitions. And it also defended her from despondency and defeat." [72] It was during her early teens that she first conceived the romantic version of her heredity. By eavesdropping, she learned that her father was the son of Dr. Jessie Manning, and that her mother was the daughter of an Irish overseer and an Indian slave. She embellished the story, and the resultant tale had her father as the son of Dr. Manning and a beautiful octoroon, the most beautiful woman in the entire state, whose own father had been an English aristocrat. Lillian's mother, in the new version, was the granddaughter of a United States president and an octoroon who was the daughter of a Confederate army general. Himes tells us that Lillian Taylor "created the fiction of being 1/32nd Negro deliberately. It symbolized her contempt and disdain for all the Negroes she felt had tried to hurt her. It was her final rejection of all the people who would not recognize her innate superiority. . . . She possessed the very maximum of white blood a Negro can possess and remain a Negro. . . . She wanted to impress on . . . [her children] that in their veins flowed the blood of aristocrats." [73]

Lillian Taylor's hatred of blacks and blackness, together with the Oedipal relationship her sons have with their mother, eventually destroys the entire family. It is Charles and his mother upon whom Himes focuses—and upon Charles's spiraling self-destructive behavior, in particular. Sections of the novel are powerfully drawn; however, the novel is irreparably flawed because Himes undermines the cause-effect relationship he himself has established. Rather than showing us that the destruction of the family arises from Mrs. Taylor's obsessions, Himes piles one tragedy upon the next. As a work of art, therefore, *The Third Generation* is not always successful. Nevertheless, as a treatment of the mulatto character by a major black novelist, this work deserves our attention.

The mulatto as race leader (Chapter 8), a very important topic to Negro writers of the late nineteenth and early twentieth centuries, is also the subject of several recent novels by white and black authors. Willard Savoy's *Alien Land* (1949) tells the story of a black (mulatto) race leader and his son who decides his own identity by joining the white group. *Quality* (1945), by Mrs. Cid Rickette Sumner, concerns, "Pinkey," a mulatto nurse who returns to the South in order to "help her people." In spite of the intentional burning of the house that she and a young Negro doctor are planning to turn into a hospital, the novel concludes on an optimistic note: Pinkey builds the hospital with the help of some friendly whites. She dedicates herself to this work, rather than to a life with her white fiancé, who is willing to marry her even after she reveals her Negro blood. *Daughter of Strangers* (1950), by Elizabeth Coker, takes place in the years shortly before and after the Civil War. The beautiful mixed-blood heroine of this novel achieves happiness and a sense of her own identity only after years of struggle. Her ultimate solution to her marginal status is to become a race leader and to try to raise the status of the lower-caste group with which she identifies.

Sinclair Lewis's Neil Kingsblood *(Kingsblood Royal,* 1947) ultimately takes his stand with the black group and is willing to fight against the whites he has known all his life in order to maintain his right to be free and black (even if only 1/32 black!). In addition to attacking racial ideology and its institutionalization in practically every form, Lewis's treatment of Neil's mental state—his need to find an identity in a world suddenly turned chaotic—is more skillful than that of many other novelists of mulatto fiction. Even more sophisticated is Robert Penn Warren's treatment of his heroine's identity crisis in *Band of Angels* (1955). In spite of the weaknesses of *Band of Angels,* Warren delves into the problem of marginality and its existentialist implications in a way that few novelists have been able to manage.

Peter Feibleman is one of the few modern authors who has written a genuinely complex and sophisticated literary study, one in which the sociological and psychological concerns are elements in a work of literature and do not serve as ends in themselves. *Place Without Twilight* (1957) is an extremely well written novel. The author is in control of both the humorous tone, and the dense existentialist musings of his protagonist, Cille. The novel is the study of the slow, painful destruction of a family (particularly Cille and her two brothers, Dan and Clarence) as a result of their race and their light skins: their mother was so fearful for her children's future that she destroys two of her three children and maims the third.

> Mama says our blood and our color made the cross which God put on us in this life. And she said if we could just *get through* this life, we should have a home in the next one. She was trying to teach us not to expect a rightful home in this world . . . so we wouldn't need the world any more than it needed us; trying to teach us not to care about this life—just to live it—not to care.
>
> And how can a mother teach her kids *not* to care?
>
> . . . It was the first lesson you had, when you didn't belong to either part: when you didn't *belong* anywhere. We learned to

be outsiders everyplace we went, and we only had ourselves to grow up with.

... I guess I'll never know what would of come to pass if Mama had just let the world teach us our lesson. It would of been hard, sure—only not as hard as what she did. But Mama couldn't let us find out from the world how to live. She was too scared. So much, she wrapped us in her wings and crushed down. So scared we might get hurt, she did the hurt herself. Sometimes, broken love can be worse than the thing that breaks it—and sometimes it can be worse than no love at all.[74]

Toward the end of the novel, Cille thinks that her salvation will be in leaving her home. This, she thinks, will finally bring her freedom. But in the end she decides that freedom lies in remaining to face her old ghosts, herself, and her world. Exactly how she achieves this final peace is not entirely clear—a flaw in an otherwise fine novel.

Shirley Ann Grau's *The Keepers of the House* (1964) is an effectively written study of the tortured relations of the white and black members of a southern family. The burden of the white South—the guilt, fear and deep attraction for blacks—is excellently embodied in the novel's protagonist, Abigail Howland. The children born of the legal union of a mulatto woman and wellborn white man suffer from their rejection by their mother who wants them to be "white." The interrelationships of the mulatto woman, Margaret; Abigail, the white granddaughter of Margaret's husband; and Margaret's children are all handled well. The doom under which both whites and blacks must live is skillfully realized in Miss Grau's novel.

In the 1970s, several works of mulatto fiction by blacks demonstrate a continuing interest in the issues involved in this fiction. One section of Ernest J. Gaines's *The Autobiography of Miss Jane Pittman* (1971) deals with the tragic love affair between a young white aristocrat who cannot accept the code of the South and the beautiful Creole schoolteacher whom he loves. In *The Cotillion or One Good Bull Is Half the Herd* (1971), John Oliver Killens writes scathingly of the black bourgeoisie but rather joyously and hopefully of the unity of all black people. The brotherhood of blacks is John A. Williams's theme in *The Junior Bachelor Society*

(1976), as he explores the histories of a diverse group of black men united by their adolescent experiences in a club they called "the Junior Bachelor Society." Finally, in another novel from 1976 entitled *The Bloodworth Orphans,* Leon Forrest turns to the familiar material of mulatto fiction: the fate of the mulatto and white children of a southern slaveowning family named Bloodworth, their incestuous connections, their torment and pain.

Delta Blood (1977), Barbara Ferry Johnson's gothic romance, is about Leah Bonvivier, a beautiful octoroon born of a quadroon woman and a Creole gentleman who were joined in the "marriage" relationship called *plaçage.* Set in New Orleans before, during, and after the Civil War, *Delta Blood* tells the familiar story of the beautiful free all-but-white woman who encounters many adventures and loves. The novel is no different from others written years earlier. Leah is very much aware of her class and third-caste position and yearns to go north and pass. However, circumstances and the love of a handsome Creole gentleman involve her, like her mother, in the *plaçage* relationship. At the end of *Delta Blood,* Leah is offered love and marriage to a white northern lawyer. We are left uncertain as to whether she will leave the "husband" she loves for the legitimacy she desires with a man she says she can come to love.

Archetypal Themes in Mulatto Fiction

According to Robert Penn Warren, some of our best novelists have finally abandoned "the fantasy construct of the stereotype" which removed the Negro "from human consideration to a kind of psychological and moral no-man's land" and now interpret "him and his situation as archetypal, as 'an image of man's fate.' " [75] But, contrary to Robert Penn Warren, the archetypal approach is also dangerous to criticism. In fact, the old stereotype of the brute Negro (to take just one example) may also be seen as an archetype: a figure from a nightmare so ugly, so horrible, and so threatening as to be the incarnation of all that is evil. If Jung's concepts of "archetypes" and the "collective unconscious" have any applicability, it would be here. The modern archetypal treatment of the mulatto poses an identical problem. If he is regarded as the embodiment of social misunderstanding, of the dislocation of modern life, of the search for the father, of the suffering of all mankind, as the conscience of mankind, and so forth, this figure can also lose his significance as a character with moral and psychological dimensions. The key to whether or not the mulatto character (or the Negro character in general) has meaning on the archetypal and human planes is very likely the issue of his identity. With the rejection of the stereotype as a means of explaining the character, some authors have turned to the Negro's search for identity as their basic theme: "Once the role-playing is abandoned, then the man has a time of self-consciousness when he is paralyzed for fear that any desire or action may be in conformity with the abandoned image. He wants a racial or cultural identity and is unsure how to attain it while avoiding the old clichés about his race." [76] Thus, Joe Christmas, Lucas Beauchamp *(Intruder in the Dust)*, and Charles Bon all have reality for us on both levels; whereas Jim Bond *(Absalom, Absalom!)* and Nancy Mannigoe *(Requiem for a Nun)* exist almost exclusively on the symbolic level. Witness the deep psychological pain experienced by Joe Christmas as he tries to find a place, a state of being, he can endure; Charles Bon's single-minded drive for recognition by his father; and Lucas Beauchamp's anger toward the man who was like a brother, his assertion of dignity and pride, and his puzzling over the code of the South: "How to God can a black man ask a white man to please not lay down with his black wife? And even if he could ask it, how to God can the white man promise he won't?" [77]

The search for identity and the archetypal aspects of mulatto fiction are interrelated in another way. Incest, fratricide, patricide, the search for the father, and the evil and good sons are all archetypal themes. From one culture to the next, from one historical era to the next, authors have returned again and again to man's fundamental biological relations and explored their meaning with respect to man's own sense of identity. Authors of mulatto fiction have returned to these themes again and again because the historical reality of miscegenation has given rise to these phenomena within the context of that literature.

In *Killers of the Dream*, Lillian Smith writes of the triangulation of "sin, sex, and segregation." She argues that there are "three ghost relationships . . . haunting the mind of the South and giving shape to [their] lives and [their] souls." One of these, the relationship between the white father and his mixed-blood children, is explored in the mulatto fiction of the nineteenth and twentieth centuries by both black and white authors. These children, according to Smith, are "little ghosts playing and laughing and weeping on the edge of the Southern memory. . . . Surely one can reject a child only by rejecting an equal part of one's psychic life."[78]

In nineteenth-century literature, the emphasis is on the fact that a man may be both a child's master and his or her father. This dual role of the white man infuriated abolitionist authors and seemed to them to be one of the most heinous crimes of southern society. William Wells Brown, author of *Clotelle*, the first Negro novel in the United States, said: "Society does not frown upon the man who sits with his half-white child upon his knee while the mother stands, a slave, behind his chair." [79] In *Iola Leroy* (1892), the white aristocrat, Eugene Leroy, marries the octoroon woman he loves in spite of the sanctions society will place upon such a union. In *The Garies and Their Friends* (1857), *Iola Leroy* and *Clotelle*, the white father is unable to protect his mulatto children in spite of his attempts to do so. In Robert Penn Warren's *Band of Angels*, Amantha's father never freed her, being unable to admit that his flesh was enslaved in the first place.

The mixed-blood children yearn for the love of their white fathers. Some obtain this love, but it is never the unmixed affection and pride of the white father for his white children. Harry Gordon says in *Dred* that "when the fathers of such as we feel any love for us, it isn't like the love they have for their white children. They are half-ashamed of us; they are ashamed to show their love, if they have it; and, then, there's a kind of remorse and pity about it, which they make up to themselves by petting us. They load us with presents and indulgences. They amuse themselves with us while we are children, and play off all our passions as if we were instruments to be played on." [80] In *The Autobiography of an Ex-Coloured Man* (1912), the narrator does not know his father, and he is embittered by this void in his identity. In *The Chinaberry Tree* (1931), Laurentine Strange says that she is "nobody, not only illegitimate . . . but a child of a connection that all America frowns on. I'm literally fatherless." [81]

In "Father and Son" (1933), in *The Ways of White Folks*, a novella later adapted as a play entitled *Mulatto*, Langston Hughes depicts the tragedy of fathers and sons forever alienated from each other by the racist code under which they live. Under the warping influence of racist ideology and institutions, the emotional and spiritual affinity between father and son is not permitted to grow but must be denied and destroyed.

Hughes tells the story of Col. Thomas Norwood and his mulatto son Bert, the oldest of the five children born to Coralee Lewis, the Colonel's mistress for thirty years. Bert, who is now a twenty-year-old college man in Atlanta, has already been "the brightest and best of the Colonel's five children, lording it over the other children, and sassing not only his colored mother, but his white father, as well." [82] The tall, handsome, well-dressed light-skinned young man, who is also an excellent athlete, has been courted by the black bourgeoisie of Atlanta. But Bert cannot forget that he has grown up as one of Colonel Norwood's "yard-niggers" (a term used by field hands for the mulatto children of white planter). He cannot forget that "all of the other kids in the quarters were named after their fathers, whereas he and his brother and sisters bore the mother's name, Lewis. He was Bert Lewis—not Bert Norwood.[83] We are told that Bert felt he has no home because he had always slept in a "nigger cabin" while his brown-skinned mother and white-skinned father slept in the Big House. By virtue of the color of his skin, Bert has been rendered homeless, nameless, and fatherless.

Yet this father and son are much alike. During one of their confrontations, Hughes describes Bert as he stood before his father, "looking as the Colonel must have looked forty years ago—except that he was a shade darker." [84] The white father and his mulatto son also have intense feelings of love and hatred toward each other. As the novella opens, Colonel Norwood is seen waiting anxiously for Bert to return from college. Hughes says that the Colonel would never have admitted that he was waiting for Bert, and in fact the Colonel goes into the study before Bert comes in order to indicate his indifference to the homecoming.

Throughout his lifetime Bert seeks the father who feels compelled to deny him. Once as a child, he called the Colonel "Papa" in front of white people. The Colonel became furious and beat the boy severely. As an adult, Bert tells some white people in town that his name is Norwood and that the plantation will be his when the

Colonel dies. The Colonel is shocked and furious when he hears of the incident.

Hughes suggests that Colonel Norwood's beating of his son for calling him "Papa" creates "a barrier of fear—a fear that held a certain mysterious fascination for Bert's sense of defiance, a fear that Bert from afar was continually taunting and baiting." [85] Thus, because of his father's strict orders against the use of the front door by blacks, Bert often darts out the forbidden door when his father is away or unaware. Again, both because of his yearning for recognition from his father and because of his defiance, Bert willfully challenges the code of the South. Where he arrives home, he and his father walk up to each other and say hello. Then Bert offers his hand. His father looks at the strong, light-skinned hand and makes no effort to take it. Their eyes meet; then the Colonel turns and, without a word, walks into the house. " 'The bastard,' Bert said, 'Why couldn't he shake hands with me? I'm a Norwood, too.' " [86]

This paternity is precisely what Colonel Norwood can never admit. We are told on the opening page of the novella that Colonel Norwood has "no real son, no white and legal heir to carry on the Norwood name." [87] Should the child's purity of blood be the only prerequisite for recognition by his own father? By adhering to the racist code of the South, the Colonel turns away from his own humanity and, finally, from his own salvation. As the summer goes by, father and son continue to confront each other, to attract and repel each other. Finally, they can go on no longer. Their last conversation conveys the utter hopelessness of the situation: " 'Fatherless?' Bert asked. 'Bastard,' the old man said." [88] Moments later Bert strangles his father.

Retaliation comes quickly, and Bert kills himself before he can be lynched. His innocent brother Willie, who had always been "docile and good-natured and nigger-like, bowing and scraping and treating white folks like they expected to be treated," [89] is indiscriminately lynched. In the newspaper account of Colonel Norwood's murder, we are told that "the dead man left no heirs." [90] The last line of the novella, this remark understates the obvious tragic irony of the situation.

In *Keepers of the House,* as in many of the other novels that deal with the relationships between a white father and his mixed-blood offspring, the interaction between the white and black half brothers and half sisters is also important. After Abigail Howland's mother dies, Margaret (the mulatto wife of Abigail's grandfather) serves as both mother and grandmother to Abigail. Abigail carries inside herself an unquenchable fury toward Margaret's mulatto children, who were like her siblings. She is angry at Margaret for having denied them so that they could be white; yet she is also furious at them simply for existing and for feeling the pain of their isolation. Like many of Faulkner's characters, she must bear the burden of southern history. The novel ends with Abigail and Robert, Margaret's son, locked in bitter conflict. Ultimately, Abigail is destroyed because she cannot find an answer to the question she poses to her grandfather's ghost: "Why, why did you have children, for them to tear each other apart?" [91]

In Charles Chesnutt's *The Marrow of Tradition* (1901), Janet Miller, a mulatto woman, has always loved the white sister she has never known. "All her life long she had yearned for a kind word, a nod, a smile, the least thing that imagination might have twisted into a recognition of the tie between them." [92] But the recognition never comes. In fact, Janet's white sister, Olivia, has a veritable phobia about Janet. She cannot bear even to look at Janet or to be reminded of her. As a southern lady, Olivia cannot accept the fact of this Negro sister or her parentage. In the relations between Harry and Tom Gordon *(Dred)* and between Tom Driscoll and Valet de Chambre *(Pudd'nhead Wilson)*, reviewed in the preceding chapter, the white boys treat their black brothers with a hatred born of guilt.

Even when the relationship between black and white characters starts off well, a day comes when the intimacy is broken. Communication and love become subordinated to the code of the South. Lucas Beauchamp and Roth Edmonds lived together "until they were both grown almost as brothers lived. They had fished and hunted together, they had learned to swim in the same water, they had eaten at the same table at the white boy's kitchen and in the cabin of the negro's mother. . . ." [93] But inevitably, white boy and black boy must separate. Only as innocents do they fail to see the heritage of sex, sin, and segregation that surround and ultimately doom them.

Faulkner also writes of what Lillian Smith calls another of the "ghost relationships" of the South—that between the "black mammy" and the white male child. Faulkner says of Roth Edmonds's son, Carothers, and Lucas Beauchamp's son, Henry:

> Still in infancy, he [Carothers] had already accepted the black man [Lucas] as an adjunct to the woman [Molly Beauchamp] who was the only mother he would remember, as simply as he accepted his father as an adjunct to his existence. Even before he was out of infancy the two houses had become interchangeable: himself and his foster brother sleeping on the same pallet in the white man's house or in the same bed in the negro's and eating of the same food at the same table in either, actually preferring the negro house. [94]

Then slowly, he realized that he was a white boy; and that Lucas, Molly, and Henry were black. One night he makes it clear to Henry that the white boy will lie in the bed, the black on the pallet. That night Carothers lay "in a rigid fury of the grief he could not explain, the shame he would not admit. . . . They never slept in the same room again and never again ate at the same table. . . . Then one day he knew it was grief and was ready to admit it was shame also, wanted to admit it only it was too late then, forever and forever too late." [95]

Faulkner and the Mulatto Character:
Intruder in the Dust, "The Fire and the Hearth," and Absalom, Absalom!

The works of William Faulkner capture the "southern mystique," the spirit of the South. The fictional world he has created certainly does not always, or even often, correspond to the reality of southern life. But the myths, the lore, the secret repulsions and attractions are brilliantly articulated in Faulkner's novels. How much he is in control of this material and to what degree he himself is a victim of the mythology of the South are probably unanswerable questions.

Absalom, Absalom! (1936), *Go Down, Moses* (1940), *Light in August* (1932), and *Intruder in the Dust* (1948) contain important mulatto characters. In *Go Down, Moses* and *Intruder in the Dust,* Faulkner creates the saga of the McCaslin clan. To be a McCaslin is to have an almost mystical relationship—through biology and heredity—with the best of Faulkner's southerners: a deep understanding of the guilt of the white South and the need for atonement for the sins committed against the red man and the black man; a closeness to the land, to the South as a place, as a way of life; a deep respect for the best of the past and a commitment to a sinless future; and finally, a fierce dignity of spirit and pride in self.

Lucas Beauchamp, one of the central figures in both *Go Down, Moses* and *Intruder in the Dust,* is one of the mulatto members of the McCaslin family. In "The Fire and the Hearth," both Lucas and Edmonds—who were reared as "brothers" until racist ideology forced them apart—respect the fact that Lucas's McCaslin blood came through male descent and reached the black man a generation sooner, while Edmonds's had come to him from a woman. Lucas's countenance is said to be "composed, inscrutable, even a little haughty, shaped even in expression in the pattern of his great-grandfather McCaslin's face." [96] Lucas dresses in the faded overalls of a Negro but wears a heavy gold watch chain, uses a gold toothpick, and wears a hat of handmade beaver—all of which are not part of the usual, or even acceptable, appurtenances of black men. [97] In "The Fire and the Hearth," Lucas, now grown old, is just as fierce in his dignity as he was nearly a half century before. He is "erect beneath the old, fine, well-cared-for hat, walking with that unswerving and dignified deliberation which every now and then, and with something sharp at the heart, Edmonds recognized as having come from his own ancestry too as the hat had come." [98]

Of Lucas's racial mixture, Faulkner says:

> It was not that Lucas made capital of his white or even his McCaslin blood, but the contrary. It was as if he were not only impervious to that blood, he was indifferent to it. He didn't even need to strive with it. He didn't even have to bother to defy it. He resisted it simply by being the composite of the two races which made him, simply by possessing it. Instead of being at once the battleground and the victim of the two strains, he was a vessel, durable, ancestryless, noncon-

ductive, in which the toxin and the anti stalemated one another, seetheless, unrumored in the outside air.[99]

Of himself, Lucas says, "I'm a nigger. . . . But I'm a man too. I'm more than just a man. The same thing made my pappy that made your grandma." [100] What makes Lucas "more than just a man" is his McCaslin spirit. The mere existence of white skin carries no honor so far as Lucas is concerned: "to Lucas the sheriff was a redneck without any reason for pride in his forbears nor hope for it in his descendants." [101] What makes Lucas a man is his refusal to bow low before the code of the South. It is Lucas's imperviousness to the rituals of his culture that infuriates the whites around him. Lucas refers to Zack Edmonds as Mr. Edmonds rather than Mr. Zack, as the other blacks do, and he avoids calling Roth Edmonds by any name at all. He says "ma'am" to women just like any white man does, and says "sir" and "mister," but does not mean either. When the narrator of *Intruder in the Dust*, Charles Mallison, Jr., tries to pay Lucas 70 cents for a meal Lucas gave the boy, Lucas makes the boy learn once and forever that the mulatto is a man.

Lucas is not lynched for the crime he did not commit. Indeed, as Charles Nilon points out, he is actually guarded by the symbol of white womanhood: "When Miss Habersham and Charles's mother, mending their laundry, sit on the porch of the jail, they are saying in effect that the whole symbolic structure around which bi-racial living coheres in the South is false." [102] Throughout the search for the actual murderer, Lucas remains calm and inscrutable. He is always, as Gavin Stevens tells his nephew, a "gentleman." The last scene in *Intruder in the Dust* is a final testimonial to Lucas's inflexible dignity: Lucas does not grovel with thanks before the white lawyer but offers lawyer Stevens his fee—anything within reason. Stevens says that Lucas owes him nothing because the white man had not believed in the black man's innocence. Back and forth they bargain; finally, Stevens tells Lucas he can pay two dollars in expenses for the broken point of a fountain pen. Lucas says that it does not sound like enough, but Stevens is the "lawing man." So Lucas carefully counts out the money, pennies and all. Everything is conducted in an orderly, businesslike way, as if the amount of money being passed from black man to white were two hundred, rather than two, dollars. When the transaction is completed, Lucas still does not leave.

" 'Now what?' his [Charles Mallison's] uncle said. 'What are you waiting for now?' 'My receipt.' Lucas said." [103]

"The Fire and the Hearth" is the story of confrontation between two men—one white, one black—who had been like brothers but are driven apart because of their need to fight for their honor. When Zack Edmonds's wife dies in childbirth, Molly Beauchamp, Lucas's wife, goes with her own baby to the "big house" and stays there as a wet nurse for six months. It is only when Lucas goes to Zack and says, "I wants my wife. I needs her at home" that he even realizes that he is "furious, bursting, blind." That night, Molly returns to her husband. Then Lucas realizes that he must kill Zack or leave, even though he will never know if his wife and the white man had cuckolded him. Many years later, Zack's son Roth realizes that his father and Lucas had fought over "a nigger woman." And he understands, too, that the mulatto bastard of the McCaslins had beaten his father, who is merely an Edmonds whose McCaslin blood is "woman-made." *"Yes, Lucas beat him, else Lucas wouldn't be here. If father had beat Lucas, he couldn't have let Lucas stay here even to forgive him. It will only be Lucas who could have stayed because Lucas is impervious to anybody, even to forgiving them, even to having to harm them."* [104]

Lucas's dress, speech, and bearing all add up to an unspoken denial of profound significance: Lucas refuses to be a "nigger." The narrator, Charles Mallison, learns what every other white man had been thinking about Lucas for years: *"We got to make him be a nigger first. He's got to admit he's a nigger. Then maybe we will accept him as he seems to be intended to be accepted."* [105] Gavin Stevens tells his nephew that Mr. Lilley, one of the white townspeople, has nothing against "niggers." But he wants them to act like "niggers." According to Lilley, Lucas murdered a white man, which Mr. Lilley thinks all black men want to do; the whites should burn Lucas, which everyone white and black expects—"both of them observing implicitly the rules: the nigger acting like a nigger and the white folks acting like white folks and no real hard feelings on either side once the fury is over." [106] In fact, Stevens says, Mr. Lilley would probably be the first to contribute toward Lucas's funeral and the care of his family!

In no way, then, does Lucas fit the old stereotype of the mulatto torn by his warring bloods. Rather, in his handling of Lucas Beauchamp, Faulkner invests him with archetypal significance. In *Intruder in the Dust*, Gavin Stevens tells his nephew that now that everyone knows of Lucas's innocence they will watch right here in Yoknapatawpha County "the ancient oriental relationship between the savior and the life he saved turned upside down; Lucas Beauchamp once the slave of any white man within range of whose notice he happened to come, now tyrant over the whole county's white conscience." [107] In "The Fire and the Hearth" Lucas is explicitly spoken of as a "principle" embodying the spirit of his region: *"He's more like old Carothers than all the rest of us put together, including old Carothers. He is both heir and prototype simultaneously of all the geography and climate and biology which sired old Carothers and all the rest of us and our kind, myriad, countless, faceless, even nameless now except himself who fathered himself, intact and complete, contemptuous, as old Carothers must have been, of all blood black white yellow or red, including his own."* [108]

In *Absalom, Absalom!* William Faulkner tells an incredible tale of the South in which all of these relationships—between black woman and white man, white man and his black half brother, black man and his white half sister, white father and black son—are explored in an elaborate gothic tale full of doom, destruction, and death. Conceived of as a tragedy not unlike those of ancient Greece, the story of Thomas Sutpen's fall symbolizes the fall of the South. In one traumatic moment, young Thomas Sutpen is shown the vast differences among white men—distinctions based upon wealth, power, and culture. From that instant forward, he devotes himself—single-mindedly, ruthlessly, and regardless of human decency—to the selfish pursuit of his own rise up the social and economic ladder. When he discovers that the wife he has married as a stepping-stone to this end is part Negro, he abandons her and their son immediately and without reconsideration. He builds his empire upon slave labor and the plantation system. Ilse Dusoir Lind has spelled out the relationship between Sutpen's personal tragedy and the collective doom of the South: "Sutpen had two sons: one white, the other Negro. he denied the Negro; fratricide resulted. The Civil War, too, was a fratricidal conflict caused by denial of the Negro. Sutpen's sin, his failure of humanity, is the equivalent in personal terms of the sin of plantation culture, its failure to accept the brotherhood of all mankind." [109]

The story is told through the distorted perceptions of four narrators whose interactions with the characters in the tale weave a complex tapestry of the anguished soul of the South. As with much of Faulkner's writing, it does not matter whose version is true—in fact, there can be no true version of the events narrated, given the subjectivity of the points of view. What is significant to each of his characters and, indeed, to ourselves, is the search for an understanding of reality each of us undertakes. Ultimately, nothing else matters. Fact and myth, past and present all blend in Faulkner's works—nowhere more brilliantly than in *Absalom, Absalom!* It is not my purpose to offer a full analysis of the novel, but rather to look at the results of Sutpen's marriage to an all-but-white woman. For Sutpen's destiny is determined by the fathering of a mulatto child and his denial of that child. Faulkner makes clear that Sutpen realizes that his doom is sealed by his repudiation of his own flesh and blood, although he is not actually able to understand the enormity of his sin. "Mr. Compson explains; even though he [Sutpen] knew that Bon and Judith had never laid eyes on one another, he must have felt and heard the design—house, position, posterity and all—come down like it had been built out of smoke, making no sound, creating no rush of displaced air and not even leaving any debris. And he not calling it retribution, no sins of the father come home to roost; not even calling it bad luck, but just a mistake." [110]

Charles Bon, the mulatto son of Thomas Sutpen, seduces the minds and bodies of Henry and Judith Sutpen, Sutpen's white children. Bon is a fascinating figure, and neither Henry nor Judith can help themselves. He is, as Mr. Compson describes him, "a young man of a wordly elegance and assurance beyond his years, handsome, apparently wealthy ... a personage who in Mississippi of that time must have appeared almost phoenix-like, fullsprung from no childhood, born of no woman and impervious to time ... a man with an ease of manner and a swaggering gallant air in comparison with which Sutpen's pompous arrogance was clumsy bluff and Henry actually a hobble-de-hoy." [111] How ironic that the cast-off, partly Negro son of the largest plantation owner in the area should have more culture, more polish, than his self-made father or that father's legitimate heir. This is a tale of love as well as of hatred. The love Judith and Henry feel toward Bon is returned. But Bon is compelled to destroy his family when his father refuses to grant his son the recognition he so desperately needs. Sutpen must deny Bon's marriage to his daughter, Judith. Because of Henry's love for Bon, the white son renounces his own birthright and rides off with Bon. And even after Henry knows that he and Judith are Bon's half siblings, Henry can allow the incest between them. His own incestuous feelings toward Judith are made clear as well. Bon's morganatic marriage to an octoroon woman, however, and Bon's own tainted blood are more than Henry can bear. The ceremony with the Negro woman, the legitimizing of the relationship (even though no court in the South would recognize such a union)—this Henry could not stand. Miscegenation, first between Sutpen and Bon's mother and Sutpen and Clytie's mother, and later contemplated between Judith and Bon, cannot be tolerated. Bon will not renounce his marriage; Henry cannot allow Bon to marry Judith. Thus Henry commits fratricide, "practically fling[ing] the bloody corpse of his sister's sweetheart at the hem of her wedding gown." [112]

And still the tale is not complete; the reparations have not been made in full—and indeed they never can. For Charles Bon and his octoroon wife have a child, Charles Etienne Saint-Valery Bon, who is brought to Sutpen's Hundred when he is twelve years old, six years after his father's death. There he is cared for by Judith and Clytie, Thomas Sutpen's mulatto daughter. Ten years later, after an absence of a year, he returns to Sutpen's Hundred with "a coal black and ape-like woman and an authentic wedding license. . . . [He] rode up to the house and apparently flung the wedding license in Judith's face with something of that invincible despair with which he attacked the negroes in the dice game." [113] General Compson said that it would have been better had Charles Etienne Bon never been born. The latter must have agreed since he tried in every way possible to kill himself—by fighting when he knew he would be beaten insensible and by constant drinking. And he was dead by the age of twenty-five, but by smallpox, not through his own fury.

And still the tale is not finished. Charles Etienne Bon's ape-like wife births the last heir of Thomas Sutpen: Jim Bond, who grows up to be "a hulking . . . light-colored negro . . . , his arms dangling, no surprise no nothing in the saddle-colored and slack-mouthed idiot face." [114] In 1910, fifty-one years after Henry and Charles Bon had met, Clytie kills herself and the dying Henry (who had returned to Sutpen's Hundred): Thomas Supten's dream is consumed in the nightmare of the social system which spawned it. But the South can never escape its guilt, the burden of its past. For Jim Bond, "the scion, the last of his race" howls at the fire. "But they couldn't catch him. They could hear him; he didn't seem to ever get any further away but they couldn't get any nearer and maybe in time they could not even locate the direction any more of the howling." [115] Shreve McCannon, the young Canadian who is Quentin Compson's roommate at Harvard, and who has listened to Quentin's whole anguished tale, understands that the whole ledger is clear except for one thing. "You've got one nigger left. One nigger Sutpen left. Of course you can't catch him and you don't even always see him and you never will be able to use him. But you've got him there still. You still hear him at night sometimes. Don't you? . . . I think the Jim Bonds are going to conquer the western hemisphere." [116]

And that is the end of the tale. But it is not the end of the social reality which it reflects. Whether Rosa, or Quentin, or Mr. Compson, or Shreve is more or less accurate in reconstructing the story of Sutpen is largely irrelevant, because the composite vision they produce is true to the racial history of the South.

The mulatto as lover, husband, son, brother; wife, mistress, sister, daughter; the mixed-blood character as the object of passion and fascination or irrational fear and nightmarish fantasy; as the white man's burden and curse or as the index of our best selves—this figure has been an extraordinarily powerful one in the American novel. Mulatto fiction is not always good. In fact, much of it is quite weak. But if we study our literature for content as well as style, as social history as well as art, as a means of learning something about our most secret selves, then we cannot afford to ignore it.

NOTES

1. Richard Wright, "The Literature of the Negro in the United States," in *Black Expression: Essays by and About Black Americans in the Creative Arts,* ed. Addison Gayle, Jr. (New York: Weybright & Talley, 1969), p. 200.
2. Nancy Tischler, *Black Masks: Negro Characters in Modern Southern Fiction* (University Park: Pennsylvania State University Press, 1969), p. 102.
3. Alain Locke, "American Literary Tradition and the Negro," *Sociology and Social Research,* 22 (1937), 217.
4. Leslie Fiedler, *Love and Death in the American Novel,* rev. ed. (New York: Stein & Day, 1966), pp. 200-201.
5. Ibid., p. 206
6. Penelope Bullock, "The Treatment of the Mulatto in American Fiction from 1826-1902," master's thesis, Atlanta University, 1944, pp. 50-51.
7. William Stanley Braithwaite, "The Negro in American Literature," in Gayle, ed., *Black Expression,* p. 169.
8. Summary from Helena M. Smith, "Negro Characterization in the American Novel: A Historical Survey of Work by White Authors," diss., Pennsylvania State University, 1959, p. 178.
9. Bullock, "The Treatment of the Mulatto in American Fiction from 1826 to 1902," p. 54.
10. Harriet Beecher Stowe, *Uncle Tom's Cabin: or Life Among the Lowly* (1852; rpt. New York: AMS Press, 1967), 2 vols., I, 142.
11. Ibid., I, 19.
12. Ibid., I, 24.
13. Ibid., I, 145.
14. Ibid., I, 151.
15. Stowe, *Uncle Tom's Cabin: or Life Among the Lowly* (1852; rpt. New York: AMS Press, 1967), 2 vols., I, 236, as quoted in Jean Fagan Yellin, *The Intricate Knot: Black Figures in American Literature, 1776-1863* (New York: New York University Press, 1972), p. 136.
16. Yellin, *The Intricate Knot,* p. 136a.
17. Garrison, in *The Liberator,* March 26, 1852, as quoted in Fredrickson, *The Black Image in the White Mind: The Debate on Afro-American Character and Destiny, 1817-1914* (New York, Evanston, San Francisco, London: Harper & Row, Publishers, 1971), p. 118.
18. Yellin, *The Intricate Knot,* p. 172. See her chapter devoted to Brown, pp. 154-81, for a complete discussion of the origins and development of the numerous versions of the novel.
19. Ibid., p. 167.
20. Ibid., p. 172.
21. Ibid., p. 193.

22. In *The Way of the New World,* p. 197, Addison Gayle, Jr. shows that Delaney had specifically attacked *Uncle Tom's Cabin* and speculates that he probably began writing a novel in response to her version of black life.
23. Addison Gayle, Jr., *The Way of the New World: The Black Novel in America* (Garden City, N.Y.; Anchor Press, 1975), p. 21.
24. Fredrickson *The Black Image in the White Mind,* pp. 112-13.
25. Locke, "American Literary Tradition and the Negro," p. 215.
26. Thomas Nelson Page, *Red Rock: A Chronicle of Reconstruction* (New York: Scribner's, 1909), pp. 291-92.
27. Braithwaite, "The Negro in American Literature," in Gayle, *Black Expression,* p. 169.
28. Frances E. W. Harper, *Iola Leroy: or Shadows Uplifted,* 3d ed. (Boston: James H. Earle, 1892), p. 44.
29. Robert A. Bone, *The Negro Novel in America,* rev. ed. (New Haven, Conn.: Yale University Press,1968), pp. 24-25.
30. Ibid., p. 27.
31. Beulah Johnson, "The Treatment of the Negro Woman as a Major Character in American Novels 1900-1950," diss., New York University, 1955, p. 121.
32. Hugh M. Gloster, *Negro Voices in American Fiction* (Chapel Hill: University of North Carolina Press, 1948), p. 89.
33. Ibid., p. 118.
34. Sterling Brown, *The Negro in American Fiction* (Washington, D.C.: The Associates in Negro Folk Education, 1937), p. 143.
35. In *Selected Writings of Gertrude Stein,* ed. Carl Van Vechten (1945; rpt. New York: Random House, 1962), p. 343.
36. Ibid.
37. Ibid., p. 443.
38. I am referring only to the treatment by these authors of the mulatto. Claude McKay, for example, most often used the figure of the "vagabond," a type quite outside bourgeois life.
39. Rudolph Fisher, *The Walls of Jericho* (1928; rpt. New York: Arno Press and the New York Times, 1969), pp. 78-79.
40. Ibid., p. 74.
41. Ibid.
42. Ibid., p. 8.
43. Ibid., p. 38.
44. Ibid.
45. Ibid., p. 108.
46. Ibid., p. 13.
47. Ibid., p. 51.
48. Ibid., p. 281.
49. Ibid., pp. 282-83.
50. Gayle, *The Way of the New World,* p. 138.
51. See Nat Huggins's *Harlem Renaissance* (New York: Oxford University Press, 1971).

52. Jean Toomer, *Cane* (1923; rpt. New York: Harper & Row), p. 11.
53. Ibid.
54. Ibid., p. 27.
55. Ibid., p. 24.
56. Ibid., p. 36.
57. Ibid., p. 47.
58. Ibid., p. 145.
59. Ibid.
60. David Littlejohn, *Black on White: A Critical Survey of Writing by American Negroes* (New York: Grossman Publishing, 1966), p. 51.
61. George S. Schuyler, *Black No More: Being an Account of the Strange and Wonderful Workings of Science in the Land of the Free, A.D. 1933-40* (New York: The Macaulay Company, 1931), p. 46.
62. Ibid., p. 247.
63. Ibid., p. 249.
64. Frank Yerby, *The Foxes of Harrow* (New York: The Dial Press, 1946), p. 269.
65. Ibid., p. 259.
66. Ibid., p. 274.
67. Frank Yerby, *The Vixens* (New York: The Dial Press, 1947), p. 274.
68. Calvin C. Hernton, *Sex and Racism in America* (Garden City, N.Y.: Doubleday & Company, 1965), pp. 15, 21.
69. Zora Neale Hurston, *Their Eyes Were Watching God* (Philadelphia and London: J. B. Lippincott Company, 1937), p. 172.
70. Ibid., p. 74.
71. Ibid., pp. 215-16.
72. Gayle, *The Way of the New World,* pp. 146-47.
73. Chester Himes, *The Third Generation* (1954; rpt. Chatham, N.J.: Chatham Bookseller, 1973), p. 36.
74. Ibid.
75. Ibid., p. 12.
76. Ibid., pp. 14-15.
77. Ibid., p. 18.
78. Peter S. Feibleman, *A Place Without Twilight* (Cleveland and New York: The World Publishing Company, 1957), p. 21.
79. Seymour L. Gross, "Introduction: Stereotype to Archetype: The Negro in American Literary Criticism," p. 25 in *Images of the Negro in American Literature,* ed. Seymour L. Gross and John Edward Hardy (Chicago and London: University of Chicago Press, 1966).
80. Tischler, *Black Masks,* p. 191.
81. William Faulkner, "The Fire and the Hearth," *Go Down, Moses* (New York: Random House, 1942), p. 59.
82. Lillian Smith, *Killers of the Dream* (New York: W.W. Norton, 1949), pp. 120-21.
83. William Wells Brown, *Clotelle: A Tale of the Southern States* (1855: rpt. Philadelphia: Albert Saifer, 1955), p. 5. Originally published in Britain in 1853 under the title *Clotel;* the later and different American version is used here.

84. Stowe, *Dred,* vol. III, pp. 76-77.
85. Jessie Redmon Fauset, *The Chinaberry Tree* (New York: Stokes, 1931), p. 12.
86. Langston Hughes, "Father and Son," in *The Ways of White Folks* (1933; rpt. New York: Knopf, 1962), p. 201.
87. Ibid., p. 215.
88. Ibid., p. 224.
89. Ibid., p. 216.
90. Ibid., pp. 221-22.
91. Ibid., p. 200.
92. Ibid., p. 233.
93. Ibid., p. 219.
94. Ibid., p. 248.
95. Shirley Ann Grau, *The Keeper of the House* (New York: Knopf, 1964), p. 268.
96. Charles Chesnutt, *The Marrow of Tradition* (Boston: Houghton Mifflin Company, 1901), p. 65.
97. Faulkner,, "The Fire and the Hearth," *Go Down, Moses,* p. 55.
98. Ibid., p. 110.
99. Ibid., p. 112.
100. Faulkner, "The Fire and the Hearth," *Go Down, Moses,* pp. 70-71.
101. Faulkner, *Intruder in the Dust* (New York: Random House, 1948), p. 12.
102. Ibid, p. 129.
103. Ibid., p. 104.
104. Ibid., p. 47.
105. Ibid., p. 43.
106. Charles Nilon, *Faulkner and the Negro* (New York: Citadel Press, 1965), p. 29.
107. Faulkner, *Intruder in the Dust,* p. 247.
108. Ibid., pp. 115-16.
109. Ibid., p. 18.
110. Ibid., pp. 48-49.
111. Ibid., p. 199.
112. Ibid., p. 127.
113. "The Design and Meaning of *Absalom, Absalom!,*" in *William Faulkner: Three Decades of Criticism,* ed. Frederick J. Hoffman and Olga J. Vickery (East Lansing: Michigan State University, 1960), p. 300.
114. Faulkner, *Absalom, Absalom!* (New York: Random House, 1936), p. 267.
115. Ibid., p. 74.
116. Ibid., p. 18.
117. Ibid., p. 205.
118. Ibid., p. 370.
119. Ibid., p. 376.
120. Ibid., p. 378.

4.

The Tragic Mulatto

The figure of the tragic mulatto—the almost-white character whose beauty, intelligence, and purity are forever in conflict with the "savage primitivism" inherited from his or her Negro ancestors—is the most frequently encountered stereotype in mulatto fiction. This figure is usually a product of the white man's imagination and often expresses his deepest (usually unspoken) fantasies about the largest marginal group in our society: specifically, his assumption that the mixed blood yearns to be white and is doomed to unhappiness and despair because of this impossible dream. In this, the white author becomes a victim of his own racist ideology. While black novelists have employed the stereotype in order to gain sympathy from white readers for their "black" characters, the tragic mulatto character is much more likely to appear in white-authored mulatto fiction.

The tragic mulatto is usually a woman. Especially in the mediocre melodramas, so often the vehicle for presenting the tragic mulatto character, nothing supposedly inspires sympathy more than the plight of a beautiful woman whose touch of "impurity" makes her all the more attractive. The fact that many of these stereotyped characters are raised as white women—in fact, as aristocratic women and only discover their Negro blood as adults— allows white readers more identification with them than with full-blooded Negroes. The white reader is able to imagine how he himself would respond to such a "catastrophe." And the fact that many tragic mulatto characters try to "pass for white" as the means of solving their problems can also be titillating to white readers. Not only does the romance of the lonely passer—cut off from all others by her "desperate" secret—appeal to many white readers, but the latter can turn their speculation to those around them. Who can tell the passer?

The tragic mulatto character is an outcast, a wanderer, one alone. He is the fictional symbol of marginality. Rejected out of fear and hatred by the dominant group, he is often rejected out of envy and hatred by the lower caste as well. In addition, the tragic mulatto character is usually depicted as being ambivalent toward the two castes. He is torn between the two groups, not primarily in a psychosocial sense, but rather as the expression of his divided biological inheritance. Sterling Brown, a black critic who often wrote scathingly of white novelists' depiction of the mulatto, describes the tragic mulatto stereotype in this way: "Mathematically they [white novelists] work it out that his intellectual strivings and self-control come from his white blood, and his emotional urgings, indolence and potential savagery come from his Negro blood. Their favorite character, the octoroon, wretched because of the 'single drop of midnight in her veins,' desires a white lover above all else, and must therefore go down to a tragic end." [1] Nancy Tischler aptly describes the formula used by most authors who present the tragic mulatto character: "Supposedly the black blood and the white blood stage a gory civil war in the mind and body of the mulatto, much as the medieval writer would have had the Body and the Soul battling it out over possession of Everyman." [2] The formula is conceived in terms of racist ideology: the phrases "racial disharmony," "the clash of blood," and "unstable genetic constitution" [3] betray this racist bias.

Abolitionist authors magnified the nobility and long-suffering virtue of the tragic mulatto. William Wells Brown in his 1855 novel, *Clotelle, or The President's Daughter;* W. W. Smith in his 1860 novel, *The Yankee Slave Driver;* and Harriet Beecher Stowe in her 1852 novel, *Uncle Tom's Cabin* deal exclusively with the virtues of the tragic mulatto character. But even in the case of these authors, the mulattoes' virtues are ascribed to their "white blood." In contrast to later images of the mixed blood, the tragic mulatto character of this period is not in conflict over the warring parts of his own nature. Instead, he is at odds with a society that exploits and oppresses him as if he were a common slave or, worse, abuses him sexually in a manner rarely endured by the full-blooded field slave. Since the tragic mulatto character in these novels is often an educated and cultured individual, his oppression is all the more difficult to endure.

One of the most unforgettable portraits of the tragic mulatto character appears in *Uncle Tom's Cabin.* Cassy's history is "wild, painful, and romantic." Her face, once seen, is never to be forgotten: "There was a fierce pride and defiance in every line of her face." [4]

Cassy's history is the prototype for the history of many tragic mulatto characters in later fiction. She was brought up in luxury. When she was fourteen, however, her father died suddenly and Cassy was sold to cover her father's debts *(Band of Angels* and *Iola Leroy* follow this pattern). She became the mistress of a man whom she loved and who gave her "everything that money could buy." For seven years they were happy; two children, Henry and Elise, were born to them. Then through a series of misfortunes, she passes from one master to another and at last is sold to Simon Legree. She says to Tom that she cannot love God if he can allow such things to happen to her. But if there is a God, Cassy continues to count on him to wreak vengeance upon those who have sinned against her: "I've walked the streets when it seemed as if I had misery enough in one heart to sink the city. . . . Yes! and in the judgment day, I will stand up before God, a witness against those that have ruined me and my children, body and soul!" [5]

In spite of all that has threatened her humanity, Cassy helps a woman in the fields, aids Uncle Tom and a lovely young mulatto woman Legree has taken as a new mistress, and can still weep over Jesus' last words. Cassy's noble endurance is rewarded by eventual freedom and reunion with her daughter. Cassy is a powerful weapon in Mrs. Stowe's war against slavery and injustice.

In another early novel, *The Garies and Their Friends* (1857), by a black author, Frank J. Webb, one of the central characters is a tragic mulatto who has passed for white. Estranged from both the white and the black group, he is never free of his secret and at last he loses all through exposure of his racial heritage. Haunted by fear of detection, consumed with guilt because of his denial of the black group, Clarence Garie is an excellent example of the tragic mulatto passer.

Death through grief, murder, childbirth, abortion, and suicide; life with remorse, despair, bitterness, alienation, and insanity; this is the catalogue of tortures that are endured by various tragic mulatto characters. In "La Belle Zoraide," a story by Kate Chopin, a lovely mulatto girl is raised at her mistress's side. She has never performed more difficult labor than sewing, and she even has a black servant. Her mistress wishes Zoraide to make a "good" marriage with a mulatto, but Zoraide loves a man as black as ebony. When Zoraide's mistress shows her fury, the slave girl answers: "since I am not white, let me have from out of my own race the one whom my heart has chosen." [6] But her lover is sent away. Zoraide's one remaining happiness is the child she bears, but when that child is born, she is deceived into thinking it dead. The cost of all these foolish attempts to impose intraracial color prejudices is the girl's sanity: Zoraide lives to be an old woman, always clasping a "senseless bundle of rags shaped like an infant in swaddling clothes." [7] Even when her real child is returned to her, Zoraide will not recognize her and holds instead her "bundle of joy." Typical of many of Kate Chopin's studies in race relations, the tale is offered without authorial comment. However, her sense of the profound irony inherent in the relations between the races is apparent. This story is particularly ironic because the racial prejudice which destroys the lovely mulatto girl is not her own but her mistress's and it is not the white woman's hatred for the girl, but rather her love that destroys Zoraide. In this story, as in "Desirée's Baby," pretense results in disillusionment and death.

In the latter tale Desirée is in actuality a white woman who has a baby by her beloved husband Armand and who is rejected by him when that baby shows unmistakable evidence of Negro blood. When Desirée realized that Armand's rejection of her is total, she took her child in her arms, "disappeared among the reeds and willows that grew thick along the banks of the deep, sluggish bayou; and ... did not come back again." [8] Since Desirée's parentage was indeed unknown, both she and Armand had assumed that it was she who carried the stigma of intermixture. So Desirée enacts the final desperate act of so many tragic mulattoes. But Kate Chopin adds a wonderful twist to her story: after Desirée's death and that of his only son, Armand finds an old letter from his mother to his father. In it, his mother thanks God that her son "will never know that his mother, who adores him, belongs to the race that is cursed with the brand of slavery." [9] With savage irony, Chopin exposes the tragic folly of racial pride. Through his own actions, Armand caused the deaths of his innocent wife and the son who carried Armand's own "tainted" blood.

Charles Chesnutt's *The House Behind the Cedars* (1900) is one of the best-known novels by a Negro author utilizing the tragic mulatto theme. Chesnutt depicts the virtues of an all-but-white woman named Rena Walden—a woman who is intelligent, refined, and sensitive but who is nonetheless doomed because she cannot cross the barrier of caste. Chesnutt employed this theme because he was a member of the early Negro middle-class school: like other black authors writing during this period, he made almost all his protagonists light-skinned members of the Negro upper class in order to show the "better class of Negroes"—their culture and gentility and thus their right to be treated as the equal of whites.[10] The tragic mulatto character was most appropriate for this purpose.

There is a whole series of novels in the 1920s and early 1930s, all by white authors, in which the melodrama of the tragic mulatto plays a major role. Among these are John Bennett's 1921 novel, *Madame Margot;* Vera Caspary's 1929 novel, *The White Girl;* Evans Wall's 1929 *The No-Nation Girl* and his 1933 *Love Fetish;* Geoffrey Barnes's 1932 *Dark Lustre;* and *Gulf Stream* (1931) by Marie Stanley. The tragic mulatto protagonists of these novels are almost always all-but-white women of great beauty. They are "creatures in a half-world, belonging neither to one race nor the other ... the white in them seems never quite able to absorb the black. [It is] ... a sort of Gulf Stream; that never-ending current; a warm, vivid, vital flow of color through the white. Once it's there, it stays there, retaining its temperature, its color, no matter what alien waters surround it." [11]

In most of these novels, the mulatto figure is characterized by an inability to control his own fate. She is either a character like Cassy of *Uncle Tom's Cabin,* who does have stature and dignity but is prevented by external forces (slavery in this case) from being her own mistress; or she is the victim of her own internal struggle between her mixed blood and her own unsatisfied yearnings. Characters like Cassy more legitimately deserve to be thought of as "tragic" because they are given the stature to go along with the concept. The "no-nation" female and many of the self-divided male mulatto characters are strictly creatures of melodrama and are, at most, figures of pathos rather than of tragedy.

Although there has been a transformation of the tragic mulatto character in the direction of greater psychological and sociological complexity (e.g., William Faulkner's *Light in August* and Robert Penn Warren's *Band of Angels),* the old formula was used as late as 1950 in Elizabeth Coker's *Daughter of Strangers.* Although the protagonist of her novel eventually finds happiness by identifying with and working for the black group, her long internal struggles are described in the traditional terms of the tragic mulatto personality: "Her beauty has a strange, wild quality quite at variance with her intelligent, trained mind"; and "the idea of the mixed river of her blood was whirling in her brain and in her troubled, uneasy frame of mind she had become a stranger to herself." [12] Biological determinism seems to be a hard idea to put to rest. That, together with the fascination that white authors have had with the long suffering mixed-blood character, and the fact that the tragic mulatto character lends itself well as a subject of the "potboiler," probably insures that we have not seen the last of this formula character in the American novel.

Before leaving this subject, there are two late-nineteenth-century authors who deserve special attention as serious writers of fiction: George Washington Cable and William Dean Howells. Cable's stories and novels dealing with the tragic mulatto are considered by many critics to be the best literature on the subject; and William Dean Howells's *An Imperative Duty* is an excellent satire on the tragic mulatto character and the literature surrounding her.

One of the strengths of Cable's writing stems from his interest in the mulatto community in New Orleans and his ability to capture the ambience of that particular environment. In addition, Cable's genuine concern for the fate of the black man in America is clearly evident in his writing. Between 1880 and 1894, George Washington Cable waged virtually a one-man crusade on behalf of Negro civil rights during a period of American history when neither the North nor the South was willing to consider the issues raised by the emancipation of the slaves. In *Old Creole Days,* a collection of stories first published in 1879, Cable most clearly displayed his interest in the tragic mulatto character. In his 1880 novel, *The Grandissimes,* Cable broadened the scope of his subject to include not merely two very important tragic mulattoes, but a gallery of Negro characters who represent almost every facet of the black experience of his time (or that of 1803, when the novel takes place). And in *The Grandissimes,* Cable uses his tragic mulatto characters in a more complex and subtle fashion than he does in "Madame Delphine" and " 'Tite Poulette" *(Old Creole Days).*

Cable is representative of a group of authors of both fiction and nonfiction who have written about the quadroons of New Orleans. Prior to the Civil War, New Orleans had the largest community of free Negroes anywhere in the South, and the wealth of this community was considerable. Many of these mixed bloods were not only wealthy but very well educated. A distinct group of these mixed bloods consisted of the beautiful almost-white women who were raised with the utmost care and delicate handling in order to serve as the mistresses of the white male aristocracy. It was at the famous quadroon balls that many of these matches were arranged. In "Madame Delphine," Cable provides a lengthy description of the quadroons during the height of their splendor during the 1820s and 1830s.

This long story (sometimes called a novella) is set in New Orleans in the early 1820s. Madame Delphine's splendor has already passed; her "husband" is dead, and she lives a quiet, pious existence. In order to allow her sixteen-year-old daughter, Olive, to make a respectable match with a white man (the girl's guardian, in fact), Madame Delphine takes the only course she can think of to save her daughter from a life of unhappiness as a quadroon mistress: she goes before a lawyer and swears that Olive is not her child. Cable rounds out his story with Madame Delphine's confession to Pere Jerome that Olive is her child. With her confession, Madame Delphine dies.

" 'Tite Poulette," another story in *Old Creole Days*, is similar to "Madame Delphine." Like Madame Delphine, Zalli John—"Madame John"—is a quadroon who inherited her house from her "husband." There she and her seventeen-year-old daughter, 'Tite Poulette, live in genteel poverty. Like Madame Delphine, Madame John is bitter at the fate of her child; both Olive and Poulette are "saintly" young women who accept their fate uncomplainingly. And to both of these young girls, Cable brings happiness—at the cost of their mothers' denial of their only joy, their daughters. Yet only through Madame Delphine's and Madame John's denial of motherhood can Olive and Poulette marry their white lovers.

The issues confronted in *Old Creole Days* are peripheral. The plight of the octoroon is dealt with only as part of the traditional dilemma of the almost-white girl and her Caucasian lover. Cable's emphasis is on local color and the narration of tales is filled with pathos and charm. In *The Grandissimes*, however, he attempts to deal with many of the major problems confronting the South: with public education, segregation in public facilities, mob violence, and the denial of true freedom to blacks. Cable emphatically declared later that he had "meant to make *The Grandissimes* as truly a political work as it has ever been called." [13] This first novel was written at a point in Cable's career when he had great faith in what he later called "the Silent South," by which he meant a large minority of southerners who agreed privately with the positions to which he was publicly committing himself. When he wrote his earliest novel he was first and foremost a reformer; Cable later said that he wrote as near to truth and justice "as I knew how, upon questions that I saw must be settled by calm debate and cannot be settled by force or silence." [14] Although this study cannot examine the novel in its entirety, it is very important to see the context in which appear the two tragic mulatto characters, Palmyre Philosophe and Honoré Grandissime, free man of color (f.m.c.). In addition to his delineation of the race issue, Cable includes two other memorable Negro characters: Bras Coupé, the noble full-blooded African prince who will not submit to bondage; and

Clemence, the figure who represents the black masses, a character Philip Butcher has called "one of the most realistic Negro characters in American literature." [15]

Like many other authors of mulatto fiction, Cable uses the history of two brothers, alike in everything save a drop of Negro blood. In fact, Honoré Grandissime, f.m.c., and his brother, Honoré Grandissime, have been treated more as equals than any other pair of siblings in mulatto fiction. Their father had sent both his sons to Paris to be educated, but Honoré, f.m.c., inherits most of the fortune. Even so, the position of the *gens de coleur* in New Orleans is intolerable. Joseph Frowenfeld, Cable's spokesman in the novel, describes the plight of the quadroons on more than one occasion. He says to Honoré that they "want a great deal more than free papers can secure them. Emancipation before the law, though it may be a right which man has no right to withhold, is to them little more than a mockery until they achieve emancipation in the minds and good will of the people—'the people,' did I say? I mean the ruling class." [16] Honoré agrees with Joseph. Of his brother's life, he says, "what an accusation, my-de'-seh, is his whole life against that 'caste' which shuts him up within its narrow and almost solitary limits! . . . I am am-aze at the length, the blackness of that shadow! . . . It drhags us a centurhy behind the rhes' of the world! it rhetahds and poisons everhy industrhy we got!" [17]

On yet another occasion, Joseph speaks directly to Honoré, f.m.c., and urges him to go among his people, to work for their "moral elevation, their training in skilled work, . . . [and] public recognition of the rights of all. . . ." Joseph tells Honoré, f.m.c., that the free quadroons

are the saddest slaves of all. Your men, for a little property, and your women, for a little amorous attention, let themselves be shorn even of the virtue of discontent and for a paltry bit of sham freedom have consented to endure a tyrannous con-tumely which flattens them into the dirt like grass under a slab. I would rather be a runaway in the swamps than content myself with such a freedom. As your class stands before the world today—free in form but slaves in spirit—you are—I do not know but I was almost ready to say—a warning to philanthropists! [18]

Cable's concern for the political and social status of the mixed-blood character is quite unusual. Rather than bemoaning the fact that the quadroon or octoroon is not "lily white," Cable assumes that all people should be accorded the human rights and dignity which are their due, and he urges the mixed blood to be proud and forceful in fighting for his rights.

Honoré, f.m.c.'s, fate is that of the conventional tragic mulatto. After an unsuccessful attempt at suicide, he succeeds in killing himself for love of Palmyre Philosophe, the beautiful quadroon. She, however, loves Honoré, f.m.c.'s, brother and is unhappy because he does not return her love. Palmyre is far different from Olive and Poulette. In type, she is closer to Cassy of *Uncle Tom's Cabin.* Palmyre is described as having "a femininity without humanity—something that made her with all her superbness, a creature that one would want to find chained." [19] Much wronged, Palmyre tries to take revenge upon the man who wronged her. Joseph Frowenfeld attends to the bullet wound inflicted on Palmyre, and Cable uses the occasion to compare his kind treatment of the mulatto woman with the harsh treatment she has endured all her life. In an eloquent passage. Cable writes of the injustices done to Palmyre, abuse which helps to explain her "femininity without humanity":

Frowenfeld, even while his eyes met hers, could not resent her hostility. This monument of the shame of two races—this poisonous blossom of crime growing out of crime—this final, unanswerable white man's accuser—this would-be murderess— what ranks and companies would have to stand up in the Great Day with her and answer as accessory before the fact!
... This woman had stood all her life with dagger drawn, on the defensive against what certainly was to her an unmerciful world. With possibly one exception, the man before her was the only one she had ever encountered whose speech and gesture were clearly keyed to that profound respect which is woman's first, foundation claim on man. And yet by

inexorable decree, she belonged to what we used to call "the happiest people under the sun." We ought to stop saying that.

So far as Palmyre knew, the entire masculine wing of the mighty and exalted race, three-fourths of whose blood bequeathed her none of its prerogatives, regarded her as legitimate prey. The man before her did not. There lay the fundamental difference that, in her sight, as soon as she discovered it, gloried him.[20]

Eventually, Palmyre leaves the country and remains abroad, a wealthy woman. But she is forever alienated from the man she loves as well as from her country.

As unusual as George Washington Cable was in presenting the tragic mulatto not only as a figure of romance and melodrama but also as a social and political being, William Dean Howells's treatment of the theme was even more creative. A great realist of late-nineteenth-century American fiction, Howells was intensely devoted to social change in America. As Everett Carter points out, Howells was a satirist who believed in "the significance of the social organism of which he [was] a part"; he was an artist who tried "to make this organism even healthier." [21] Howells opposed romanticism precisely because it did not promote the clear understanding and insight needed to understand and change the social structure. In *Criticism and Fiction*, he argued against romantic novels because "they are idle lies about human nature and the social fabric, which it behooves us to know and to understand, that we may deal justly with ourselves and with one another." [22]

In *An Imperative Duty*, Howells dealt with certain racial beliefs of his day, with segregation, and with miscegenation. Edwin H. Cady claims that the novella dealt with these issues "in their most immediate, crucial aspects—in Northern, urban, and what were then modern circumstances, though in terms which permitted no Howells reader to shield his prejudices from its impact." [23] Cady is probably too generous to Howells. As with Twain's evasion of the racial issue by making Roxy and Valet de Chambre so light as to be indistinguishable in appearance from whites, so Rhoda Aldgate's white skin and manners, foreign residence, and well-kept secret make Howells's work less daring than Cady's statement would have us believe. Nonetheless, Howells's exposition of the tragic mulatto theme is significant in itself.

According to Cady, the impulse for this work

> came out of the author's time of painful reconstruction of his childhood. Now it is significant that there are no such intimate images of Negro playmates and personalities in Howells's memoirs as in Mark Twain's. Offhand, one recalls no Negroes at all in *A Boy's Town*. And it is not likely that there were many in bitterly proslavery, pro-Southern, anti-freedman Butler County, Ohio, during Howells's boyhood there. [But] . . . sympathy for the slave had been cardinal in Howells's childhood morality. For that his family had been hounded out of Hamilton, had suffered and failed in Dayton, had fought triumphantly in Ashtabula County.[24]

Howells's hero, Dr. Edward Olney, is sensitive to the race issue when he returns to the United States after an extended period abroad. Howells says that Olney was agreeably struck by "the race which vexes our social question with its servile past, and promises to keep it uncomfortable with its civic future." Furthermore, when Olney reflects upon the social relations between Negroes and whites, he remembers "that one would be quite as likely to meet a cow or a horse in an American drawing-room as a person of color." [25]

While Howells skillfully handles the racist attitudes of his characters, the author is himself not entirely free from the racist ideology of his day. In describing the blacks of Boston, Howells says: "Their environment had made as little impression on the older inhabitants, or on the natives [of Boston], as Time himself makes upon persons of their race." [26] Much of Rhoda's conflict he ascribes to her mixed blood. Yet he includes a fine satiric passage in which Dr. Olney laughs at the notions of atavism and lets the cold light of reason shine upon the myth of the "black baby." He tells Rhoda's aunt and guardian, Mrs. Meredith, that such an idea persists because "it's so thrilling to consider such a possibility that people like to consider it. Fancy is as much committed to it as prejudice is." [27]

Rhoda Aldgate is the offspring of the legal union of a white-physician and an octoroon woman. When they die, the physician's sister and brother-in-law, the Merediths, take the girl into their home and rear her as a lady. They do not intend to keep the girl's origins a secret from her, but they can never seem to find a means to tell the girl. When Rhoda seems likely to accept an offer of marriage from a young clergyman, Mrs. Meredith feels "an imperative duty" to tell Rhoda the truth at last.

Rhoda is a beautiful young woman, her rich complexion olive and her eyes and hair an inky black. Her face is said to be "of almost classic perfection." Olney thinks of her as wearing a "family face, with its somewhat tragic beauty, over a personality that was at once gentle and gay." [28] She is a happy woman, for she has been raised as a young lady in the care of her doting aunt and uncle. The secret of her birth has *not* been hers to carry. In fact, she unknowingly upsets her aunt because of her patronizing affection for Negroes. Mrs. Meredith's imagination is so concerned with the secret that she bears that she cannot see Rhoda's racist condescension for the blacks for whom she claims affection. During Mrs. Meredith's disclosure of her secret to Dr. Olney, Rhoda comes bursting into the room and tells her aunt: "There's one of those colored waiters down there that even *you* couldn't have anything to say against my falling in love with, Aunt Caroline. He's about four feet high, and his feet are about eighteen inches long, so that he looks just like a capital L. [So] . . . I've decided to call him Creepy-Mousy; . . . he's so small and cunning. And he's so sweet! I should like to *own* him, and keep him as long as he lived. Isn't it a shame that we can't *buy* them, Dr. Olney, as we used to?" Mrs. Meredith's reaction is: "You see! It is the race instinct! It must assert itself sooner or later." Olney's response makes much more sense: "I should say it was the other race instinct that was asserting itself sooner." [29]

One of the strengths of *An Imperative Duty* is the double edge of Howells's satire. While Dr. Olney is at times the "voice of reason and rationality" in the novella and is therefore an effective foil for both Mrs. Meredith and Rhoda, he is himself satirized by Howells on one significant occasion. As he listens to Mrs. Meredith's rambling preamble to her disclosure, Olney's feelings are those of superiority. He imagines a catalogue of woes that could have befallen Rhoda. Here Howells's satire is turned both upon Olney and upon romantic novels and plays:

"Olney believed that he began to understand. There was some stain upon that poor child's birth. She was probably not related to Mrs. Meredith at all; she was a foundling; or she was the daughter of some man or woman whose vices or crimes might find her out with their shame if not their propensity some day. . . . He was not shocked; he was interested by the fact; and he did not find Miss Aldgate at all less charming and beautiful in the conclusion he jumped to than he had found her before." Olney's "objective," disinterested liberality is swept away by Mrs. Meredith's next words, "My niece is of negro descent." Olney "recoils" and is "in a turmoil of emotion for which there is no term but disgust. His disgust was profound and pervasive, and it did not fail, first of all, to involve the poor child herself. He found himself personally disliking the notion of her having negro blood in her veins; before he felt pity he felt repulsion; his own race instinct expressed itself in a merciless rejection of her beauty, her innocence, her helplessness because of her race. The impulse had to have its course; and then he mastered it, with an abiding compassion and a sort of tender indignation." [30]

Olney's reaction is similar to that of Rena Walden's white lover, George Tryon, and to the response of many other white characters who are faced with this same news about their lovers. Nor is Rhoda's reaction to the news surprising to the student of mulatto literature. She registers the same disbelief, shock and anguish that have characterized the responses of so many other mixed bloods to the crisis experience: "Don't you understand that it tears my whole life up, and flings it out on the ground? But you *know* it isn't true. . . . I don't know what you're doing this for. It can't be true—it can't be real. Shall I *never* wake·from it. . . ?" [31]

The melodrama continues as Rhoda goes out for a walk, tormented by her newly discovered identity. She is appalled by the deference the blacks pay her; she examines them and feels them to be hideous "burlesques of humanity." Like so many other mulatto characters, Rhoda feels bitterness and regret that she did not always know of her racial origins so that she could be one with the dark-skinned people she assumes must be her folk. Sometimes "she grovelled in self-loathing and despair." At other times, she feels she must acknowledge her kinship with the blacks. All during this frenzied walk, she feels as if there are "two selves of her, one that lived before that awful knowledge, and one that had lived as long since, and again a third that knew and pitied them both." [32] Then Rhoda meets an old mulatto woman and goes to a colored church with her. While observing the service, Rhoda thinks to herself: "I can endure them if I can love them, and I shall love them if I try to help them." [33]

What distinguishes Howells's work from that of other authors who have written about the tragic mulatto character is that the melodrama is Rhoda's, Mrs. Meredith's, Olney's—not their author's. In each case, Howells distances himself from his characters' romantic notions. Sometimes he uses one character to deliver his criticisms against another character; at other points, the author delivers the satire himself. Olney discounts Mrs. Meredith's foolish racist ideas; Howells shows up Olney's pretensions to objectivity; and once Olney has realized how wasteful and foolishly romantic Rhoda would be to devote herself to living out her "tragic fate," Olney deflates Rhoda's tragic pose.

When Olney confesses his love for Rhoda, she says that she can never marry him. He, of course, already knows her secret and has been waiting to see if she will share it with him. Then, in a passage which is an outstanding illustration of Howells's brand of realism and the way in which he believed realism could help us to keep human nature and the social order in some rational, healthy perspective, Olney destroys Rhoda's great moment—and saves the woman:

> "I love you! I ask you to be my wife!"
> ... "Never!" She sprang to her feet and gasped hoarsely out, "I am a negress!"
> Something in her tragedy affected Olney comically. . . . He smiled. "Well, not a very black one. Besides, what of it, if I love you?"
> "What of it?" she echoed. "But don't you *know?* You *mustn't!*"

The simpleness of the words made him laugh outright; these she had not rehearsed. She had dramatized his instant renunciation of her when he knew the fatal truth.

"Why not? I love you, whether I must or not!"

As tragedy the whole affair had fallen to ruin. [So] ... it must be treated in no lurid twilight gloom, but in plain, simple, matter-of-fact noonday.[34]

When she protests to Olney that she *ought* to devote her life to elevating the blacks, Olney says she should devote fifteen-sixteenths of herself to his race and him; and the other one-sixteenth can be given to her colored connections. When she falls back upon the language of melodrama (she is one of them, she says; it is branded into her), he answers that she belongs far more to the oppressors than the oppressed. He insists that he is not ashamed of her, but she begs him to keep her secret. Olney agrees, but only so long as Rhoda does not believe him afraid to tell it. Howells concludes his work on an ironic racist note. If Olney ever had any regret, Howells tells us, it was that "the sunny natured antetypes of her mother's race had not endowed her with more of the heaven-born cheerfulness with which it meets contumely and injustice. His struggle was with the hypochondria of the soul into which the Puritanism of her father's race had sickened her, and which so often seems to satisfy its claim upon conscience by enforcing some aimless act of self-sacrifice."[35]

In *An Imperative Duty*, then, Howells manages to transcend the formula literature of the tragic mulatto and produce a genuine satire which exposes the racist assumptions and ideology of the tragic mulatto novel. The "liberal" pose of the white lover is exposed *as* a pose in the scene in which Olney is shocked to find himself horrified at the fact of Rhoda's heritage. Without the rejection by society and lover that is the stock-in-trade of the beautiful, tragic heroine, Howells removes the logical possibility of suicide for his heroine. Indeed, Howells rejects not only tragedy, but also melodrama, as a means of resolving his story. Using deflation as his major technique, he reduces Rhoda's posturing to absurdity. Finally, although Howells does allow Rhoda to be "long suffering," he adds a final irony when he attributes the cause of her suffering not to her mixed-racial heritage but rather to the Puritanism of her father's race. Considering the intellectual milieu in which Howells produced this "small" work, and viewing *An Imperative Duty* in the context of the racist stereotypes and ideology of tragic mulatto fiction, his achievement in this work was indeed considerable.

NOTES

1. Sterling Brown, *The Negro in American Fiction* (Washington, D.C.: The Associates in Negro Folk Education, 1937), p. 144.
2. Nancy Tischler, *Black Masks: Negro Characters in Modern Southern Fiction* (University Park: Pennsylvania State University Press, 1969), p. 97.
3. Everett V. Stonequist, *The Marginal Man: A Study in Personality and Culture Conflict* (1937; rpt. New York: Russell & Russell, 1961), pp. 147–48.
4. Harriet Beecher Stowe, *Uncle Tom's Cabin: or Life Among the Lowly,* 2 vols. (1852; rpt. New York: AMS Press, 1967), p. 408.
5. Ibid., p. 425.
6. Kate Chopin, "La Belle Zoraide," *The Complete Works of Kate Chopin,* ed. Per Seyersted (Baton Rouge: Louisiana State University Press, 1970), p. 305.
7. Ibid., p. 307.
8. Kate Chopin, "Desirée's Baby," *The Complete Works of Kate Chopin,* ed. Per Seyersted (Baton Rouge: Louisiana State University Press, 1970), p. 244.
9. Ibid., p. 245.
10. Chesnutt also was capable of satirizing the "blue-vein" circles and their pretensions, as in his "Wife of His Youth."
11. Marie Stanley, *Gulf Stream* (New York: Coward-McCann, 1931), p. 96.
12. Elizabeth Boatwright Coker, *Daughter of Strangers* (New York: E. P. Dutton and Company, 1950), pp. 164, 144.
13. Louis J. Rubin, Jr., *George Washington Cable* (New York: Pegasus, 1969), p. 78.
14. Ibid.
15. *George W. Cable* (New York: Twayne Publishers, 1962), p. 115. Characters like Bras Coupé, Clemence, and Honoré Grandissime, f.m.c., do not appear in Cable's later fiction. Unfortunately, he resolved the conflict between his reformist impulses and his desire to be a socially acceptable writer of the Genteel tradition by succumbing to the latter alternative.
16. George Washington Cable, *The Grandissimes* (New York: Scribner's, 1898), p. 185.
17. Ibid., p. 201.
18. Ibid., p. 225.
19. Ibid., p. 89.

20. Ibid., p. 173.
21. Everett Carter, *Howells and the Age of Realism* (Hamden, Conn.: Archon Books, 1966), pp. 19–20.
22. Howells, *Criticism and Fiction,* ed. Clara Marburg Kirk and Rudolph Kirk (New York: New York University Press, 1959), pp. 46–47.
23. Edwin H. Cady, *The Realist at War: The Mature Years, 1885–1920, of William Dean Howells* (Syracuse, N.Y.: Syracuse University Press, 1958), p. 156.
24. Ibid., p. 157.
25. Howells, *An Imperative Duty* (New York: Harper & Brothers, 1892), p. 5.
26. Ibid., p. 6.
27. Ibid., p. 38.
28. Ibid., p. 17.
29. Ibid., pp. 55–56.
30. Ibid., p. 34.
31. Ibid., p. 75.
32. Ibid., p. 87.
33. Ibid., p. 95.
34. Ibid., p. 139.
35. Ibid., p. 149.

Part II

5.

The Crisis Experience

When "Master Tom Driscoll" is told by Roxy that he is in reality her son—a "black" man and a slave—he calls her a lying devil and a beast and raises a club against his new-found mother. When he is finally convinced that he is indeed her son, his anguish is terrible. Her revelation, if made public, would strip him literally, of everything. By relegating him to the colored caste in American society, Roxy could take power, pride, wealth, dignity, security, and physical well-being itself from her son, Valet De Chambre. The magnitude of "Master Tom Driscoll's" loss is made clear from the fate he suffers at the end of *Pudd'nhead Wilson:* he is sold down river to a life of brutal, unremitting slave labor.

The discovery of Negro blood in one's veins would be a shattering experience for most white Americans. Many Caucasians have been conditioned to fear, distrust, and often to hate blacks, for the myths, lies, and superstitions about blacks have been potent in molding the racial attitudes of the white caste. And, to the white racist, discovering that one is literally kin to a darkly "mysterious" race of people whose origins are in the "primeval jungle" is

119

traumatic. However, it is the expected social repercussions of the public exposure or revelation of Negro "blood" that are most to be feared, according to those authors who deal with this topic. Suddenly, the caste system is seen by the "new black man or woman" as being horribly unjust. The prejudice against blacks developed over a lifetime may not be completely erased; but for some characters, the "crisis experience" brings freedom from prejudice and misconceptions as well as pain and confusion. For others, the acceptance of their Negro heritage may be so greatly feared and abhorred that the "white" individual loses his sanity. Still others choose to "remain white" by passing. In any case, virtually all the fictional characters who undergo "the crisis experience" also undergo profound social and psychological changes in their lives. This "soul-shaking" experience, as reflected in American fiction, is the subject of this chapter: the nature of the revelation itself, the individual's immediate reactions, and his decisions regarding his racial and individual identity. (The mixed blood's permanent response to the crisis experience is, as I have indicated in Chapter 1, the subject of Chapters 6 through 9.)

According to Everett Stonequist, the crisis experience is the point in the mixed blood's life when he becomes conscious of his own racial and social marginality. Before the crisis experience, he is unaware, or is only dimly cognizant, of his own difference from the dominant white caste. At a critical moment in his life, however, an event occurs that shows him conclusively that he can no longer think of himself as belonging to the "superior" majority; he discovers that he in fact belongs to a despised minority and that even his identity and place within the lower caste are problematic. Due to such factors as his physical appearance and cultural and educational attainments, the mixed blood has been conditioned to feel more comfortable among the upper caste. During the period of crisis, when the individual is trying to understand the meaning of his marginality, the habits and attitudes of a lifetime, to some extent, break down. Even if he seeks identification with the lower caste, the distrust and envy of the full-blooded lower-caste members must be overcome. Furthermore, there is "an important change in his conception of himself, although the total transformation may come only after a prolonged and painful process, especially if the crisis has been severe. The individual must then 'find himself' again. He must reconstruct his conception of himself as well as his place or role in society. The two are interrelated; they are two aspects of the personal-social process." [1]

Mark Twain likens Tom Driscoll's crisis experience to the geophysical rending of the earth's surface:

> A gigantic eruption . . . changes the face of the surrounding landscape, beyond recognition, . . . making fair lakes where deserts had been and deserts where green prairies had smiled before. The tremendous catastrophe which had befallen Tom had changed his moral landscape in much the same way. Some of his low places he found lifted to ideals, some of his ideals had sunk to the valley, and lay there with the sack-cloth and ashes of pumice stone and sulphur on their ruined heads.
>
> For days he wandered in lonely places, thinking, thinking, thinking—trying to get his bearings. It was new work. If he met a friend, he found that the habit of a lifetime had in some mysterious way vanished—his arm hung limp, instead of involuntarily extending the hand for a shake. It was the "nigger" in him asserting its humility, and he blushed and was abashed. . . . Under the influence of a great mental and moral upheaval, his character and habits had taken on the appearance of complete change, but after a while with the subsistence of the storm, both began to settle toward their former places.[2]

Tom Driscoll returns to his former habits; even the knowledge that Roxy could expose him as an "ignominious" black man cannot remake this scoundrel. Yet Tom feels the magnitude of Roxy's revelation. Having no moral reserves upon which to call, Tom responds to the crisis experience in what is for him, a characteristic fashion: he ignores it, as he does all other unpleasant realities.

Tom Driscoll's history illustrates another significant element in the individual's reaction to the crisis experience. He has not only been white; he has belonged to the upper class within the upper caste. His exposure as a Negro would thus remove from him the privileges accorded to a white gentleman, to a Virginia aristocrat. Tom's privileges have obviously been far greater than those of a white sharecropper, whose only social esteem comes through the color of his skin. If the "cracker" were to lose his caste privileges, his greatest loss would, more than likely, be psychological in nature: to become a "black" would be to become less than human. But for ruling-class whites, the loss would be far greater.

According to Everett Stonequist, the degree of trauma associated with the crisis experience reflects the extent to which the individual has assimilated the culture and values of the dominant group: "The more completely the individual assimilates the culture of the dominant group the greater are his confusion and difficulty when he finds himself excluded.... The extent of his assimilation measures the depth of his psychic identification, and this in turn measures the severity of the mental shock when he experiences the conflict of cultures as it bears upon his own acceptability." [3] Using this measuring rod, we can see that some lower-class individuals facing the crisis experience might respond with less shock and disgust than some upper-class members. One difference between the two types of individuals is the number of material objects and the social and monetary accouterments of wealth and status that the upper-class individual stands to lose.

The crisis experience, as depicted in the American novel, is usually a single shattering experience that irrevocably transforms the mixed-blood—always with respect to his psychological well-being, and often also with respect to his social standing. He is faced with the existential crisis of redefining himself in terms of his social and psychological environment. How he meets this challenge is the subject of much mulatto fiction.

One who survives the crisis experience eventually achieves a permanent adjustment. Before this, however, he usually passes through a period of ambivalence toward himself, his society, and his marginal position in that society. According to Everett Stonequist, the marginal man "is torn between two courses of action and is unable calmly to take the one and leave the other. The unattainable white world ... continues to haunt his imagination and stir his emotions. At one moment it may be idealized and longed for; at another moment despised and hated. The other world to which he has been assigned has the same contradictory character: at times it appears as a beloved place of refuge, solace and recognition: again it may seem like a prison—something cursed and hateful, or even shameful." [4] This ambivalence is suggested in

Imitation of Life (1933), where Fannie Hurst's Peola, a mulatto girl, tells her dark-skinned mother that she has "prayed same as you, for the strength to be proud of being black under my white. I've tried to glory in my people. I've drenched myself in the life of Toussaint L'Ouverture, Booker Washington, and Frederick Douglass. I've tried to catch some of their spark. But I'm not that stuff." [5]

Of Mimi Daquin, the mixed-blood heroine of *Flight*, Walter White wrote: "At times this [her consciousness of being black] created within her moods of introspection which veered dangerously near the morbid. At other times it inculcated a deep and passionate scorn of those who were her own and her race's oppressors. She chuckled when she read or heard of or saw their imbecilities, their shortcomings. She looked with scorn upon their provincialism, their stupidity, their ignorance. Conversely, she found herself magnifying the virtues, the excellencies of her own people and, at the same time, she tried to explain away through a process of subtle sophistry all their faults." [6]

Most of the mulatto characters who undergo the crisis experience have no previous knowledge of their Negro blood. Their immediate reactions reveal their attitudes toward race, status, and self-esteem. An individual character may experience more than one reaction in the first period after the discovery of his Negro background. For some mixed-blood characters, there occurs a brief symbolic death. The world reels; consciousness is lost, or a dazed state ensues; in *Iola Leroy,* the result is even serious "brain fever." The sense of living in a nightmare, of losing touch with reality, common to those who undergo the crisis experience, is also evident in Robert Penn Warren's *Band of Angels* (1955) and Elizabeth Coker's *Daughter of Strangers* (1950).

In *Kingsblood Royal* (1947), Sinclair Lewis narrates Neil Kingsblood's crisis experience and the resolution of the dilemma that this creates for him. Here a priggish young banker discovers his family's Negro blood in a genealogical search for English royal blood. From this point on, Lewis describes the transformation of the mental state of this cocky, provincial member of the Anglo-Saxon elite of Grand Republic, Minnesota. His moral landscape having just suffered an irreversible shock, Neil spends the next six months of his life trying to come to terms with his new identity. He must fight against the prejudice of a lifetime, and he considers several courses of action. Before he can decide upon his racial and personal identity, he realizes that he must understand that he is indeed a Negro. Neil says to himself: "If you *are* a Negro, you be one and fight as one. See if you can grow up, and then fight. —But I've got to learn what a Negro is; I've got to learn, from the beginning, what I am!" [7] Neil thus understands the fundamental existentialist dimension of his dilemma. He must find out *who* he is before he can assert his being.

In order to find out who they are, many mulatto characters search for the visible signs of their "damnation." Charles Chesnutt's John Walden *(The House Behind the Cedars)* and Elizabeth Coker's Charlotte Le Jeune *(Daughter of Strangers)* gaze at themselves in the mirror to detect signs of their "black blood." Abby Clanghearne, the protagonist of Edith Pope's novel *Colcorton* (1944), and Neil Kingsblood dejectedly study their fingernails to see whether they have the supposedly telltale blue half-moons of the black.

Just as an accident victim often wonders why he "deserves" such a fate, so the individual who undergoes the crisis experience often agonizes over the reason for his trauma. Why must I be a Negro? he asks. Tom Driscoll asks himself, "Why were niggers *and* whites made? What crime did the uncreated first nigger commit that the curse of birth was decreed for him?" [8] Accepting the stereotype of the lower-class Negro as the only identity open to a member of the oppressed caste, the mulatto often cannot imagine what role he will play as a "Negro." To Harry Leroy, the consequences of being a Negro are clear: "On one side were strength, courage, enterprise, power of achievement, and memories of a wonderful past. On the other side were weakness, ignorance, poverty, and the proud world's social scorn. He knew nothing of colored people except as slaves, and his whole soul shrank from equalizing himself with them. He was fair enough to pass unchallenged among the fairest in the land, and yet a Christless prejudice had decreed that he should be a pariah." [9] For Neil Kingsblood the thought of being a Negro evokes only the white racist stereotypes:

> To be a Negro was to live in a decaying shanty or in a frame tenement like a foul egg-crate, ... to sleep on unchanged

bedclothes that were like funguses, and to have for spiritual leader only a howling lecherous swindler.

There were practically no other kinds of Negroes. Had he not heard so from his Georgia army doctor?

To be a Negro, once they found you out, no matter how pale you were, was to work in kitchens. . . .

It was to be an animal physically. It was to be an animal culturally, deaf to Beethoven and St. Augustine. It was to be an animal ethically, unable to keep from stealing and violence, from lying and treachery. It was literally and altogether to be an animal, somewhere between human beings and the ape.[10]

And, indeed, when Neil stands up in front of the "best class of men" at the Federal Club's Auld Lang Syne Holiday Stag and tells them that he is happy to be a Negro, he finds out that some of his assumptions about being black in white America are true. He is rejected by many of his friends, moved to a position in the bank where his "black" presence cannot disturb the white customers, later fired from his job, turned down for other jobs because of his race, treated as a oddity, asked insulting questions, threatened, asked to move from his home, and finally shot at because he refuses to be "run out."

In order to destroy the old identification with the white caste, in order to learn more about blacks as individuals and not merely as stereotypes, Neil Kingsblood and Rhoda Aldgate, heroine of Howells's An Imperative Duty, like other mulatto characters, go to Negro churches to observe members of the Negro race. Rhoda is fascinated, but also repulsed, and her final adjustment to her small portion of black blood is less comfortable than that of Neil. He goes to Evan Brewster's church and is greatly impressed with the minister, who is an eloquent, gentle, highly trained theologian from Harvard Divinity School. Neil is moved by the sermon (having half expected a lot of "jungle" primitivism, he is happy to hear Brewster's restrained presentation) and the reading of the Scriptures. Of Neil's pilgrimage to the church, Lewis says: "He was not an amused tourist; it was desperate for him to know his own people." After hearing the service, Neil's reaction is: "This is my history. . . . This is my people; I must come out." [11] After the service, Neil gets himself introduced to a black family (he had known the son at school) and goes home with them. He has no intention of revealing what he has found out about his ancestor, Xavier Pic. But he finds himself liking the Woolcapes so much and so wants them to feel that he is not an outsider that he confesses his secret. From this point on, for the next six months, Neil sees his new friends often and learns a great deal about his race. Now a marginal man, he is tormented by feelings of ambivalence. He is now aware of his white friends' racism, of their bigoted arrogance, but he does not feel ready to "come out." His black friends advise him not to; he himself cannot fathom how he could reject his identity as a member of the local elite. And how can he force his "innocent" mother, wife, and daughter to bear with him the cross of Negro birth? Yet when he sees a Negro couple turned away from a hotel, he approaches them and tells them of other accommodations. The man says that most members of Neil's race do not show much courtesy toward blacks, whereupon Neil finds himself saying: "I'm not white. I'm colored, thank God!" [12] When he finally does reveal his black ancestry at a family council, he realizes that he may lose his wife Vestal and daughter Biddy. They return home and there Neil, a changed man and yet the same man, a white man and yet, somehow, a member of a despised minority, confronts Vestal: "the unknown Negro, Neil, faced his white wife, and he had no allies." [13]

Neil feels so much admiration for his black friends that he tells Vestal that he would *volunteer* to be a Negro even if the Xavier Pic story turned out to be a mistake. Yet when one of his black friends suggests that he find a job with a black business, Neil thinks to himself that he will not "go down that far, and then, considerably shocked, understood that Mayo Street and Negro businessmen still *were* far down, to him, and that Hack Riley had been right in scolding that he was playing at being a Negro." Here we can observe the ambivalence, the divided loyalty, to which Stonequist alludes. Neil has come to despise white racists; the doctrine of Anglo-Saxon superiority; and the failures of the American political, economic, and social system. He greatly admires his black friends who fight discrimination and maintain their dignity. Yet his spontaneous reaction to working in the Negro section of town, for a Negro employer, is one of repugnance. Then his new identification and new outlook reassert themselves, and he stifles his negative feelings. Lewis wants us to recognize Neil's sincerity in trying to establish a black identity, for he tells us that Neil "was not playing [at being a Negro], even if he was slightly confused as to what he wanted to do, in the unceasing job-hunt." [14]

Neil's shock at discovering that he is a "black" man in a predominantly white culture, his attempt to accept his black inheritance and mold a new identity, and his inconsistency and ambivalence are all aspects of the crisis experience. Throughout the novel he tries to learn what a Negro is, what he himself is. When a black friend points out to Neil that he would be ashamed to bring her home, he answers, "I can't take you home till I can take my own self there!" [15] But by the conclusion of the novel, Neil has come to accept and to feel proud of his new black identity.

With greater power than other novels discussed in this chapter, Robert Penn Warren's *Band of Angels* provides a profound insight into role-playing; the meaning of self-definition, loneliness, and alienation; freedom and responsibility; and the human condition itself. Although Warren is a southern white outsider who writes about a "black problem" (as our caste definitions might style it), and although he is not and could not possibly be entirely free of racist ideology himself, his subject is Amantha Starr's existentialist dilemma. He is not, as so many black writers have said of William Styron's *Confessions of Nat Turner,* just writing about himself. Warren works with familiar material, much of it historically verifiable. [16]

Warren's heroine, Amantha Starr, has been raised on her father's plantation, Starrwood, primarily by her "black mammy," Aunt Sukie. Her warm and loving father is a dominant figure in the child's life. Treated as a white aristocrat, she knows no other existence. Her assimilation into the white culture of the ante-bellum South is complete. Her father is a slaveholder, and her conception of blacks has been formed by her knowledge of Aunt Sukie; Shaddy, a black carpenter who works on the plantation; and the black field hands. Manty's existence prior to her crisis experience is happy except for one significant trauma. Shaddy had been a beloved figure in her childhood and had made her a doll, Bu-Bula, her favorite toy. She had been used to sitting on the carpenter's lap, talking to him and playing with him. This practice continued unbroken until one day Aunt Sukie turned on Shaddy and told him to stop fondling the now adolescent Manty. Shaddy became angry, and looking at Manty with revulsion he said, "Yeah, what she?—ain't nuthin', no better'n nuthin'—yeah, what she?" [17] Like any other mulatto character, "she ain't nuthin'. She ain't house dog and she ain't rabbit dog. She ain't nuthin'. She ain't nigger and she ain't white. She born tangled up—she ain't nuthin'." [18]

Utilizing another convention, Robert Penn Warren eliminates the white father (who, in this case, is still technically his daughter's master). Because of his untimely death, because he never manumitted his daughter, *and* because he died in debt, his daughter Amantha is plunged into a nightmare. The situation is unreal: "Little Manty" stands by her father's grave, having been unexpectedly called back from Oberlin; the Edenic scenes of her childhood surround her; "and in the timeless flicker of my consciousness I felt myself a child again, lying on my back in that little embracing trough, safe, under the sunny sky and cedars, safe—." [19] Then, suddenly, dreamlike, grotesque, the sheriff grabs at her, tears her out of this innocence and plunges her into the waiting, malevolent, post-Edenic experience. You're worth $1200, at least, she is told, the sum of her father's debts. Manty's flesh becomes the means to pay off an unredeemed debt to society.

Unlike Tom Driscoll and some of the other mixed bloods discussed here, Manty does not cry out her denial. She has never been free of the memory of Shaddy's accusation and of her father's punishment of the faithful slave (he was sold). "I knew it was true," she tells us; true that she is a Negro and a slave. "I knew it as truly as though I had known it all my life, and with some unformulated surge of emotion, a hope, a despair, a yearning, I swung toward the other grave [of her mother], the old grave over yonder by the cedars." [20] When Manty later thinks of her mother, she feels joy because *"oh, she loved me.* Then suddenly [Manty] thought: but she was a nigger." [21]

The conflict between love and self-definition in this novel is powerful. Manty yearns for love from others, yet that love is always based on the denial of her black roots. Furthermore, she wants these loved ones (her father; then her first (or should we say second?) master, who is also her first lover, Hamish Bond; and finally, her husband, Tobias Sears, to define her. Yet how can their definition of her identity be anything but false since she can no longer be defined as she was in her state of innocence? It is this understanding that she finally reaches; and with this awareness, she can begin the task of self-definition.

Although Manty knows that she is a Negro, she cannot actually accept the fact of her degradation. "Amantha's problem," as Leslie Fiedler has pointed out, "is that she cannot will to say the words, 'I am a Negro.' " [22] She actually sees "the stain of the black blood swelling through[her] veins—yes, I actually saw some such picture in my head, a flood darkening through all the arteries and veins of my body—no, a stain spreading in a glass of clear water." [23] This image threatens her stability, perhaps not as melodramatically as that which disorients Helen Phillips in *The Call of the South,* but with just as much psychological significance. But if Amantha is not a Negro, then, in our society, she is nothing—for the culture refuses to let her define herself as white. And she herself cannot pretend that she belongs to the upper caste. But if she is a Negro, then she is indeed nothing, for she has been reduced to chattel, "a non-person . . . suspended in the vacuum of no identity." She tells the slave trader that everything is a mistake: "it can't be true, it can't happen to me, not to me, *for I'm Amantha Starr—I'm Amantha Starr!"* [emphasis added].[24] It is as if she hopes to exorcise the evil that menaces her by repeating her name: she is Amantha, who, by definition, is white. But the trader understands her desperate hope and answers, "Yeah, you're Amantha Starr, all right. And that's why you are here, because you are you, gal." [25] Later, as she looks at the other slaves on board the ship that is taking them to market, she protests: "I was not one of them, I was no nigger, I was I, I was Amantha." [26]

But who is, who was, Amantha? The answer to the first question is what Warren's heroine searches for throughout her life. The answer to the second question is easy. Amantha Starr was the white daughter of a southern aristocrat, mistress of her father's plantation, since her mother (presumed to be white) and her father's second wife were both dead; a young lady taken to Oberlin to be educated. And then Manty finds out that she is no longer that white girl but an undefined Negro and that her identity has been predicated upon the person that she and others had created:

> Who had I, Amantha Starr, been before that moment? I had been defined by the world around me, by the high trees and glowing cookhearth of Starrwood, and the bare classrooms and soaring hymns of Oberlin, by the faces bent on me in their warmth and concern, the faces of Aunt Sukie, Shaddy, Miss Idell [her father's mistress], . . . my father, Seth Parton [a boy with whom she was involved at Oberlin]. But now all had fled away from me, into the deserts of distance, and I was, therefore, nothing.
>
> For in and of myself, or so it seemed, I had been nothing. I had been nothing except their continuing creation. Therefore, though I remember much of that earlier time, my own feelings, my desires, my own story, I do not know who I was. Or do we ever come to know more? Oh, are we nothing more than the events of our own story, the beads on the string, the little nodes of fear and hope, love and terror, lust and despair, appetite and calculation, and the innermost sensation of blood and dream?" [27]

This is the problem that Sartre and other existentialists have pondered: How can the human being define himself? How can he separate his own self-concept from the concept of him created by others? How can we distinguish the "thing-in-itself" from the "thing-for-itself"? The task of the existentially cognizant human being is to establish his identity as a subject—as the person he thinks himself to be, and, more important, as the person whose actions establish his being. What he must be aware of and must fight against is the objectification of his being—the tendency to see himself as an "object" created out of others' consciousness rather than as a subject emanating his essence, an assertion of will in an indifferent universe. And although his assertion of will requires an acceptance of great responsibility, it is only through the acceptance of responsibility that freedom is won.

It is precisely this establishment of her own identity that Amantha cannot achieve. For many years she fails to find an identity for herself that she can accept, for she cannot accept being Negro as *any* part of her self-concept; thus she cannot take upon herself the responsibility for her life or win the inner freedom for which she yearns. For most of her life, Amantha's crisis experience dominates her and she literally remains in a state of trauma. Her nightmare at the grave remains a continuous felt reality rather than a past experience with which she has come to terms. The knowledge she gains at her father's grave *could* have been the means to her freedom (and finally is), for she has been given an opportunity to face herself and the universe, not in ignorance, but with greater understanding. Warren shows us this through a vision Manty has throughout her life. She sees a grave with the word "Renie" and the dates 1820-1844 and sees herself as a child, playing there. She says: "Sometimes this real spot and the spot of my imagination, of my dream of freedom and delight, seem to become the same spot. But how can that be, when the place in my dream is a place of beginnings and the place in my true recollections has a grave, the mark of endings? When the dream place is a place of freedom, the real place a place of immobility and constrictions?" [28]

Before Manty is able to unify the "dream place" and the "real place," she journeys through her own personal hell, a universe in which the word "nothing" reverberates. Her identity torn from her, she loses control of her life. Taken from her father's grave to a boat bound for the New Orleans slave market, Amantha loses contact with reality. There were times when she would say her own name over and over again, "trying, somehow, to make myself come true." [29]

She is sold to Hamish Bond, who treats her with kindness and respect. She is made to do no work except needle work (the pastime of aristocratic white women). Black servants attend her, and she is given much freedom of movement, although her attempt to run away is thwarted. Although Hamish Bond and Amantha eventually become lovers, the relationship is voluntary on both sides. They are very close, until an incident convinces her that she is no more "real" to Hamish in her role as his mulatto lover and confidante than she was as the white daughter of a southern gentleman. And if she is not "real" to him, then she is not real to herself. Having looked to Hamish to define her, she becomes "nothing" when he turns her into an object and distorts what little sense of self she has. Manty repulses the unwanted attentions of Bond's cousin, Charles Prieur Denis, with the aid of a courageous and highly intelligent black man named Rau-Ru. After Hamish defeats Charles in a battle of "brains and brawn," the master lover confesses to his slave mistress that he had known that sooner or later Charles would make sexual advances toward Amantha and that he, Hamish, had felt a need to see what the girl (she is only seventeen or so) would do. Hamish, the man who was to have given her a sense of her own concrete reality—and with this reality, a sense of freedom—had himself acted under compulsions which proved that he could never have granted *her* freedom. Manty explains:

> He [Hamish] had not been real, just a dream I was having, a dream I had to have and cling to.
> And now, all at once, something was beginning to come real. . . . If Hamish Bond had been nothing but a dream I was having, that was like finding out, of a sudden, that I myself was nothing but a dream which he had been having, and had to have for his own need. So I was nothing, and alone in the middle of nothing. It was the feeling of that old nightmare of mine, of being in the middle of a desert and the horizon fleeing away in all directions.[30]

Manty distinguishes the two kinds of nothingness she fears: "the kind which is being only yourself, lonely as the distance withdraws forever, and the kind when the walls of the world come together to crush you. . . . If I could only be free, I used to think, free from the lonely nothingness of being only yourself when the world flees away, and free from the closing walls that would crush you to nothingness." [31] These words: "nothing" and "nothingness" and along with them, "freedom," "loneliness," "will," and "the nightmare of history," echo and reverberate throughout *Band of Angels* like so many voices in a Bach fugue. One is reminded of E. M. Forster's use of refrain in *Howard's End*, or perhaps even of Joyce's *Ulysses*, although Warren's technique never reaches this level of complexity. As these words and ideas are repeated throughout the novel, singly and in groups, the pattern of ideas in the novel becomes clear: self-definition is achieved through the assertion of will and the acceptance of responsibility for our own actions. Through this lonely assertion of self—"lonely" because no one else can truly define another individual or his responsibility because no one else can actually *be* another human being—the individual can win his freedom, and with this freedom, his measure of humanness. In "Miscegenation as Symbol: *Band of Angels,*" John Longley says that Manty "learns that only through separateness is identity earned and is permission finally granted to rejoin the body of those equally distinct and, because innocent of self-inflicted error, equally fulfilled. Between two absolutes, rejection and subjection, she achieves her station." [32] Until "Little Manty"—a name she casts off when she ceases to be a "victim"—can recognize that her black blood is only one kind of burden and that every human bears some burden, she isolates herself from the rest of humanity. Depending upon others to define her, she demands absolute strength from them and is afraid of their weaknesses. (If others must accept responsibility even in their present imperfect human state, then how can it be right for her to subjugate her will to that of others?) Immediately after Manty is horrified to perceive that to Hamish she has been "nothing," she learns an important lesson in compassion that bears upon her own unity with humankind. At first she had been repulsed by Hamish's admission of weakness (that he wanted to know her response to Charles). But when he tells her that he had somehow *wanted* Manty to accept Charles's advances, when he cries out to her that it is awful for a man to be this way, "She jumps up and kisses him; the tenderness or pity [having] caught her unawares." [33] This assertion of her kinship with all people looks forward to her final questions and answers, to her truce with man and God. Ultimately she realizes that her blackness is only a symbol of the loneliness and alienation of the human condition. She had used her nightmare to try to make herself more than mortal and, at the same time, less than human (by exempting herself from human responsibility for her actions): "Oh, did you always need your old nightmares? Did you need them to hide something? To hide what? To hide the common light of day? To hide, I knew, with an ebbing of the heart, my sad humanness. . . . [I] thought how people had their own humanness, and therefore had to have their nightmares and the world had its nightmare, and history had its nightmare, but people put things out of the mind and went on living." [34] At an earlier time, Manty had wondered whether "we want happiness, or is it pain, pain as the index of reality, that we, in the chamber of the heart want? Oh, if I knew the answer, perhaps then I could feel free?" [35] Do we want to escape our nightmare, or embrace it, or merely recognize it as fact? What is the relationship between one's private nightmare and the nightmare of history? If individuals collectively "make" history, then the question of whether we have been seeking happiness or pain can be asked of our entire species. Manty says:

> You live through time, that little piece of time that is yours, but that piece of time is not only your own life, it is the summing-up of all the other lives that are simultaneous with yours. It is, in other words, History, and you do not live your life, but somehow, your life lives you, and you are, therefore, only what History does to you? . . .
> You feel that if you can answer the questions, you might be free.
> What I started out to say, however, was this: how do you know how you yourself, all the confused privateness of you, are involved with that history you are living through? [36]

Critics of the novel have praised Warren's union of history—of the outer "impersonal" events—with Manty's personal, individual history. Charles H. Bohner observes that "The decisive public events are transmitted by Warren into symbols of personal histories. The conflicts that rage on the battlefield, the emancipation of the slaves, the horrors of Reconstruction—all have their counterparts in the soul of the novel's heroine, Amantha Starr." [37] Viewed from this perspective, Manty's childhood can be regarded as a symbol of the antebellum South. Her life at Starrwood epitomized the leisurely aristocratic life built upon slavery. When she goes to Oberlin, she is made to develop an awareness of the "sins" of slavery. When she begs her father to free his slaves, he says that he cannot, for such an action would be his economic ruination. So the false Eden of Starrwood lives on until Aaron Starr's death. At this time, the other side of the antebellum South is revealed when the dark secret of miscegenation is brought to light in the hell-like scene at Aaron's grave.

Hamish Bond treats Mandy with kindness (he had kindness like a disease, his former quadroon mistress tells Manty), and he eventually asks the girl to marry him. But before his death, Hamish Bond, who had made a fortune as a slave trader, calls Manty a "nigger." In many ways, he is presented as having been a "good" man. Yet Bond was tied inextricably to the ideology of the South, whereby the white was blessed and the black cursed. His death occurs as the Confederacy falls.

The third phase of Manty's story concerns her life with Tobias Sears. He is a northern army captain, who, for a long time after their marriage, does not know of Manty's parentage. She explains to us that she thought he had been told by Seth Parton. While there is some reason for Manty to believe that Tobias knows her secret, I think that Warren would have us see the incident as another example of Manty's escapism. When she finally realizes that Tobias is completely unaware of her mixed blood, she tells him. Tobias's answer is: " 'You are what my deepest heart desires. More now than ever. More now than ever.' At that he kissed me, but once lifted his head to say: 'You are given to me for a sign.' " [38]

But Tobias cannot really accept Manty's "curse," and she comes to feel that she has only been an occasion for Tobias's magnanimity, that her life with him meant nothing. He had made all of the northern liberal gestures, and more, having led a black regiment and later having worked for the Freedman's Bureau. When, however, Tobias leaves Manty on the night of her revelation because he wants to try to prevent interracial bloodshed, she sees his leaving as a betrayal. That night she makes a desperate attempt to leave the white race and identify with the blacks. Through a series of complicated events, she meets Rau-Ru, the black man who had been Hamish Bond's trusted overseer. When he and Manty make love to the background of a bloody race riot, she feels that she has found the answer to her crisis experience. She will go with Rau-Ru; she will be black. Yet when whites appear on the scene, she cannot bear to be a Negro: "It was as though a strong galvanic current had been passed through my being to jerk me out of my torpor, to jerk me scrambling up, not in fear, in some deeper necessity, uttering the unplanned words, the words that burst out of me. The words were: 'I'm not nigger, I'm not nigger— I'm white, and he [Rau-Ru] made me come—oh, he made me!' " [39]

"I'm not nigger!" Manty cannot even say "I'm not a nigger," because blacks are still not people but only a hated state of being. Manty cannot yet take responsibility for her actions. She must make herself Rau-Ru's victim in order to justify her actions, just as she sees herself as the victim of her father, Bond and Tobias. It is not until she is a middle-aged woman that she can stand in front of the mirror and say "nigger" to herself, and it is at this time that she exorcises Shaddy and Rau-Ru from her soul. She has always felt responsible for the fates of these two black men—having betrayed them—and has carried her guilt all her life. It is at this time also that she suddenly—and finally—realizes that no one else can ever set her free—not her father, Rau-Ru, Hamish, or Tobias. No one can set her free except herself:

> This was more awful than the thought of dying. It was more awful because it was the thought of living. Except yourself, except yourself: and that thought meant that I had to live and know that I was not the little Manty—oh, poor, dear, sweet little Manty—who had suffered and to whom things happened, with all its sweet injustice. Oh, no, that thought, by implying a will in me, implied that I had been involved in the very cause of the world, and whatever had happened corresponded in some crazy way with what was in me, and even if I didn't cause it, it somehow conformed to my will, and then somehow it could be said that I did cause it,[40] and if it had not been for me then nothing would ever have happened as it happened, Hamish Bond would never have plunged from his cotton bale, Rau-Ru would never have waited in the ruined house while Jimmee pleaded with him to leave, Tobias would never have become the sad, sardonic slave of bottle and bitterness, the betrayer of women, and the thought of my involvement in all things was awful.[41]

As others have noted, this statement represents Manty's emancipation. She has at last answered her tortured questions about the nature of the individual in history: her life does not live her and she is not only what history does to her; rather she has an active will that somehow affects everything around her. By asserting her will, she accepts awesome responsibility but achieves the "awfulness of joy": "The drama enveloping her impersonates and reveals her inner conflict: the Civil War, the whole social fretwork based on the myths of miscegenation—these are projections of her own self-division. The northern reformers, armed with righteousness and bayonets, do not constitute a band of angels. Reform is a matter for the individual soul, whose health or disease society merely reflects; it cannot be imposed, any more than freedom can be absolutely given or denied, or can even be defined absolutely from without." [42]

The end of the novel finds Amantha and Tobias middle-aged failures in the eyes of the world. He has become a drunkard and barely makes a living from his law practice in a dusty Kansas town. But Warren concludes the novel on a double epiphany. Manty's sudden understanding coincides with Tobias's ability to admit to just how degraded he has become. In helping a black millionaire find and rescue his father from the "slop heap," in giving the filthy old man a bath with the gentleman-son, with a black man who does *not* try to escape his past but who has sought it out in the form of an illiterate, dirty piece of flesh, Tobias Sears finally achieves a genuine sense of the brotherhood of man. Having recognized their "sad humanness," Amantha and Tobias are able to win some measure of freedom.

While there is much of the old "blood warfare" found in the cruder novels that contain this theme, *Band of Angels* goes far beyond them into questions—and answers—grounded in the very ambiguities of the "human condition." A brilliant dramatization of the mulatto's anguished search for self-definition, Warren's novel offers a superior instance of the crisis experience.

NOTES

1. Everett V. Stonequist, *The Marginal Man: A Study in Personality and Culture Conflict* (1937; rpt. New York: Russell & Russell, 1961), pp. 121-22.
2. Mark Twain, *Pudd'nhead Wilson and Those Extraordinary Twins: Harper and*

Brothers Edition (New York: P. F. Collier & Sons Company, 1922), pp. 76-77.

3. Stonequist, *The Marginal Man,* pp. 130, 139-40.

4. Ibid., p. 146.

5. Fannie Hurst, *Imitation of Life* (New York: Harper & Brothers, 1933), p. 297.

6. Walter White, *Flight* (New York: Knopf, 1926), p. 77.

7. Sinclair Lewis, *Kingsblood Royal* (New York: Random House, 1947), p. 65.

8. Twain, *Pudd'nhead Wilson,* p. 74.

9. Frances E. W. Harper, *Iola Leroy,* rev. ed. (Boston: James H. Earle, 1892), p. 125.

10. Lewis, *Kingsblood Royal,* pp. 66-67.

11. Ibid., p. 97.

12. Ibid., p. 202.

13. Ibid., p. 214.

14. Ibid., p. 277.

15. Ibid., p. 190.

16. Some critics have called the material "hackneyed" and melodramatic. Charles H. Bohner refutes the validity of this label in *Robert Penn Warren* (New York: Twayne Publishers, 1964).

17. Robert Penn Warren, *Band of Angels* (New York: Random House, 1955), p. 16.

18. Elizabeth Boatwright Coker, *Daughters of Strangers* (New York: E. P. Dutton & Company, 1950), p. 121.

19. Warren, *Band of Angels,* p. 58.

20. Ibid., p. 58.

21. Ibid., p. 64.

22. Leslie Fiedler, as quoted in Bohner, *Robert Penn Warren,* p. 133.

23. Warren, *Band of Angels,* pp. 227-28.

24. Ibid., p. 52.

25. Ibid., p. 64.

26. Ibid., pp. 74-75.

27. Ibid., p. 62.

28. Ibid., p. 4.

29. Ibid., p. 3.

30. Ibid., p. 163.

31. Ibid., p. 3.

32. In John Lewis Longley, ed., *Robert Penn Warren: A Collection of Critical Essays* (New York: New York University Press, 1965), p. 148.

33. Warren, *Band of Angels,* p. 163.

34. Ibid., p. 365.

35. Ibid., p. 13.

36. Ibid., p. 134.

37. Bohner, *Robert Penn Warren,* pp. 128-29.

38. Warren, *Band of Angels,* p. 291.

39. Ibid., p. 332.

40. See Jean-Paul Sartre's "Freedom and Responsibility," in his *Being and Nothingness,* in which he says that "from the instant of my upsurge into being,

I carry the weight of the world by myself alone without anything or any person being able to lighten it." Further on he says, "I find myself suddenly alone and without help, engaged in a world for which I bear the whole responsibility without being able, whatever I do, to tear myself away from this responsibility for an instant. For I am responsible for my very desire of fleeing responsibilities." Reprinted in *Hard Rains,* ed. Robert Disch and Barry N. Schwartz (Englewood Cliffs, N.J.: Prentice-Hall, 1969), p. 373.

41. Warren, *Band of Angels,* p. 364.
42. Longley, *Robert Penn Warren,* p. 147.

6.

The Novel of Passing; or Black No More

Langston Hughes is the author of a story which takes place in a well-known club in Harlem. There, Caleb Johnson, "a colored social worker [who] was always dragging around with him some nondescript white person or two," [1] is entertaining three whites when they are joined by several black artists, one of whom is the narrator of the piece. After one of the whites leaves, the party of blacks is left entertaining a couple who appear to be typical unenlightened whites. Unexpectedly, the woman leans forward and says that she and her husband have been passing for fifteen years. Caleb and the artists are taken aback, and then all respond with gales of laughter: "We almost had hysterics. All at once we dropped our professionally self-conscious 'Negro' manners, became natural, ate fish, and talked and kidded freely like colored folks do when there are no white folks around. We really had fun then." [2]

After an evening of camaraderie, the woman makes a second startling revelation: she and her husband are *not* colored after all, but are whites who decided to pass for colored—just as the black

140

artists had told them that Negroes sometimes pass for white. The blacks are dumbfounded, for they do not know now *which* way they have been fooled. "Were they really white—passing for colored? Or colored—passing for white?" [3] Although a humorous satire, this story illustrates a response to the crisis experience which has profound psychological and societal implications for those who attempt it: passing for white.

In terms of the way one relates to society and to others, every black American must make a choice between an assimilationist attitude and some form of black nationalist sentiment, or he must elect a position which lies between these two extremes. For those light-skinned marginal figures who undergo the crisis experience, the need to choose is intensified. In the preceding chapter, we have seen the anguish of the crisis experience, with its ensuing sense of dislocation and alienation. Since very light-skinned blacks are often treated as white by the dominant caste, they often identify with the latter's culture and many are unwilling or unable to give up this identification and form another. They choose or have been driven to choose to continue that identification and assimilate into the dominant caste by passing for white.

Crossing the racial barrier is titillating, as well as threatening, to many whites. And to blacks, passing may arouse ambivalent feelings of envy and disapproval, contempt and admiration. Gunnar Myrdal summarizes these attitudes in the following statement:

> As a social phenomenon, passing is so deeply connected with the psychological complexes—built around caste and sex—of both groups that it has come to be a central theme of fiction and of popular imagination and story telling. The adventures of the lonesome passer, who extinguishes his entire earlier life, breaks all personal and social anchorings, and starts a new life where he has to fear his own shadow, are alluring to all and have an especially frightening import to whites. There is a general sentimentality for the unhappy mulatto—the "marginal man" with split allegiances and frustrations in both directions which is especially applied to the mulatto passer. From all we know about personality problems there is

probably, as yet, substantial truth in the picture of the passer
which our literary phantasy paints for us.[4]

Black and white novelists of the nineteenth and twentieth centuries
have dealt with this topic, and if we take careful note of the biases
held by these authors, perhaps we can learn something about the
genuine fears and problems of the complete passer.

As might be expected, passing occurs more frequently among
male mulattoes than among their female counterparts. There are
several reasons for this phenomenon. There is a greater likelihood
for males to have the occupational skills needed to leave the black
caste; light-skinned black women are desirable marriage partners
and have the opportunity to marry into the upper class of the
lower caste, and therefore have less motivation to pass; and finally,
the female "passer" has more difficulty in white society as a solitary
woman with no family than does the male mulatto.

Not all passing is "complete" or "total"; sometimes it is
"partial" in that it occurs only in particular public areas of the
passer's daily existence. Some passing is done for cultural reasons.
Light-skinned Negroes were able to attend theaters, concerts,
lectures, to dine in fine restaurants, and to use a public library—
only if they used these facilities in the guise of being white. Passing
for such cultural reasons has been extensively fictionalized. Nella
Larsen's *Passing* (1929), Jessie Fauset's *Plum Bun* (1928), and
Willard Savoy's *Alien Land* (1949), provide three interesting
illustrations of the black novelists' depiction of this phenomenon.

Another type of temporary passing occurs at educational
institutions. At school, the child learns a great deal more than how
to read or solve mathematical problems. He learns the moral
values of his culture as well; and he learns what place he is to have
within that culture. For the mixed-blood child, the marginal child,
the racial attitudes of his classmates may be painful to him. Since
the knowledge that he belongs to the lower caste is bitter, it is not
surprising to find a fictional example of even a young child passing
at school. In Fannie Hurst's *Imitation of Life* (1933), Peola, a child of
eight, goes to a school outside her neighborhood and passes for
white. She tells no one, not even her mother. Jessie Fauset's *Comedy,
American Style* (1933), *Alien Land* and *The Garies and Their Friends*

(1857) (all by black authors) contain comparable examples of educational passing.

Comedy, American Style, also presents two blacks who pass professionally but maintain an identification with black culture. In another of her novels, *There Is Confusion* (1924), Fauset presents a young mixed-blood character who passes in order to fight racial discrimination. This character travels in the South in order to discover—in a way that no black person could—the truth about the treatment of black soldiers stationed in the South. One immediately thinks of John Griffin's odyssey as a "black" man in *Black Like Me.* Fauset has also provided one of the best fictional accounts of complete passing in her 1928 novel, *Plum Bun.*

The most basic fear of the passer is that he will suddenly be exposed. One black character in *The Garies and Their Friends* formulates the peculiar anxiety of the passer in this way: "An undetected forger, who is in constant fear of being apprehended, is happy in comparison with that coloured man who attempts, in this country, to hold a place in the society of whites by concealing his origin. He must live in constant fear of exposure; this dread will embitter every enjoyment, and make him the most miserable of men." [5] Neil Kingsblood realizes that if he chooses to pass, he will forever wonder if there were some telltale mark on his fingernails. Abby Clanghearne's reaction (in Edith Pope's *Colcorton*) is similar: she spends agonizing hours searching for kinks in her hair. The fear of exposure by other Negroes is also a factor, as *God Is for White Folks* (1947), by Will Thomas, and *Alien Land* (1949), by Willard Savoy, suggest.

The "black-baby myth" also haunts many a passer. Even if he does not fear the birth of a dark-skinned baby with kinky hair, a wide nose and bulbous lips, he may fear exposure through the birth of a baby that does not look quite white. In Nella Larsen's *Passing,* this fear is discussed by two women who have gone through the experience. There is even one fictional example of a woman who sterilizes herself in order to avoid giving birth to a dark-skinned child. Peola, in *Imitation of Life,* explains to her mother that her action is only fair, since a dark-skinned child could be a terrible blow to a husband who thinks she is white.

If a dark-skinned child is born to a woman (or man) who is

passing, this child may sometimes have to be disowned. In Sutton Griggs's *The Hindered Hand,* Arabelle Seabright sends her dark-skinned daughter away from the rest of the family, all of whom can pass. In *Flight,* Mimi Daquin is forced to keep her son's existence a secret. This rejection of a loved one can take a terrible toll, both on the passer and on his alienated relatives and friends. In *Imitation of Life,* it is the daughter, Peola, who rejects her dark-skinned mother, thus causing the good-hearted simple black woman to "die brokenhearted." Angela Murray in *Plum Bun* finds that she has to reject her own sister—her only family—to keep from losing her white lover. The experience is so jarring for Angela that "For the first time in the pursuit of her chosen ends she began to waver. Surely no ambition, no pinnacle of safety was supposed to call for the sacrifice of a sister." [6] And later, Angela pays dearly for this denial of her race.

In *The House Behind the Cedars,* both brother and sister must reject their darker-skinned mother. Because Rena Walden cannot maintain the estrangement from her mother, the beautiful mulatto ultimately meets her death. Other characters meet death either through their own passing or because of someone else's crossing of the racial barrier. In *The Hindered Hand,* Arabelle Seabright's son dies as a result of his racial deception. In *Comedy, American Style,* Oliver, the youngest child born to Olivia Cary, is rejected because of his dark skin. In the company of several white women, she refuses to recognize her own child when they meet on the street. On another occasion, Olivia pretends that Oliver is playing a game with her—the game consists of Oliver's dressing up, pretending he is a Filipino butler, and serving her company, never letting on that he is her son. The boy had never understood what was wrong with him, but he was terribly hurt by his mother's attitude. When Oliver mistakenly believes that his beloved sister has also rejected him, he kills himself.

Sometimes, loved ones relinquish their hold over the passer, no matter how painful that may be. We have already seen how Madame Delphine and Madame John denied their relationships with their daughters in order to make possible their marriages to white men. In Shirley Ann Grau's novel *The Keepers of the House* (1964), Margaret gives up her three children so that they can establish white identities. While she gives up her claim on her children in a spirit of love and selflessness, her decision is charged with ambivalence: the cost of the children's being able to enjoy the privileges of white society is the tremendous psychological damage they suffer by virtue of their mother's denial of them. Abby Clanghearne, Edith Pope's beautifully drawn protagonist in *Colcorton*, makes the same kind of sacrifice. Yet her renunciation is seen as heroic.

What of the varying reactions to passing by the two racial groups? It would appear that blacks experience more ambivalence toward the phenomenon than do many whites, to whom "passing is an insult and a social and racial danger." [7] In addition to this difference, most whites have only heard about passing but have no firsthand experience with the phenomenon. This ignorance can lead to distortions and stereotypes that are fed by beliefs in racial atavism. The following fascinating illustrations suggest, *not* the way in which whites react to the discovery that a loved one is actually black, but how two black authors have attempted to understand how whites would react to such knowledge.

In *The Garies and Their Friends*, a tormented Clarence decides that he must reveal his secret to his fiancée. The day that he goes to tell "little Birdie," she tells him of a terrifying dream: "I thought you held my hand; I felt it just as plain as I clasp yours now. Presently a rough ugly man overtook us [the specter of racial hatred?], and bid you let me go; and that you refused, and held me all the tighter. Then he gave you a diabolical look, and touched you on the face, and you broke out in loathsome black spots, and screamed in such agony, and frightened me so, that I awoke all in a shiver of terror, and did not get over it all the next day." [8]

The situation is much the same in Chesnutt's *The House Behind the Cedars*. George Tryon, Rena's estranged lover, has a dream in which his knowledge of Rena's mixed blood turns her into a monstrosity. Both Chesnutt and Webb use these nightmares to capture the primitive, subrational aspect of racial prejudice. A Jungian might assign these images to the collective unconscious; but such irrational cerebration is in fact socially indoctrinated—the unconscious mental baggage of many white Americans. In George's dream, Rena appears before George: "In all her fair young beauty she stood before him, and then by some hellish magic she was slowly transformed into a hideous black hag. With agonized eyes he watched her beautiful tresses became mere wisps of coarse wool, wrapped round with dingy cotton strings; he saw her clear eyes grow bloodshot, her ivory teeth turn to unwholesome fangs. With a shudder he awoke." [9] Like little Birdie, George's love for Rena conquers these nightmare visions. What whites actually feel about passing, we may never know. But these two imaginative visions by black writers can tell us something of black perception (during the latter half of the nineteenth century) of the dominant group's deepest response to passing.

Black attitudes toward passing are easier to pinpoint, although some of the information comes from white sources. To the extent that individual blacks want to escape their caste but cannot, they may have feelings of envy and jealousy as well as contempt for, and disapproval of, those who do escape. In Nella Larsen's novel, *Passing*, one of the characters says: "It's funny about passing. We disapprove of it and at the same time condone it. It excites our contempt and yet we rather admire it. We shy away from it with an odd kind of revulsion, but we protect it." [10] On the opposite end of the spectrum are those blacks who are appalled by passing because of their identification with the black community (virtually all of the mixed-blood characters in *Iola Leroy* are of this persuasion). In two Harlem Renaissance novels, *Plum Bun* and *Flight*, the passers return to the black communtiy and, in so doing, achieve happiness and fulfillment. Like several other passers, the protagonists of these two novels visit Harlem several times; they cannot remain away from "their people." These female mulatto characters learn that they are not free, that so long as their lives are based upon a lie, they cannot be free. Rather than achieving self-realization, passing has actually impeded self-development.

In contrast to *Plum Bun* and *Flight*, two novels by black authors, both from the late 1940s, depict the mixed-blood heroes' self-realization through identification with the white caste. In *Alien Land* and *God Is for White Folks*, Kern Adams and Beau Beauchamp, who have lived as members of the black and the white groups, decide to pass. In both instances, their wives know of their racial backgrounds.

The sacrifices of Margaret Howland, Madame Delphine, Madame John, and Abby Clanghearne are intended to arouse the reader's sympathy and compassion. Rebecca Harding Davis takes

this theme of sacrifice one step further and transforms her hero—
one of the "lonesome passer" types—into a black Christ. In giving
his life for his people, John Broderip achieves peace and self-
realization. What is most interesting about him is that he does not
fit the stereotype of the black Christ by virtue of his being lynched
or otherwise crucified.

In *Waiting for the Verdict* (1867), Davis portrays Broderip as a
"queer, unhappy, brilliant little man" whose few drops of black
blood have nearly ruined his life. Just as he is about to claim
happiness by marrying the white woman he loves, his brother
appears. Since John had been raised as a Caucasian, this mulatto
slave brother is a stranger to him. Yet he cannot quite deny the
relationship. At this point, his thoughts parallel those of many of
the marginal characters who undergo the crisis experience. There is
"no middle ground," Broderip thinks. "Let him acknowledge the
mulatto as his brother; and he stood alone, shut out from every
human relation with the world in which he belonged. A negro—no
wealth, no talent, no virtue could wash out that." With this
reasoning as his justification, John Broderip, a surgeon, almost kills
his own brother on the operating table. He rationalizes that he
"had a right to his manhood—a right. How could he bring his
faculties and needs into the bounds allowed this negro's life? It was
self-murder."

But Broderip concludes that it would be self-murder to *deny* the
relationship with his brother Nathan, for in spite of all attempts to
brutalize this black man, the brother is determined to return to the
South and fight against slavery. Broderip is stunned by this
man's—this brother's—nobility. This poor slave had hardly been
given the latitude to develop his "white" brother's sensibility and
yet would die like a man:

> "Brother, brother," he said aloud, testing the sound. For
> twenty years there had been no such tie between him and any
> other creature. He laughed as he said it—an eager credulous
> laugh. He was not ashamed of this sleeping wretch, of the
> coffee-colored skin and clown's clothes. They had used him as
> a brute, but they could not hinder him from discovering what
> true manhood was. "Better than I," said John Broderip—
> "better than I.".... Having touched shore, whatever of this

life's hope might be taken from him tonight forever, the lie in which he had lived was gone, and his feet were firm. Black or white—Margaret his wife or taken from him—these he felt were outside trifles: in his soul he faced God, at last, an honest man.[11]

Finally, in "Near-White" (1932), Claude McKay tells the story of a woman who passes successfully but faces torment when she falls in love with a white racist who would, if he knew of her "black blood," regard her as less than human. McKay's protagonist is Angie Dove, a beautiful twenty-year-old mulatto Harlemite who has always faced the world as an attractive, confident black. It is not until she meets Eugene Vincent, a blue-eyed octoroon who pronounces his name in the French way, that she is introduced to someone who passes and would not have it any other way. Together, they go to all of the fashionable spots of white New York.

Just when Angie has come to need these diversions, Eugene leaves and "the magic portal swung suddenly back into place." [12] Angie is no longer contented to live within the Harlem community: "The city was held a vast pleasure-world to which she felt she was entitled by right of feeling, of birth, and by right of color . . . now she was no more just a pretty, irresponsible girl of the Belt. In a few weeks she had developed into a very discontented woman." [13]

As Angie grapples with her extreme dissatisfaction, she longs to pass and regards with envy men like Vincent. She expresses the restraints against female passing that Myrdal was to record later: "in a man-fashioned world a woman could not cut herself off from home and relations to make her way alone." [14]

In spite of her reservations, however, she does meet a white man and begins to date him, all the while lying about her family. She is uncomfortable with her behavior and worries especially about two interrelated problems that haunt many other passers—fear of exposure by friends and family, and guilt over the necessary denial of her connections if the deception is to remain effective. Unlike Angela Murray *(Plum Bun),* Angie Dove is never forced to act out, face to face, the denial of her black family and friends.

Angie and her mother discuss the phenomenon of passing in a conversation much like that between Janet Murray and her daughter Angela. The older women, both of whom are light enough to pass, do not identify with whites or desire to be "pretend" Caucasians. Angie's mother says, "what's the use of selling your birth-mark for a mess of pottage that might turn bitter-gall in your mouth afterwards?" [15] Angie's mother explains further: "Why, we hate [whites] more because we are so close to them and yet so far from them. We hate them more because we are *not* black." [16] This is the same attitude exhibited by Fred Merrit, the upper-class mulatto lawyer in Rudolph Fisher's *The Walls of Jericho.*

Angie clearly does not share her mother's feelings. Like so many of the beautiful all-but-white female characters of white-authored mulatto fiction, Angie pines for her white lover. She hopes that love is stronger than racist ideology. But she discovers how wrong she is. The nightmares of Little Birdie *(The Garies and Their Friends)* and George Tryon *(The House Behind the Cedars)* are turned into, reality in "Near-White." Angie's lover John firmly rejects Angie's comment that respectable colored people ought to be able to go places where whites amuse themselves. When she asks him the key question—could he love a quadroon or octoroon girl—he answers: "Me! I'd sooner love a toad!" [17] It is on the words "A toad! O god! a toad!" [18] that McKay ends his story. Knowing what we do of McKay's strong sense of identification with the black proletariat, it is no surprise that he severely punishes a foolish young woman who had come to feel that she was "sick, pining, wilting, dying of that tight-roped-in life of the Belt." [19] As her mother told her, and as the "Ex-Coloured Man" of James Weldon Johnson's famous novel learned, the price of a mess of pottage is never worth one's birthright.

Whether or not the passer can achieve a healthy identity, then, is a central motif in the literature about this phenomenon. Some, like Rena Walden, are destroyed when they try to cross the racial barrier. Others, like Mimi Daquin (heroine of *Flight*) and Angela Murray *(Plum Bun)* return to their race and thus achieve self-fulfillment. Still other passers, like Kern Adams *(Alien Land)*, achieve a full life as members of the Caucasian caste. In the best-known and the most artistically satisfying novel of passing, *The Autobiography of an Ex-Coloured Man* (1912), by James Weldon Johnson, the question of self-realization is central.

As Sterling Brown, Hugh Gloster, and Edward Margolies have all pointed out, Johnson's novel was ground-breaking for several reasons. *The Autobiography of an Ex-Coloured Man* deals not only with passing but with the Negro artistic world and the urban and European scenes.[20] In its assertion of black cultural pride, this novel is a precursor of the Harlem Renaissance school.[21] Furthermore, as Hugh Gloster noted in his discussion of the novel, it is "more impartial and more comprehensive than any earlier novel of American Negro life." [22] Carl Van Vechten has best captured *The Autobiography*'s most outstanding quality in the following comment: "it reads like a composite autobiography of the Negro race in modern times. [We see that] ... his young hero, the ostensible author, either discusses (or lives) pretty nearly every phase of Negro life, North and South and even in Europe, available to him at that period." [23] The novel is a brilliant study of the marginal man: his place in the white and black cultures; his ambivalent feelings toward his role as a mixed blood in a caste-oriented society; the crisis experience that ineluctably changes his life; his attempt to identify with the black group and his genuine admiration for certain achievements of that group; and finally, his crossing of the racial barrier to live out his life as a cynical, remorseful white man. While it may be true that there is too much discussion and not enough dramatization in the novel, Sterling Brown's assertion that "the novel seems to exist primarily for the long discussions of race, and the showing of the Negro in different milieus" [24] is debatable. The protagonist is sufficiently "complex and interesting," to use Brown's own phrase, to call the novel an artistic success.

Johnson's narrative structure is one of the strengths of the novel. The "Ex-Coloured Man"—like the "Invisible Man" of many years later—narrates his own story, and like the protagonist of Ellison's novel, Johnson's central figure looks back upon his life. Johnson juxtaposes dual perspectives: that of the older man—experienced, cynical, despairing—with the innocence of the boy and young man he no longer is. Primarily because of this narrative structure and the skillful characterization of the protagonist, *The Autobiography of an Ex-Coloured Man* has a contemporary tone. The Ex-Coloured Man is a prototypical figure: he is the alienated modern hero.

Johnson's protagonist is characterized by a perversity born of despair and disillusionment: "I know that I am playing with fire [in revealing his story], and I feel the thrill which accompanies that most fascinating pastime; and back of it I think I find a sort of savage and diabolical desire to gather up all the little tragedies of my life and turn them into a practical joke on society." [25] Johnson's protagonist has other reasons, however, for wanting to tell his story. He has an irresistible need to divulge the secret he has "guarded more carefully than any of [his] earthly possessions." [26] He needs respite from the burden of his deceit: "And, too, I suffer a vague feeling of unsatisfaction, of regret, of almost remorse, from which I am seeking relief." [27] Johnson's nameless protagonist is not unlike Amantha Starr, for he is tormented by the question of identity throughout the novel. Like Amantha and many of the mixed-blood characters who undergo the crisis experience, the Ex-Coloured Man has spent a happy childhood as one of the elect. He knows nothing about race except that a black boy in his school, a boy who was "the best at everything," who won "the majority of the prizes for punctuality, deportment, essay writing, and declamation . . . was in some way looked down upon." [28]

The protagonist has no idea that he is anything but white until a traumatic incident in school brings him an understanding of his position in American society. The simple, everyday set of circumstances that Johnson forms into the protagonist's crisis experience is as effective as Robert Penn Warren's melodramatic graveside scene in *Band of Angels*. Indeed, the fall from grace is all the more chilling precisely because it occurs during the course of everyday experience.

When the protagonist stands with the white students upon a request from the principal of the school, he is told, kindly, to sit down and rise with the others. "I sat down dazed. I saw and heard nothing. When the others were asked to rise, I did not know it. When school was dismissed, I went out in a kind of stupor." [29] Like other mulatto characters, he is catapulted into a state of shock. Like them, too, he rushes home and examines himself in the mirror. Then he runs to his mother and asks her: "Mother, mother, tell me, am I a nigger?" [30] And then, he tells us, he looks at her critically for the first time. Their little Eden is gone; even his conception of his mother has been tarnished. She is still beautiful to him, but he now sees that her skin is almost brown in color; her hair is not as soft as his. The older narrator, looking back upon this scene, understands very well what he had felt that day: "I had thought of her in a childish way only as the most beautiful woman in the world; now I looked at her searching for defects." [31]

She tells him that he is not black; that he is as good as anybody—as if being good and being black are mutually exclusive. Then her son wisely asks her: "Well, mother, am I white? Are you white?" She says that she is not white, but that his father—his father!—"is one of the greatest men in the country—the best blood of the South is in you." [32] (We have seen this attitude, this pride in the white lover, in other mulatto women.) Now the boy must know the answer to another question that is almost as important to him as the issue of his racial identity: "I almost fiercely demanded: 'Who is my father? Where is he?'" [33] To whom do I belong? What role in society am I to play? Is it my fate to be a member of the inferior caste?

On the day that the protagonist had discovered his caste status, he asked his mother about his father; but she would tell him nothing. So the word "father," the protagonist tells us, "had been to me a source of doubt and perplexity ever since the interview with my mother on the subject." [34] When his father comes to visit, the boy meets a handsome, prepossessing man—the kind of father a boy would like to have, the narrator says. But he cannot rise to this "melodramatic" scene. "Somehow," he says, "I could not arouse any considerable feeling of need for a father." [35] Many of the mulattoes discussed in this study have seen their white fathers as strangers (Rena Walden in *The House Behind the Cedars* and Laurentine Strange of *There Is Confusion* are two examples); this feeling of "fatherlessness" is a contributing factor to their sense of isolation and uprootedness.

In the following passage, the Ex-Coloured Man analyzes the feelings of that younger self who had undergone the crisis experience:

> Since I have grown older I often have gone back and tried to analyse the change that came into my life after that fateful

day in school. There did come a radical change, and, young as I was, I felt fully conscious of it, though I did not fully comprehend it. Like my first spanking, it is one of the few incidents in my life that I can remember clearly. In the life of everyone there is a limited number of unhappy experiences which are not written upon the memory, but stamped there with a die; and in the long years after, they can be called up in detail, and every emotion that was stirred by them can be lived through anew; these are the tragedies of life. We may grow to include some of them among the trivial incidents of childhood—a broken toy, a promise made to us which was not kept, a harsh, heart-piercing word—but these, too, as well as the bitter experiences and disappointments of mature years, are the tragedies of life.

And so I have often lived through that hour, that day, that week, in which was wrought the miracle of my transition from one world into another; for I did indeed pass into another world. From that time I looked out through other eyes, my thoughts were coloured, my words dictated, my actions limited by one dominating, all-pervading idea which constantly increased in force and weight until I finally realized in it a great, tangible fact.

And this is the dwarfing, warping, distorting influence which operates upon each and every coloured man in the United States. He is forced to take his outlook on all things, not from the view-point of a citizen, or a man, or even a human being, but from the view-point of a *coloured* man.[36]

In the protagonist's first period of adjustment, like others who have undergone the crisis experience, he begins to identify himself with the black group. He reads *Uncle Tom's Cabin* and is very much impressed. He is moved by Shiny's graduation speech on Wendell Phillips's "Toussaint L'Ouverture." Pride in Negro accomplishments, which the narrator expresses here for the first time, becomes one of his dominant attitudes. "Shiny, it is true, was what is so common in his race, a natural orator; but I doubt that any white boy of equal talent could have wrought the same effect. The sight of that boy gallantly waging with puny, black arms so unequal a battle touched the deep springs in the hearts of his audience, and they were swept by a wave of sympathy and admiration." [37] The protagonist becomes interested in Dumas. Since the discovery of his racial identity, he says he has been a loner; he reads a great deal and plays the piano (a gift from his father).

When he has the choice of going to Harvard or to a university in Atlanta, he chooses the school in the South, a region which fascinates him. Here he comes into contact, for the first time, with large numbers of blacks. His response is typical of others who have been in his situation. He is repelled by their "unkempt appearance, the shambling, slouching gait and loud talk and laughter of these people." [38] But even then, at seventeen years of age, alone in a strange city, surrounded by people who were very different from him in educational and cultural backgrounds, even then he is interested in their dialect, the richness of their language, and the power of their humor: "These people talked and laughed without restraint. In fact, they talked straight from their lungs and laughed from the pits of their stomachs." [39] His attitude is ambivalent: he admits that he is both fascinated and repelled by the loud talk and laughter of the blacks.

The narrator is proud of many of the achievements made by American Negroes, and he feels respect for the black man and pride in his connection with the Negro race even after he has crossed the racial barrier. He tells us that blacks have "originality and artistic conception, and, what is more, the power of creation that can influence and appeal universally." [40] It is precisely because he has powerful emotional ties with the black caste that he feels contempt for himself and remorse for having left his race and their struggles. He regards the cakewalk, the Uncle Remus stories, the Jubilee Songs, and ragtime music as four Negro achievements "which refute the oft-advanced theory that they are an absolutely inferior race.... These are lower forms of art, but they give evidence of a power that will someday be applied to the higher forms." [41]

After a series of adventures, the protagonist has the opportunity to go to Europe as the companion and friend of a white millionaire. Nonetheless, he feels that he is wasting his life. He wants to return to his music, to compose seriously, to work for his people by using their music. The millionaire says that the Ex-Coloured Man is foolish to think he can be happy living as a

Negro. His argument is a powerful one. He says that as a black man, the narrator will be forced to maintain a marginal position in American society. He is too educated, his sensibilities have been too finely developed for him to take his place among the black masses. Once more, we face the question: What distinguishes a black man from a white? The protagonist is probably only one-fourth Negro, and, as his friend says:

My boy, you are by blood, by appearance, by education, and by tastes a white man.... This idea you have of making a Negro out of yourself is nothing more than a sentiment; you do not realize the fearful import of what you intend to do. What kind of a Negro would you make now, especially in the South? If you had remained there, or perhaps even in your club in New York, you might have succeeded very well; but now you would be miserable. I can imagine no more dissatisfied human being than an educated, cultured, and refined coloured man in the United States.[42]

The narrator, however, feels that he must return to the United States in order to speak for black people by transforming their own music into formal composition. He has a commitment to his people that is not uncommon in the marginal person. So he travels in the South making transcriptions of the slave songs and getting to know more about the "black folk." His response to a revival meeting he attends is wholly enthusiastic. He seems to feel no strangeness or alienation toward the blacks and is profoundly moved by the experience: "Any musical person who has never heard a Negro congregation under the spell of religious fervour sing these old songs has missed one of the most thrilling emotions which the human heart may experience. Anyone who without shedding tears can listen to Negroes sing 'Nobody knows de trouble I see, Nobody knows but Jesus' must indeed have a heart of stone." [43]

Just at the point when the protagonist is feeling good about his new-found commitment and pride in his Negroness, he has an experience that is as disruptive to his life and as shattering to his ego and self-directedness as was the shock he endured that day in school when he discovered he was a member of the lower caste: he sees a black man burned to death. Because of this traumatic incident, as he travels from the South to the North he debates with himself whether or not to forsake his race. He finally decides to "let the world take me for what it would. . . . It was not necessary for me to go about with a label of inferiority pasted across my forehead." [44] He is not being honest with himself when he says that he will "neither disclaim the black race nor claim the white race; but [decided] that I would change my name, raise a moustache, and let the world take me for what it would." [45] After all, the hard lesson that he had learned in school and during the intervening years, when he had lived as a black man, was surely that he *would* be categorized as either black or white. And since he does not look like a Negro, according to the conception of most whites, he must know that he will be treated as a white man. Once that occurs, he will have to practice some conscious deception in order to maintain his upper-caste status. So the Ex-Coloured Man would seem to be lying to himself and to us.

His reasons for crossing the racial barrier are significant. Like most other passers, he is more concerned with his status as an inferior being than with his difficulty in "bettering himself": "it was not discouragement or fear or search for a larger field of action and opportunity that was driving me out of the Negro race. I knew that it was shame, unbearable shame. Shame at being identified with a people that could with impunity be treated worse than animals. For certainly the law would restrain and punish the malicious burning alive of animals." [46] Johnson's literary skill is evident when he juxtaposes the narrator's rapturous description of the Negro spirituals with the burning—the crucifying—of a black man, an event which leads directly to the narrator's decision to pass. The rejection of his status as a black man is made all the more poignant because of our knowledge that he has been genuinely moved by the black experience in America. He had hoped to capture that experience through the use of its cultural expressions: the anguish of bondage (the old slave songs that he went South to collect) and the resistance to anonymity and noncreativity (ragtime music, the humor of the Negro). He had given up a life of ease as an expatriate and returned to his homeland. Because the narrator's shame is not only for himself, but for all blacks who are oppressed by American society—"the great example of democracy to the world, [which is] the only civilized, if not the only state on earth, where a human being can be burned alive"; [47] because he feels shame for the white Americans who perpetrate this oppression and shame for the tarnishing of the American dream; because Johnson uses his protagonist's life as a means of exemplifying the quality of American Negro life, and more particularly that of a mulatto, I cannot agree with Edward Margolies's statement that the protagonist's "weaknesses are shown to stem chiefly from his own character and not essentially from the society that terrifies him." [48]

The remainder of the novel concerns the protagonist's life as a white man. He works his way through business college and seems very proud of his accomplishments. He appears to have accepted the "Protestant Ethic" and the pursuit of materialism, and he bears little resemblance to the younger, more sensitive man he had been. He does not completely lose his acuteness as a social observer or his analytical powers, however, particularly with regard to his own position in society: "The anomaly of my social position often appealed strongly to my sense of humour. I frequently smiled inwardly at some remark not altogether complimentary to people of colour; and more than once I felt like disclaiming 'I am a coloured man.' Do I disapprove the theory that one drop of Negro blood renders a man unfit? Many a night when I returned to my room after an enjoyable evening, I laughed heartily over what struck me as the capital joke I was playing." [49]

Then, however, he falls in love with a white woman, "and what I regarded as a joke was gradually changed into the most serious question of my life." [50] The desire to marry precipitates the necessity of crucial decisions by the passer: Peola must ask her mother to give up her only child; she sterilizes herself as well; Rena Walden and John Broderip become convinced of the need to tell their lovers; Clarence Garie is tormented by the fear that his lover will find out, yet he also desires to unburden himself; Kern Adams breaks his engagement with the white woman he adores, although he finally reveals his secret to her. Johnson's Ex-Coloured Man is also tormented by the need to tell his lover. When he finally does reveal his racial background, her reaction is one of horror: "I felt her hand grow cold, and when I looked up, she was gazing at me with a wild, fixed stare as though I was some object she had never seen. Under the strange light in her eyes I felt that I was growing black and thick-featured and crimp-haired." [51] Like George Tryon and little Birdie, the protagonist's lover is a victim of the racial myths of American culture.

Eventually, however, she is able to transcend those prejudices and agrees to marry the Ex-Coloured Man. Years pass; his wife dies, and he devotes himself to his two "white" children. Above all, he does not want the mark of inferiority to fall upon them. His marriage, he says, had been wonderful, although he says he had an unfounded fear that haunted him: "I was in constant fear that she would discover in me some shortcoming which she would unconsciously attribute to my blood rather than to a failing of human nature." [52] More racial myths.

The Ex-Coloured Man is bitter about his life and feels self-contempt. "I feel that I have been a coward, a deserter, and I am possessed by a strange longing for my mother's people." [53] He says that he feels "small and selfish" beside the great leaders of the black group: "I am an ordinarily successful white man who has made a little money. They are men who are making history and a race. I, too, might have taken part in a work so glorious." [54] Furthermore, he has never entirely lost the feeling that he is an outsider when he is among both whites and blacks: "Sometimes it seems to me that I have never really been a Negro, that I have been only a privileged spectator of their inner life." [55]

In the end, the protagonist has very little in his life. He says: "My love for my children makes me glad that I am what I am and keeps me from desiring to be otherwise." [56] But what is he? Edward Margolies's description of what the Ex-Coloured Man has lost is insightful: "The main character, sympathetic but poignantly cowardly, shies away from making the decisions that would give substance to his life." [57] The Ex-Coloured Man "has a little money," he says, and two children he wishes to protect. But what he has given up is described beautifully in the closing words of the novel: "when I sometimes open a little box in which I still keep my fast yellowing MS, the only tangible remnants of a vanished dream, a dead ambition, a sacrificed talent, I cannot repress the thought that, after all, I have chosen the lesser part, that I have sold my birthright for a mess of pottage!" [58]

The fictional treatment of the passer found in James Weldon Johnson's *Autobiography of an Ex-Coloured Man* is representative of the handling of this subject in the American novel. Of the twenty works discussed in this chapter, fifteen are by black authors. But despite the fact that black novelists have treated this subject with more frequency than whites, there is much similarity in the approach of the authors of both races. In no instance does a novelist, white or black, show contempt for, or cruelty toward, the passer. These authors are sensitive to the psychological, social, and economic reasons for passing and, to a greater or lesser extent, they discuss and dramatize these complex motivations. They recognize the appeal that outstanding black leaders have for their mulatto characters: Kern Roberts *(Alien Land)* and the Ex-Coloured Man *(The Autobiography of an Ex-Coloured Man)* in black-authored novels, and John Broderip *(Waiting for the Verdict)*, Neil Kingsblood *(Kingsblood Royal)*, and Peola *(Imitation of Life)* in white-authored novels all recognize the nobility of those black people who devote their lives to the advancement of their race. Interestingly enough, mulatto characters who are unable to identify with *any* members of the black group, and so become permanent passers in an attempt to resolve their identity crises, appear in both a white-authored novel *(Imitation of Life)* and a black-authored work *(Alien Land)*.

The primary difference between the treatment of the subject by whites and blacks is the emphasis in black novels on racial pride. Harlem Renaissance authors (Fauset, McKay, Larsen, and White) fictionalize the lesson that happiness is the reward of those mulattoes who remain within or return to the Negro group. Many mulatto characters who at one time deny their heritage—Angela Murray *(Plum Bun)*, Mimi Daquin *(Flight)*, John Broderip *(Waiting for the Verdict)*,[59] among others—return to the Negro group in the end and thus find some measure of happiness. But in other novels—*Comedy, American Style; The Garies and Their Friends;* and *The Autobiography of an Ex-Coloured Man* are notable examples—the mulatto character is unable to accept identification with the black group and, at least in the eyes of these authors, sells his birthright "for a mess of pottage." He trades his spontaneity, creativity, and personal and racial pride for an uneasy—and often unfulfilling—identification with white middle-class America.

NOTES

1. Langston Hughes, "Who's Passing for Who?" *The Ways of White Folks* (1933; rpt. New York: Knopf, 1962), p. 40.
2. Ibid., p. 44.
3. Ibid., p. 45.
4. Gunnar Myrdal, *An American Dilemma: The Negro Problem and Modern Democracy* (New York and London: Harper & Brothers, 1944), p. 688.
5. Frank J. Webb, *The Garies and Their Friends* (1857; rpt. New York: Arno Press and the New York Times, 1969), pp. 274-75.
6. Jessie Fauset, *Plum Bun* (London: Elkin Mathews & Marrot, 1928), p. 160.
7. Myrdal, *An American Dilemma*, p. 687.
8. Webb, *The Garies and Their Friends*, p. 329.
9. Charles W. Chesnutt, *The House Behind the Cedars* (Cambridge, Mass.: The Riverside Press, 1900), pp. 146-47.
10. Nella Larsen, *Passing* (New York: Knopf, 1929), pp. 97-98.
11. Rebecca Harding Davis, *Waiting for the Verdict* (1867; rpt. Upper Saddle River, N.J.: Gregg Press, 1968), pp. 301-4.
12. In Claude McKay, *Gingertown* (1932; rpt. Freeport, N.Y.: Books for Libraries Press, 1972), p. 81.
13. Ibid.
14. Ibid.
15. Ibid., p. 94.
16. Ibid., p. 96.
17. Ibid., p. 104.
18. Ibid.
19. Ibid., p. 83.
20. Sterling Brown, *The Negro in American Fiction* (Washington, D.C.: The Associates in the Negro Folk Education, 1937), p. 105.
21. Edward Margolies, *Native Sons: A Critical Study of Twentieth-Century Negro American Authors* (Philadelphia: University of Pennsylvania Press, 1968), p. 26.
22. Hugh M. Gloster, *Negro Voices in American Fiction* (Chapel Hill: University of North Carolina Press, 1948), p. 80.
23. Introductory comments to James Weldon Johnson's *The Autobiography of an Ex-Coloured Man* (1912; rpt. New York: Knopf, 1970), pp. vii-viii.
24. Brown, *The Negro in American Fiction*, p. 105. In fact, the debate about Johnson's intentions in the novel, particularly with regard to how we are to view the Ex-Coloured Man, continue. Addison Gayle regards the Ex-Coloured Man as expedient above all else and says that in the fiction of Johnson the tragic mulatto is an image of the past (*The Way of the New World: The Black Novel in America* [Garden City, N.Y.: Anchor Press, 1975], p. 92]).

Roger Rosenblatt is in essential agreement with Gayle, although he is more concerned with the causes of the Ex-Coloured Man's behavior and attitudes: "The Ex-Coloured Man is the epitome of the adaptable man. As such he indicts himself, and at the same time his existence indicts the world that encourages or necessitates his adaptability" *(Black Fiction* [Cambridge, Mass.: Harvard University Press, 1974], p. 183).

25. James Weldon Johnson, *The Autobiography of an Ex-Coloured Man* (1912; rpt. New York: Knopf, 1970), p. 3.
26. Ibid.
27. Ibid.
28. Ibid., p. 16.
29. Ibid.
30. Ibid., p. 17.
31. Ibid., p. 18.
32. Ibid., p. 19.
33. Ibid.
34. Ibid., p. 33.
35. Ibid.
36. Ibid., pp. 20-21.
37. Ibid., p. 45.
38. Ibid., p. 56.
39. Ibid.
40. Ibid., p. 87.
41. Ibid.
42. Ibid., pp. 144-45.
43. Ibid., p. 181.
44. Ibid., pp. 190-91.
45. Ibid.
46. Ibid.
47. Ibid., p. 188.
48. Margolies, *Native Sons,* p. 26.
49. Johnson, *The Autobiography of an Ex-Coloured Man,* p. 197.
50. Ibid.
51. Ibid., p. 204.
52. Ibid., p. 210.
53. Ibid.
54. Ibid.
55. Ibid.
56. Ibid.
57. Margolies, *Native Sons,* p. 26.
58. Johnson, *The Autobiography of an Ex-Coloured Man,* p. 211.
59. Both Angela Murray and John Broderip almost sell their birthrights—like Esau—but they are shown the way back to the Negro group by their siblings.

7.

The Mulatto as Black Bourgeois

Passing, as we have seen, is the most extreme form of the impulse toward assimilation. The identification with the white race—with the caste that is considered superior—is complete. The desire to be white has been translated into a spurious reality. But the American dream of upward mobility can be sought through another form of identification with white middle-class America. The existence of a bourgeois class among the Negro group, a class that imitates the values, standards, and life-style of the white middle class, may fulfill the needs of another group of black Americans who yearn for acceptance by, and assimilation into, white society. This form of assimilationism, according to Robert Bone, "is a kind of psychological 'passing' at the fantasy level." [1]

Like those blacks who literally pass for white, those who pass psychologically are also drawn heavily from the mixed-blood group. Because of this biological factor in the makeup of a large portion of the black bourgeoisie, familiar sociopsychological patterns of mulatto behavior are in evidence. There is the almost unconditional acceptance of "the values of the white bourgeois world—its morals and its canons of respectability, its standards of beauty and consumption." [2] If recognition of the mixed bloods as a separate caste will not be granted by the white man, then recognition of the achievements of the black bourgeoisie as a class may be conceded. So goes the logic of these black aspirants. Business success, professional stature, the accouterments of culture, the outward display of wealth, and strict codes of personal conduct are tools used by the black middle class to "make it" in white racist America. It seeks to protect itself from the full force of collective feelings of rejection and self-hatred. Since most whites do not make careful class distinctions among blacks, the black middle class turns inward. It seeks comfort in the frantic-paced social life of the black bourgeoisie. This is, in outline, the destructive pattern followed fictionally by a wide section of the largely mixed-blood Negro middle class. Franklin Frazier, Nathan Hare, and others believe that fictional accounts of the black bourgeoisie that adhere to the pattern described have a corresponding historical reality.

The roots of this behavior and these attitudes are to be found in the historical development of the Negro middle class. Miscegenation, as we have seen, produced a mixed-blood population in the United States which sometimes received favored treatment by whites. Feelings of superiority based upon light color, family connections, and educational or occupational advantages were found among the free men of color of New Orleans and some other urban centers as well as among the mulatto slave population of the largest plantations. In the class structure that emerged in the nineteenth century, the mulatto group was securely at the top of the social pyramid. Mulattoes, by color alone, were more easily admitted to the upper class than were full-blooded blacks.

These patterns we see in the literature about mulattoes, for the authors of this fiction were reflecting historical developments. However, the hostility between black and mulatto slaves and between free Negroes (many of them mulatto) and urban slaves has, according to Eugene Genovese, been exaggerated. The relationships among these groups were characterized more by fraternity than by hostility.[3] There was hostility toward mulattoes "who claimed and received privileges based on their color and relationship to the white family and who put on airs in the quarters." [4] But (as Chapter 1 indicates) except on some of the very large plantations and townhouses in cities like New Orleans and Charleston, not many mulattoes claimed or received such privileges.

The postbellum period brought changes in the attitudes of mulattoes and darker-skinned blacks and some changes in status as well. While the slaves valued white "as the color of those with power and accomplishment . . . [they] did not despise their own blackness. Evidence of a thirst for whiteness comes largely from the war years and long after, when new forces come into play within and without the black community." [5] While it is true that a disproportionate share of the political leadership within the black community that emerged after the war was mulatto, the cause is that better-educated mulattoes were in the best position to step out in front. "They did so, however, by strengthening their ties to their black brothers and sisters—a task made easier by previous associations." [6]

It was not until after World War I that new criteria for membership in the upper class became important, when professional standing and occupation, as opposed to color and family background, became primary:

> In the larger cities during the late nineteenth century upper-class status was accorded to a group that ranged from headwaiters, Pullman porters, coachmen, and butlers in prominent families, through draymen, blacksmiths, tailors, barbers, and postal employees, to coal dealers, hotel owners, caterers, and physicians, lawyers, teachers and certain ministers. By the twentieth century the artisan-entrepeneur and domestic servant group were passing from upper-class status (though as late as the 1920s Pullman porters in many places enjoyed considerable social status if they were of good family background, and older postal workers of good family are accorded some respect in certain cities at the present time [the early 1960s]).[7] . . . The Negro doctors, dentists, lawyers, and businessmen, who could not boast of white ancestors or did not know their white ancestors, were becoming the leaders of Negro "society." Even if they did not act like "gentlemen," they were able to imitate white "society" in their standards of consumption and entertainment. In fact, they tended to

ridicule the so-called "culture" and exclusiveness of the older Negro "society." [8]

When Gunnar Myrdal wrote *An American Dilemma*, he noted that the blue-veined societies (elitist communities based particularly on very light skin color—light enough to show the "blue veins" beneath the surface of the skin) were breaking up. One of the reasons he gave for their dissolution, in addition to greater opportunities for social mobility, was increased race consciousness: "it is no longer proper to display color preferences publicly." Still, "the primary tendency, which has always been to regard physical and cultural similarity to white people with esteem and deference," [9] had not been supplanted significantly by racial nationalism in 1944, nor, for that matter, has it completely disappeared today. The pages of *Ebony* still depict male and female models with "good" features and straight hair in advertisements for skin bleaches and hair straighteners. In an effort to be "relevant," Madison Avenue's "new Negro" may sport an Afro. The publishers of *Ebony*, however, cater to the black bourgeoisie. So just to be safe, they balance the "new" look with aspects of the old.

While black nationalism is a potent force in the Negro community today, the history of the black man in America—Marcus Garvey, Elijah Muhammed, and the Harlem Renaissance notwithstanding—shows clearly that the thrust toward assimilationism has been extremely powerful. The black bourgeoisie, especially the mulatto element that has had the greatest physical and cultural similarities with the white middle class, has placed the greatest emphasis upon white Anglo-Saxon Protestant characteristics. The desire for biological assimilation to be translated into actuality through intermarriage with whites and through marriage between mixed bloods is displayed in *Comedy, American Style* (1933); *The Blacker the Berry* (1929), by Wallace Thurman; and *Pointing the Way* (1908), by Sutton Griggs, to name but a few. The hoped-for result was to be a race of lighter- and lighter-skinned Negroes. Negroes, so the theory went, would find greater acceptance by whites; then, as the process continued, their children and grandchildren could pass for white; ultimately, their great-grandchildren and their children could be "reborn" as virtually 100 percent genuine Caucasians.

Since physical attributes—light skin color, straight hair texture, and thin nose and lips—have played such a significant role in class determination from pre-Civil War days until the second quarter of the twentieth century,[10] the perpetuation of these attributes has been regarded by the black bourgeoisie as essential. Marriage selection among the aspiring and already established upper class was based largely on color (light); family background (some white, preferably aristocratic white forebears); and what, on the level of culture, these usually implied. As Nella Larsen's protagonist in *Quicksand* discovers, Negro society "was as complicated, and as rigid in its ramifications as the highest strata of white society. If you couldn't prove your ancestry and connections, you were tolerated, but you didn't 'belong.' " [11]

For the most part, white society has not been cognizant of the class structure within the lower caste, or naturally, of the psychological and social reasons for the existence of this structure. In writing of Charleston in the 1920s, the novelist DuBose Heyward made the following comment on this subject:

> In the old city that was so strong in its class consciousness among the whites, it was singular that there was so little realisation of the fact, that, across the colour line, there existed much the same state of affairs. There were, in the opinion of most of the white residents, two general classes of negroes— those who knew their place, and those who did not. . . . If they thought at all of the innumerable distinct segments that comprised negro society it was apt to be with mild and, on the whole, indulgent amusement . . . In the set in which Lissa [the upper-class mulatto heroine] moved she seldom met a full-blooded negro—the barrier of mistrust and prejudice that rose between her fellow members of the Reformed Church and Mamba's friends [Mamba is her grandmother] on East Bay was scarcely less formidable than that separating white from black.[12]

As in any social system, education played a vital role in the inculcation of values and social behavior, and the education of the upper class—whether formal or otherwise—provided the bourgeoisie with the values and sense of status that was needed to maintain themselves as a separate class within the lower caste. According to Frazier, "From its inception the education of the Negro was shaped by bourgeois ideals." [13] These naturally included the Yankee virtues of industry and thrift, good manners, neatness—"the outward sign of a conscious Respectability" [14]—and the ideals of Puritan morality. Booker T. Washington, who always seemed to make particularly revealing comments about his social and political values, said that "the toothbrush ... was one of the world's greatest agencies of civilization." [15] In discussing the criteria for membership in the bourgeoisie of Victorian England, Treitschke once told a class in Berlin that "The English think Soap is Civilization." [16] The difference between the two comments is, of course, that the Negro leader was in dead earnest while Treitschke's opinion of this bourgeois attitude was one of contempt.

In *Quicksand,* Nella Larsen places her heroine, Helga Crane, in various modes of black life—from association with the Harlem intelligentsia during the Renaissance to entrapment among the poor and ignorant black "folk" of Alabama. We first see her at Naxos, a fictional version of Tuskegee. It is an all-Negro institution of higher education, but Larsen shows clearly the lack of concern for genuine learning. Repression reigns at Naxos, repression of teacher and student alike. The tradition of piety, of Puritan morality, and of the bourgeois values of an education "suited" to the Negro, are strong at Naxos. The school, Helga thinks, is "a big knife with cruelly sharp edges ruthlessly cutting all to a pattern, the white man's pattern. Teachers as well as students were subjected to the paring process, for it tolerated no innovations, no individualism." [17]

Certain standards of appearance must be adhered to rigidly. Many staff members at Naxos are of the opinion that dark-complexioned people should not wear bright colors. Standards of personal beauty are naturally patterned on Caucasian models. Helga notes with considerable disfavor that a friend and fellow teacher has "turned what was probably nice live crinkly hair, perfectly suited to her smooth dark skin and agreeable round features, into a dead, straight, greasy, ugly mass." [18]

The puritanical New England teachers and their black assistants work diligently to mold sexual attitudes and behavior to the white middle-class pattern. Male and female students are told to live chaste lives. One found guilty of immoral sexual behavior is expelled from school. Chastity is to be used as one more weapon to win the battle for respectability and acceptance by white society. It was only "common Negroes who engaged in premarital and unconventional sex relations. The graduates of these schools were to go forth and become the heads of conventional families. Was this not the best proof of respectability in the eyes of the white man, who had constantly argued that the Negro's 'savage instincts' prevented him from conforming to Puritanical standards of sex behavior?" [19] The small bourgeois upper class knew that the maintenance of the white pattern of family life would help them to be more "American," more like the dominant whites whose approval they sought.

Respectability could be displayed in many ways. The elitist communities of Charleston, New Orleans, Washington, D.C., and elsewhere were extremely self-conscious of their "culture." Fastidious in their speech habits, they cultivated an interest in English literature and music and sometimes established literary and musical societies and other exclusive clubs that served mainly a social, rather than an educational, function. DuBose Heyward, who considered himself a student of Negro life in Charleston, especially of its class structure, reported that "in the Monday Night Music Club ladies were ladies, those who were pale enough blushed, a leg was still a limb—and gentlemen asked permission to smoke cigarettes." [20] In addition to the literary societies and music clubs, church affiliation provided another exclusive activity. Mulattoes were to be found in the Episcopal, Congregational, Presbyterian, and Catholic churches, while the Negro masses were affiliated with the Baptist and Methodist churches. Robert Bone's succinct analysis of this phenomenon is the best I have seen: "Having just arrived, the Negro middle class took pains to conceal its lowly origins, above all from itself." [21]

In a bourgeois culture, the individual gains respectability in large part through the acquisition of wealth and by the maintenance of the prescribed bourgeois life-style. Thus, while chastity, piety, honesty, thrift, and hard work are virtues admired by the bourgeoisie, they appear to gain in value as they are associated with the visible "sign of election"—namely, wealth. Booker T.

Washington, the most influential black teacher of the Protestant ethic, told his students that "A man never begins to have self-respect until he owns a home." [22] Washington, who has been described as a "black Benjamin Franklin," [23] was undoubtedly the most important Negro advocate of what Robert Bone has aptly called the "American success ideology." [24]

In his penetrating study of Booker T. Washington and racial ideologies between 1880 and 1915, August Meier has synthesized several interlocking aspects of black bourgeois thought of the time. He observed that "To Washington it seemed proper that Negroes would have to measure up to American standards of morality and material prosperity if they were to succeed in the Social Darwinist race of life." [25] It is well known that Washington went so far as to blame the blacks for their ignorance and poverty. His answer to the Negro dilemma was "boot strapism." Those who did not have the initiative, the will, the intelligence, and the luck (although Washington would not have acknowledged this last requisite) to attain middle-class status would justly face the ignominy of bourgeois society: failure. But Washington stressed success for the individual who lived by the bourgeois values and, as the corollary to that victory, success for the race as well. George Langhorne Pryor, the black author of *Neither Bond nor Free*, a politically oriented novel from the early twentieth century, gives clear fictional expression to the Washingtonian formula for racial advancement: "Greater industry, skill, the sticking quality, honesty and reliability will open the way. . . . If we will only cultivate the saving spirit, cut loose from extravagant habits, work the year round, encourage and assist one another in business, we will acquire wealth, *and this will effectively dissipate race prejudice"* [26] [emphasis added]. By exercising "the property-acquiring virtues— thrift and industry, initiative and perseverance, promptness and reliability . . . and, a stern regard for duty," [27] blacks could presumably attain material success. They could then use this wealth to "buy" the gentility they needed for acceptance by white America.

The early Negro novel, which spanned the period from 1853, when William Wells Brown's *Clotelle* was published, to the watershed of World War I, was characterized by this "American success ideology." Stress was placed on "the property-acquiring virtues." The doctrine of deferred gratification, a term contemporary sociologists use to describe the conscious denial of self-indulgence and of any "personal habits which might interfere with the accumulation of property or the achievement of middle-class status," [28] was emphasized by the early Negro novelists. Robert Bone quotes Pauline Hopkins, author of *Contending Forces,* as saying: "We must guard ourselves against a sinful growth of any appetite." [29]

One of the best examples of the Negro novel of bourgeois life is the novel *The Garies and Their Friends* (1867), by Frank Webb. Webb presents the Ellis family, all of whom are thrifty and industrious workers who exhibit the proper decorum in their daily lives. The Ellises are firm believers in the gospel of work, and so decide to let their twelve-year-old son go into service during his summer vacation in order to learn the value of hard work. Mr. Walters, a very wealthy friend of the Ellises, advises against the plan. Like a black Benjamin Franklin, he says that the boy should sell matches or papers. The result of this policy is that "The boy that learns to sell matches soon learns to sell other things; he learns to make bargains; he becomes a small trader, then a merchant, then a millionaire. Did you ever hear of any one who made a fortune at service?" [30]

In twentieth-century novels, more than in those of a century before, we see an emphasis on status symbols: clothes, expensive homes and cars, academic degrees, servants. There is an obvious emphasis on conspicuous consumption. The "good life" is depicted in all of Jessie Fauset's novels. *There Is Confusion, Plum Bun, The Chinaberry Tree,* and *Comedy, American Style,* all contain long, loving descriptions of clothes, and to a lesser extent, of other possessions—furniture, paintings, and so on. As one reads Fauset's novels, it is apparent that she "more so than her contemporaries, spoke for the black bourgeoisie, past and present. The dream of Frank Webb, of a class midway between whites and poor Blacks, is now realized; the middle class has grown to maturity and received validation in the work of a talented writer." [31] Her family background was upper-class Philadelphia; she was raised with some of the most prestigious Negroes in America. Although Fauset sometimes wanted to *attack* bourgeois values (the ostracism of Laurentine Strange in *The Chinaberry Tree* because of her illegitimacy, for example), she was unable to do so effectively because of her belief in a basically bourgeois value structure.

Nella Larsen's two novels, *Passing* and *Quicksand,* present an interesting contrast. Like Fauset, Larsen presents numerous descriptions of clothes and other objects. At times the reader suspects Larsen of being preoccupied with "things," but in fact she is using the accouterments of wealth to highlight the preoccupations of the society in which her characters move.[32]

In Larsen's *Passing,* a clear indictment of the mulatto upper class, Irene Redfield moves in a world of refinement and luxury. Her life is filled with clothes and other objects, bridge parties and gatherings. Her husband Brian, a successful doctor who has made possible their manner of living, has been seized with periods of restlessness several times during their married life. He wants to go to Brazil to practice medicine or to do research in the United States; neither undertaking would be particularly lucrative. Irene has worked strenuously to suppress her husband's "noble" ambitions because they would bring about an end to the way of life she intends to maintain at all costs.

Inferiority feelings, self-hatred, and an obsessive need to deny their relationship to the black masses lead the black Anglo-Saxons (Nathan Hare's term for the black bourgeoisie)[33] to reject their own history and mores. Hare calls these people "Exiles" because "they are, in effect, resigning from the Negro race."[34] The novels of the Talented Tenth are noteworthy in this respect. Since these authors pressed for the defeat of the caste system through the existence of a superior class of Negroes, they were most resentful of any amalgamation of their class with the black masses. Bone points out that in several of the early novels "there is a stock situation in which a 'refined Afro-American' is forced to share a Jim Crow car with dirty, boisterous, and drunken Negroes."[35]

Almost all black writers in the 1920s, in contrast with the Talented Tenth, glorified their "Negroness" to some extent. Walter White, for example, presents the life-style of the black bourgeoisie as cold, empty, and dehumanizing. The black bourgeoisie, like their white counterparts, seem to define progress in terms of technology and quantification. These blacks are denying the gifts of their racial heritage: "Here are these colored people with the gifts from God of laughter and song and of creative instincts— . . .

and what are they doing with it? They are aping the white man—becoming a race of money-grubbers with ledgers and money tills for brains and Shylock hearts." [36]

The writers of the Harlem Renaissance came back again and again to this theme of the creative powers of black people, powers that are squandered in a wanton denial of self. Perhaps Ralph Ellison has expressed most brilliantly the reward for the individual who gives up his own identity: "I was never more hated than when I tried to be honest," says the Invisible Man; "on the other hand, I've never been more loved and appreciated than when I tried to 'justify' or affirm someone's mistaken beliefs." And the psychic cost: "Too often, in order to justify *them*, I had to take myself by the throat and choke myself until my eyes bulged and my tongue hung out and wagged like the door of an empty house in a high wind. Oh, yes, it made them happy and it made me sick. So I became ill of affirmation, of saying 'yes' against the nay-saying of my stomach—not to mention my brain." [37]

In *If He Hollers Let Him Go* (1945), Chester Himes portrays a sensitive black man in conflict with himself and his society. Like the Invisible Man, Himes's protagonist tries to say "yes" to white society—yes to being a nigger—but his manhood stands in the way. Realizing that *"there never was a nigger who could beat it"* [38] [the oppression by white society], Bob Jones moves violently between rebellion and accommodation. He almost accepts the rewards of black bourgeois life, but in the end, the price is too high.

The world of the black bourgeoisie is represented by Bob's fiancée, Alice Harrison, and her parents, who are leaders in the black bourgeois community in Los Angeles. Alice is a beautiful mulatto woman who is light enough to pass when she is with her upper-class white friends. She is a well-educated, confident woman who works as a casework supervisor in the city welfare department.

For a man who professes hatred for all things white, Bob Jones certainly has chosen "the whitest colored girl . . . [he] could find," as one of the characters points out. [39] "Rich and light and almost white," Ella Mae says of Alice. Bob is proud of her, he tells us: "Proud of the way she looked, the appearance she made among white people; proud of what she demanded from white people, and the credit they gave her; and her position and prestige among her own people. I could knock myself out just walking along the street with her; and whenever we ran into any of the white shipyard workers downtown somewhere I really felt like something." [40]

The relationship with Alice, however, bears an expensive price tag. Like Bob—like all other blacks, Himes suggests—Alice and her class have learned that they cannot beat the system. They know, Bob tells us, quoting a line from a Tolstoy story, that "There never had been enough bread and freedom to go around." [41] So the black bourgeois class has made certain that at least they get enough bread; in fact, they prosper. Bob's unsympathetic portrayal of Alice's parents, Dr. and Mrs. Harrison, reveals the immorality and social inadequacy of the black bourgeois ethic. Bob hates Alice's mother because "she looked so goddamned smug and complacent, sitting there in her two-hundred-dollar chair, her feet planted in her three-thousand-dollar rug, waving two or three thousand dollars' worth of diamonds on her hands, bought with dough her husband had made overcharging poor hard-working colored people for his incompetent services." [42]

At other times, Bob believes that he is willing to buy peace and Alice at the cost of his black manhood. However, in spite of these desires, his analysis of American racism leads him away from Alice and acceptance of the bourgeois ethic:

> No matter what had happened to them inside, they hadn't allowed it to destroy them outwardly; they had overcome their color the only way possible in America—as Alice had put it, by adjusting themselves to the limitations of their race. They hadn't stopped trying, I gave them that much; they'd kept on trying, always would; but they had recognized their limit—a nigger limit.
>
> From the viewpoint of my hangover it didn't seem a hard thing to do. You simply had to accept being black as a condition over which you had no control, then go on from there. Glorify your black heritage, revere your black heroes, laud your black leaders, cheat your black brother, worship your white fathers (be sure and do that), segregate yourself; then make yourself believe that you had made great progress, that you would continue to make great progress, that in time the white folks would appreciate all of this and pat you on the head and say, "You been a good nigger for a long time. Now

we're going to let you in." Of course you'd have to believe that the white folks were generous, unselfish, and loved you so much they wanted to share their world with you, but if you could believe all the rest, you could believe that too. And it didn't seem like a hard thing for a nigger to believe, because they didn't have any other choice.

But my mind kept rebelling against it. Being black, it was a thing I ought to know, but I'd learned it differently. I'd learned the same jive that the white folks had learned. All that stuff about liberty and justice and equality. . . . All men are created equal . . . any person born in the United States is a citizen.[43]

This chord is struck again and again throughout the novel: Bob Jones, who is, as Addison Gayle has pointed out, black everyman, wants to be both a black man and an American. He wants the American dream to be an actuality. But everywhere he turns, he encounters a white racist society that beats him back, "demonstrating that the line between the intellectual and the uneducated Black, in terms of opportunity and treatment, is thin indeed." [44] Even $3,000 carpets cannot hide the fact that "a nigger is a nigger" in the eyes of white America.

Many bourgeois blacks are too much aware of cultural nationalism to voice openly their contempt, hatred, fear of or ambivalence toward the black masses. Writing about upper-class northern mulattoes, Edward Reuter says: "In their public utterances the Negro may be idealized, but there is no desire or disposition on the part of the mulatto to have any intimate association with him." [45]

In *Quicksand,* Nella Larsen invents the character of Anne Grey in order to attack the hypocritical attitude of the black bourgeoisie toward the black masses. Anne is independently wealthy; she is witty and beautiful. She constantly talks of "the race problem" and says that she hates whites. But Larsen reveals Anne's pretensions of being a "race woman" as mere sham: Anne "aped their [the whites'] clothes, their manners, and their gracious ways of living. While proclaiming loudly the undiluted good of all things Negro, she yet disliked the songs, the dances, and the softly blurred speech of the race. Toward these things she showed only a disdainful contempt, tinged sometimes with a faint amusement." [46]

In *Mamba's Daughters,* Dubose Heyward explores even more extensively such racial hypocrisy. Lissa's bourgeois "society" friends talk a good deal about being proud of being black. But, like Anne Grey, they are busy rejecting all things Negro. Like so many other mulattoes, they are proud of their Anglo-Saxon coloring and features. Lissa examines the portraits of Negroes by a black artist and realizes that the painter's subjects give the effect "of not being negroes at all, but white people painted in darker shades—some subtle racial element was lacking." Lissa later says to Mamba that her friends "seem to spend all their time saying how glad they are to be negroes and all the time they're trying their damndest to be white." [47] On another occasion, Lissa, walking with one of her society friends, hears some spirituals being sung in a storefront church. Lissa finds the music exciting, but her companion criticizes her enthusiasm by saying that the enjoyment of spirituals is all right for ignorant Negroes but is unsuitable for such civilized people as he and Lissa. But although Lissa later goes on to sing in the Metropolitan, she never runs away from her racial origins; in fact, her singing contains "that heart-breaking pure negro quality." [48]

Like Lissa, Ralph Ellison's Invisible Man must come to terms with the fact of his race. He does this in many ways throughout the novel, but one of the most memorable is the yam-eating scene. The Invisible Man, a ginger-colored, middle-class Negro who, as Ellison shows us in the battle royal scene, is separated both by color and values from the other black boys present, has blindly striven for white approval and acceptance. By the time the yam-eating scene occurs, the Invisible Man has lost some of his naïveté regarding his college experience. Walking down a Harlem street, he passes a store displaying a sign that reads, "You too can be truly beautiful ... Win greater happiness with whiter complexion. Be outstanding in your social set." He is still feeling angry about the sign when he comes upon the old yam seller. The Invisible Man eats the yams and feels intense pleasure and freedom because he is doing what he wants to do: "to hell with being ashamed of what you liked. No more of that for me. I am what I am! ... I yam what I am!" [49] In this moment, the Invisible Man accepts his own racial heritage and begins to identify with the collective black experience. Once he is not crippled by self-hatred and the need to be the white man's "good nigger," he understands the pressure he and those like him have been under in their effort to be the living refutations of the Negro stereotype:

> What a group of people we were, I thought. Why, you could cause us the greatest humiliation simply by confronting us with something we liked. Not *all* of us, but so many. [And then] . . . I saw myself advancing upon Bledsoe [the president of the Negro college the Invisible Man had attended] . . . "Bledsoe, you're a shameless chitterling eater! I accuse you of relishing hog bowels! Ha! And not only do you eat them, you sneak them in *private* when you think you're unobserved!" . . . Why, with others present, it would be worse than if I had accused him of raping an old woman of ninety-nine years, weighing ninety pounds, blind in one eye and lame in the hip! Bledsoe would disintegrate, disinflate! With a profound sigh, he'd drop his head in shame. *He'd lose caste* [emphasis added]. The weekly [Negro] newspapers would attack him. The captions over his picture: Prominent Educator Reverts to Field Niggerism! [50]

For a bourgeois Negro ever to behave in such a way that white society associates him with the lower-class black stereotype is indeed to make himself an "untouchable" as far as the black bourgeoisie is concerned. In the Invisible Man's fantasy Bledsoe is faced with recanting or retiring from public life and washing dishes at the Automat.

On the social and psychological levels, then, we have a group of people who have felt compelled to deny their racial and cultural heritage (in so far as this heritage differs from that of white Americans). Frazier interprets the social isolation and rejection of the black heritage as a kind of self-perpetuated genocide on a group and individual level. He says that members of the black bourgeoisie in the United States "seem to be in the process of becoming NOBODY." [51] So long as the black bourgeoisie hold fast to the "genteel tradition," the educated, more affluent black Americans will not be able to eliminate the self-destructive patterns that have emerged during the last two centuries.

Franklin Frazier and his followers are particularly pessimistic about the establishment of a healthier group image and a nonschizophrenic behavior pattern for the black bourgeoisie. Frazier bases his negative assessment on his contention that "There have been only two really vital cultural traditions in the social history of the Negro in the United States: one being the genteel tradition of the small group of mulattoes who assimilated the morals and manners of the slaveholding aristocracy; and the other, the culture of the black folk who gave the world the Spirituals." [52] There is a third vital cultural tradition, however, which Frazier ignores in *Black Bourgeosie*. This third movement dates only from the Harlem Renaissance, and although there are foreshadowings of it in the 1880s and 1890s, it has a far smaller membership than the bourgeois or "folk" communities. Nonetheless, the nonbourgeois black intelligentsia has the potential to use both the best elements of black cultural history *and* of the cultural history of the West. While the writers of the Harlem Renaissance produced few, if any, great literary works; while this group was sometimes indiscriminate in praising all things Negro, and in interpreting certain traits as innately—rather than culturally—Negro (jazz, for one), they at least did escape (or begin the process of escaping) the adulation of all things white, the rigid Victorian moral standards, and the crippling self-hatred of the black bourgeoisie. The intelligentsia sought new values to replace the Protestant ethic, Washington accommodationism, and color fetishism.[53]

In *Mamba's Daughters,* Heyward depicts Lissa as moving from the lower-class folk *through* the black bourgeois society of Charleston's Monday Night Music Club to the intelligentsia. She had been excited by the spirituals she heard in the lower-class church; she had spent time with a group of lower-class blacks, going to their loud parties where she first heard jazz. She had recognized that her friends in the genteel mulatto community were ashamed of being Negro. Heyward comments that there was a third way of life, one different from either Mamba's or that of the Monday Night Music Club: "Far above, in the life of the aristocracy, the new freedom was beginning to manifest, smashing conventional usage; talking its Freud and Jung—rearranging moral standards, and explaining lapses in its pat psychoanalytical jargon." [54]

When Lissa sings the National Anthem of the American Negro at the Metropolitan Opera, Wentworth (the white protagonist) "felt suddenly the impact of something tremendously and self-consciously racial; something that had done with apologies for being itself, done with imitations, reaching back into its own origin, claiming its heritage of beauty from the past." [55] Heyward praises Lissa's accomplishment as reaching beyond the establishment of black pride and black art. It is " 'native from the dirt up—it's art—and it's ours.' 'Ours?' a voice inquired. 'Do you mean negro?' 'Negro, if you will, yes, but first, American.' " [56] Lissa has merged her "double self into a better and truer self." She has reconciled her "twoness" and has achieved a positive self-image both as a Negro and as an American.

Few of the other mulatto characters that inhabit the pages of the American novel ever lose a sense of their marginality. The complex norms and mores of black bourgeois society—many of which exist to hide the group's self-hatred and self-delusion from itself—have kept most of its members tied to this tradition. None of Jessie Fauset's characters escapes the genteel tradition, a major reason being her own inability to loosen completely the shackles of the bourgeois ethic. Her best novel, *Comedy, American Style,* is good precisely because she is *outside* Olivia Blanchard Cary, *observing* her self-hatred, her overwhelming need to "be white," rather than *sharing* Olivia's obsessions. But the novel which presents the most satisfying artistic study of the black bourgeoisie, *The Living Is Easy* (1948), by Dorothy West, shares with *Comedy, American Style,* the intellectual and moral separation of author from her central character. West's novel, in addition, is much more than an antibourgeois tract or a Renaissance glorification of Negro folk culture. As an attack on the Negro middle class, the novel is brilliant. Virtually every aspect of the black bourgeoisie comes under the author's ironic scrutiny. Through both the study of the Negro middle-class community of Boston and the protagonist of her novel, West presents a complex portrayal of the ideology of the black bourgeoisie. However, *The Living Is Easy* is not merely a work of social criticism. It is also a work of psychological complexity. As

Robert Bone has noted, "Cleo, the protagonist of the novel, is unforgettable"; she is "the most striking personality in recent Negro fiction." [57] Cleo Judson displays virtually all of the middle-class character traits described by Kardiner and Ovesey, Bertram Karon, and other students of the psychology of the black bourgeoisie. But Cleo is more than a compilation of these stereotypical traits. She is a fully rounded fictional character of sufficient stature, in my opinion, to be regarded as a tragic figure. She sacrifices—consciously and unconsciously—her vitality, spontaneity, emotional health, and much of her ability to see the absurd, to say nothing of her husband, child, sisters, and their families—in an effort to become a member of Boston society. But she is not the only one. As Robert Bone has noted, there are other characters who sacrifice—or mutilate, to use his term—their self-hood and integrity. "There is the Duchess, who buries her Catholic heart in an unsanctioned marriage, in order to pour tea for the Boston ladies who have scorned her mother. There is the Duchess's husband, Simeon, who relinquishes the editorship of a militant Negro newspaper, in order to secure his sister's social position. There is a young doctor, interested in cancer research, who turns to the abortion trade as a source of ready cash. All, like Cleo, have paid a price for belonging." [58]

Like the other middle-class Négro communities, actual and fictive, the Boston of Dorothy West's novel is concerned with color and appearance, family background, propriety, conspicuous consumption, and acceptance as a privileged minority by white society.

Black society in Boston is light skinned, of course. Society women—women who are counted among the hundred best families of Boston, New York, Philadelphia, and Washington, D.C.—consider color and significant physical attributes among the most important prerequisites for membership in their select group: "Though they scorned the Jew, they were secretly pleased when they could pass for one. Though they were contemptuous of the Latins, they were proud when they looked European. They were not dismayed by a darkish skin if it was counterbalanced by a straight nose and straight hair that established an Indian origin. There was nothing that disturbed them more than knowing that no one would take them for anything but colored." [59] Light-skinned women with "good" features are considered to be very desirable marriage partners and are valued not only for their appearance but for the expected "quality" of their offspring: Thea Binney, member of a prominent Negro family, has a complexion of "peaches and cream, and her chestnut hair was soft as silk. She could have married any man short of a Zulu, and still have had children who passed the test of color and hair." [60] Her fiancé, Cole Hartnett, who has plain features and is dark yellow in color, is himself a member of another prestigious Boston family. He is "considered a fortunate man because he had a doctor's degree and a fair-skinned wife who would give him fair children." [61] The Bostonians seem to regard Cole's light-skinned wife as at least as great an asset as his family background and professional training. One is reminded of Ralph Ellison's Invisible Man, who seemed almost as impressed by Dr. Bledsoe's cream-colored wife as by the college president's power in the black community.

Because Cleo is anxious to be accepted into society, she is very color conscious. As a child in the South, she had been made to feel miserable because of her color. She had hated her "bright skin." Her mother had made her wash her face all day in order to maintain the purity of her daughter's light coloring. Like other mulatto characters, Cleo's coloring sometimes made her the butt of spiteful comments. On occasion, her playmates had called her "yaller punkins." When Cleo came north, however, she learned to regard her color as a valuable asset. Therefore, when Cleo gives birth to her daughter Judy, who has the cocoa-brown skin coloring of her husband Bart, she is extremely upset. In the opening pages of the novel, West states that Cleo has never forgiven her child for being dark. Cleo sees Judy's color and features as an affront to her grand scheme of achieving recognition by Boston society. Cleo "worked hard" on Judy's nose, as West puts it. "She had tried clothespins, but Judy had not known what to do about breathing. Now Cleo was teaching her to keep the bridge pinched, but Judy pinched too hard, and the rush of dark blood made her nose look larger than ever." [62] Like those blacks who use skin bleaches and hair straighteners, Cleo's efforts to change her daughter's offensive nose represent a poignant denial of her race.

But Cleo's behavior does not follow the neat configurations of a case study. In one of the rare moments of tenderness she allows herself, Cleo regards Judy's face and sees her daughter through eyes unclouded by her status aspirations: "She scanned the small upturned face, and a rush of protective tenderness flooded her heart. . . . She thought she had never seen anything as lovely as the deep rich color that warmed Judy's cheeks." [63] But Cleo usually demands that her daughter meet the rigid perfectionist behavioral standards that the black bourgeoisie demand of themselves and their children. Judy must always be absolutely neat in appearance and always be "a little Boston lady," Cleo tells her.

Cleo's proper behavior is designed to win approval from white society. She thoroughly disapproves of her husband's religious affiliation with a "shouting Baptist" church, for example, and she herself goes to an Episcopalian church. Nevertheless, in spite of Cleo's efforts to remake her personality into that of a cold, genteel society matron, she cannot completely smother her "down-home" vitality. She has a double self, in effect: one half of her yearns for acceptance into what the other half of her calls "a counterfeit of the Brahmin cult." [64] At her party, "The Rabelaisian half of her mind was faithfully recording every word and gesture for devastating mimicry the moment the storm door shut behind her last guest. . . ." [65]

However, Cleo feels compelled to mutilate her Rabelaisian soul, her creativity, in order to gain acceptance into the black bourgeoisie. Perhaps it is because she knows no other form of success.[66] Like other members of the mulatto upper class, Cleo rejects identification with lower-class blacks. Indeed, she spends much of her time and energy running away from the Negro folk. She is molding Judy into the little Boston lady and does not want her daughter to go to school in the South End, a neighborhood which is deteriorating, according to Cleo's standards. The "nicer" class of Negroes, following the whites of the neighborhood, were moving out of the South End, which had been so named because of the influx of black cotton-belters. Using biblical imagery, West vividly describes the black bourgeoisie's frantic denial of their race: "For years these northern Negroes had lived next door to white neighbors and taken pride in proximity. They viewed their southern brothers with alarm, and scattered all over the city and its suburbs to escape this plague of their own locusts." [67] The Binneys, an old prestigious family, moved out of Boston to

Cambridge; in fact, "They were the first family on their street to move away because of the rapid encroachment of Negroes. They began the general exodus. Mr. Binney could say with pride, right up to the day of his death, that he had never lived on a street where other colored people resided." [68] Cleo does not have the Binney money to buy her way into white neighborhoods; but when the class of Negroes in the South End becomes objectionable to her, she looks for another place to live.

West creates a brilliant comedy of errors out of Cleo's interview with Mr. Van Ryper, the owner of the house Cleo wants to buy, as she reveals the prejudices and misunderstandings of the two characters. Mr. Van Ryper opens the interview by telling Cleo that he is sorry to give up his lovely old home; however, he is simply too old to temper his prejudices. Cleo immediately thinks that he is making reference to other colored people in the neighborhood. She considers putting on an exhibition of racial pride, but she decides to sacrifice her pride in exchange for the house. Then the thought suddenly occurs to her that her prospective neighbors "must be old second-class niggers from way down South, whom she wouldn't want to live next door to herself." [69] Cleo's locusts are pursuing her. Based upon her assumption that the family Mr. Van Ryper has mentioned is black, Cleo asks what part of the South the family comes from. When Mr. Van Ryper understands that Cleo thinks it is blacks against whom he is prejudiced, he is very angry: it is the Irish that he detests! Why, he tells her, his family were abolitionists. The *coup de grâce* comes at the end of the interview. Cleo tells Mr. Van Ryper that it has always been her dream to live in Brookline, and he replies crossly that this isn't Brookline, but Roxbury. The other side of the street is Brookline. *He's* moving to Brookline in a few days.

West is at her best as she describes the members of the upper class at Cleo's coming-out party. There were some professional men and women—a judge, a criminal lawyer with a flourishing practice, a beautiful daughter passing for white at Wellesley, and

> a young lawyer with no practice at all and a complete disinterest in the profession his father's butler-wages had bought for him; a doctor who privately hated his growing practice because his patients were the colored poor; a valet

whose dress and bearing were superior to that of all the men present; a caterer's helper, on his night off, who accepted a proffered highball with no nervous recognition of a fellow worker; and the man of talent, a violinist, handsome, poor, and gifted.

And among the ladies arriving were Miss Eleanor Elliott in old finery; an auburn-haired social worker, the first of her race at Thaw House—though hardly representative—also distinguished as a Wellesley graduate but who had no inclination to pass because her family name was honor enough; a schoolteacher, doomed to spinsterhood by Boston's ruling, but too contented with her white pupils to yearn to mother a colored child; and a brilliant teacher of piano who had a growing list of the best colored children because she had been astute enough to start her enrollment with white students selected from her neighborhood's crop and charged a modest fourth of her dollar fee.[70]

This is mulatto society. All of the qualities of the black bourgeoisie that have been noted are here: the importance of color and family background; the weak economic base of this group prior to World War I; the adherence to the mulatto upper class rather than passing for white, because among the Negroes one had a status not available in the white class structure; the adoration of the Caucasian and hatred of the Negro race, and by extension, the hatred of self (the schoolteacher who did not want a colored child); the aping of white behavior (the piano teacher's pupils); and the hatred of lower-class blacks (the doctor whose patients were lower-class blacks). As West so aptly sums up at one point in the novel: "Their lives were narrowly confined to a daily desperate effort to ignore their racial heritage." [71]

What could be the possible appeal to Cleo of membership in this world of self-delusion? West provides an answer not only through Cleo's own life and personality but also through the lives and struggles of those around her—the Duchess, Simeon, and Cole Hartnett. The primary reason for wanting "to belong," for seeking admission to the favored class, is the fundamental need for security. To belong, to be accepted, is in itself, satisfying for those in the marginal position. But, as Cleo herself wonders during one of her reflective moments: " 'What was this business of belonging? What was it worth? A tailor and a stable-owner were the leaders of society." [72]

Perhaps the answer to Cleo's question lies in the fact that membership in the mulatto upper class does not bring mere group identification, but assimilation into a favored group. The rigid rules of the Negro upper class helped enhance the sense of distinction and separateness one attained if acceptance were granted. West does show, however, that not all who are well "within the fold" are secure. As the result of an early crisis experience, Simeon had lost his sense of security. One of the children in his wealthy, virtually all-white neighborhood said that he thought Simeon was a colored boy. Later, Simeon went to the bathroom, locked himself in, and "scrubbed his hands vigorously, but it was as he had known it would be, there was no whiteness under the brown. He was not like the other boys. He was not a Bostonian." [73] The boys were evidently instructed to be friendly to him. But after that day, "He was never their equal. He was their charge, whom they were honor-bound to treat with charity. They never knew whether they liked him or not. They only knew it was something of a bother to be with him, for the feelings of a colored boy had to be coddled." [74]

The novel does present two entirely different alternatives to the life of the black bourgeoisie. One of these is represented by Cleo's husband, Bart. He is a unique black character because he is a business wizard who actually controls large amounts of money; yet he has no inclination to become part of the black bourgeoisie. He is a kind of black Benjamin Franklin: when he was one year old, the slaves were freed. On that day, his mother held out a piece of silver to the child; she closed his fist over it and "counseled him to treasure it, for money was the measure of his independency." [75] And Bart devoted his life to making money. But there is another side to the man that is Laurentian rather than Franklinesque. When he was ten years old, he saw his first banana, and was fascinated by the beautiful tropical fruit. He loves his fruit: "There was rich satisfaction in seeing it ripen, seeing the downiness on it, the blush on it, feeling the firmness of its flesh." [76] Bart himself is a warm, vital man with "The smell of fruit and earth and sweat" [77] about him. He is not a status seeker; his behavior is not regulated by status considerations. He is not afraid to smell of sweat, to laugh loudly, or to shout at the Baptist church. His emotional energy is expended on his family and business, with which is is also in love. Unlike Cleo, he is nonmanipulative, nonsecretive, and openly affectionate.

The other alternative presented in the novel is represented by Cleo's sisters and their families. They are satisfied with living the simple life of the Negro folk, close to nature and to elemental passions. It is interesting to note that neither Bart nor Cleo's sisters can be persuaded to come to her party—her entrance into society.

Cleo manipulates here sisters into coming to live with her. She has a great need to be loved and needs the love and admiration of her family. Unfortunately, this obsessive need drives her to hurt those she most deeply loves. Cleo's need to control is neurotic—and out of control. She can never tell the truth; her life consists of one petty scheme after another. As West explains, "There were so many secrets in her day that any discussion became an exposure." [78]

Cleo's sins, her tragic flaw, if you will—her inability to respect the integrity of the individual human being—finally bring a plague down upon her house. Her personal chaos is played against the international upheaval of World War I. Cleo's own needs for love, attention, and power merge with her denial of her race. Her "coming out" (or "entering into") party was given ostensibly so that Dean Galloway, a black leader, can speak for the black cause. He tells the story of a poor black man whose only crime was poverty. He was passing as white when he was sworn in as an extra policeman in order to keep some "troublesome" blacks in order. This Negro, who was hired to turn against his own people, killed a Klansman who had wantonly killed several innocent blacks and was about to reload his gun. The Negro ran, but was caught, and his father-in-law was drowned while helping him. The Negro was Robert Jones, Cleo's sister's husband, and his father-in-law was Cleo's father. Dean Galloway tells the black bourgeoisie of Boston that Robert Jones must not go on trial alone. The poverty of blacks, their oppression, must be brought out too. The people at the party are quite moved in spite of themselves. Then Cleo speaks up and says she does not see what good it will do to make Robert Jones's name a household word. People always think all Negroes are alike; why support the defense of this poor Negro? After her guests leave, Cleo breaks down. Bart agrees to support Robert's defense secretly and donates a large sum of money for this purpose. Cleo had not wanted bourgeois Boston to know of her connection with this lower-class Negro murderer. Robert is released but has lost his sanity through the entire ordeal and is last seen in a hospital for the insane.

Cleo's party is really the climax of the novel. It is during this event that she achieves her greatest social acceptance by the black bourgeoisie and immediately afterward loses her happiness because of Robert Jones. That night, too, she looks at Bart and really sees him—his tiredness and aging, the worry and strain he has been under in trying to provide for so many people.

At the end of the novel, Cleo looks pathetic in some ways and tragic in others. While she has been mistaken or blind about many things and people in her life, she shows the capacity to learn. Like most tragic figures, she learns about these things—especially about herself—too late. Also like the tragic characters of classic literature, Cleo is a giant in her own world. The world in which she moves is small; it is prejudiced and narrow, and, for some critics, this factor would deprive Cleo of her tragic stature. But I think that her imagination, her Rabelaisian gifts, her strength, and her blind needs combine to make her a figure of tragedy.[79]

The final pages of the novel find Bart bankrupt. He is leaving for New York to try to begin again. He will not let Cleo come with him because he does not want Judy uprooted. Cleo tells him to write, even if he has no money to send. But Bart would never write unless he could put money in the envelope out of fear that she would tear up the letter. As he leaves, he merely brushes his lips against her cheek. He knows that she does not like to be kissed on the lips. So at the end of the novel, Cleo has finally come to realize her love and need for Bart—but he must go, driven away in part by Cleo herself. Judy is a child who exerts a gentle influence over others and cannot be controlled by her mother. Cleo's sisters have finally picked up the broken pieces of their lives and also have moved away from Cleo's domination. Ultimately Cleo loses all she loves because of her status needs, her self-hatred and fear of the world, and because of the defenses she musters to fight that self-hatred. As Bart leaves Cleo's house, she tormentedly asks herself, "Who is there now to love me best? Who?" [80]

NOTES

1. Robert A. Bone, *The Negro Novel in America*, rev. ed. (New Haven, Conn.: Yale University Press, 1968), p. 4.

2. E. Franklin Frazier, *Black Bourgeoisie* (New York: The Free Press, 1969), p. 26.

3. Eugene Genovese, *Roll, Jordan, Roll: The World the Slaves Made* (New York: Pantheon Books, 1974), p. 430.

4. Ibid.

5. Ibid.

6. Ibid., pp. 430-31.

7. August Meier, *Negro Thought in America, 1880-1915: Racial Ideologies in the Age of Booker T. Washington* (Ann Arbor: University of Michigan Press, 1963), p. 151.

8. Frazier, *Black Bourgeoisie*, pp. 198-99.

9. Gunnar Myrdal, *An American Dilemma: The Negro Problem and Modern Democracy* (New York and London: Harper & Brothers, 1944), p. 698.

10. These factors continue to have some importance. See Nathan Hare's *The Black Anglo-Saxons* (New York: Marzani & Munsell, 1965).

11. Nella Larsen, *Quicksand* (New York: Knopf, 1928), p. 19.

12. DuBose Heyward, *Mamba's Daughters* (Garden City, N.Y.: Doubleday, Doran & Company, 1929), p. 208.

13. *Black Bourgeoisie*, p. 60.

14. G. M. Young, *Victorian England: Portrait of an Age* (London: Oxford University Press, 1936), p. 24.

15. Horace Mann Bond, *The Education of the Negro in the American Social Order* (New York: Prentice-Hall, 1934), p. 119.

16. Young, *Victorian England*, p. 24.

17. Larsen, *Quicksand*, p. 9.

18. Ibid., pp. 31-32.

19. Frazier, *Black Bourgeoisie*, p. 78.

20. Heyward, *Mamba's Daughters*, pp. 208-9.

21. Bone, *The Negro Novel in America*, p. 14.

22. From *"Black Belt Diamonds*. Gems from the Speeches, Addresses, and Talks to Students of Booker T. Washington"* (New York: Fortune & Shoot), pp. 40-41 in Frazier, *Black Bourgeoisie*, p. 76.

23. Abraham L. Harris, *The Negro as Capitalist* (Philadelphia: American Academy of Political and Social Science, 1936), p. 3.

24. Bone, *The Negro Novel in America,* p. 13.
25. Meier, *Negro Thought in America, 1880-1915,* p. 103.
26. Bone, *The Negro Novel in America,* p. 13.
27. Ibid., p. 16.
28. Ibid., p. 14.
29. Ibid.
30. Frank J. Webb, *The Garies and Their Friends* (1857; rpt. New York: Arno Press and the New York Times, 1969), p. 63.
31. Addison Gayle, Jr., *The Way of the New World: The Black Novel in America* (Garden City, N.Y.: Anchor Press, 1975), p. 119.
32. Addison Gayle, Jr., takes a somewhat different approach to Larsen's novels. While he and I agree that Miss Larsen points out the hypocrisies and pretensions of the black bourgeoisie, Gayle contends that her characters must, in the end, either find their identities in the world of the black middle class, or face disaster . . . she believes that it is far superior to the lower class" *(The Way of the New World,* p. 114). Larsen's attack in *Quicksand* on the black bourgeoisie at Naxos, the Harlem intelligentsia, and the life of the impoverished southern black seem quite even-handed. The major difference between her criticism of the black bourgeoisie and the supposed intelligentsia and the poor blacks is that members of the first two groups have lost their souls, while members of the last group have lost their freedom and sometimes their sanity as well.
33. Nathan Hare, *The Black Anglo-Saxons* (New York: Marzani & Munsell, 1965).
34. Ibid., p. 86.
35. Bone, *The Negro Novel in America,* p. 18. Chesnutt's *The Marrow of Tradition* provides an example.
36. Walter White, *Flight* (New York: Knopf, 1926), pp. 53-54.
37. Ralph Ellison, *Invisible Man* (New York: Random House, 1952), pp. 432-33.
38. Chester Himes, *If He Hollers Let Him Go* (New York: New American Library, 1945), p. 140.
39. Ibid., p. 47.
40. Ibid., p. 1.
41. Ibid., p. 141.
42. Ibid., p. 50.
43. Ibid., p. 141.
44. Gayle, *The Way of the New World,* p. 185.
45. Edward Reuter, *The Mulatto in the United States* (1937); rpt. New York: Negro Universities Press, 1961), pp. 367-68.
46. Larsen, *Quicksand,* pp. 106-7.
47. Heyward, *Mamba's Daughters,* pp. 220, 222.
48. Ibid., p. 302.
49. Ellison, *Invisible Man,* p. 201.
50. Ibid.
51. Frazier, *Black Bourgeoisie,* p. 26.
52. Ibid., p. 112.

53. Harold Cruse's view of the Harlem Renaissance (in *The Crisis of the Negro Intellectual* [New York: William Morrow & Company, 1967]), is less optimistic than that of Nathan Huggins's *Harlem Renaissance* (New York: Oxford University Press, 1971) and DuBose Heyward's *Mamba's Daughters*. Cruse claims that the creative artists of the Renaissance failed because of partial white cooptation of the movement (pp. 34-35); the failure to wed ideas to new institutional forms (p. 37); and the lack of moral, aesthetic, or financial support of the Negro bourgeois stratum (p. 38).
54. Heyward, *Mamba's Daughters*, pp. 208-9.
55. Ibid., p. 308.
56. Ibid., p. 302.
57. Bone, *The Negro Novel in America*, p. 187.
58. Ibid., p. 189.
59. Dorothy West, *The Living Is Easy* (Boston: Houghton Mifflin, 1948), p. 105.
60. Ibid., p. 94.
61. Ibid., p. 246.
62. Ibid., pp. 38-39.
63. Ibid., p. 42.
64. Ibid., pp. 112-13.
65. Ibid., p. 245.
66. When Ralph Ellison's Invisible Man left college, he says that he finally came to accept his guilt, even though he did not understand what crime he supposedly committed, because he knew of no other forms of success. Success according to bourgeois standards was all that he knew.
67. West, *The Living Is Easy*, p. 5.
68. Ibid., p. 128.
69. Ibid., p. 45.
70. Ibid., pp. 244-45.
71. Ibid., p. 105.
72. Ibid., pp. 112-13.
73. Ibid., p. 123.
74. Ibid., p. 125.
75. Ibid., p. 87.
76. Ibid., p. 35.
77. Ibid., p. 246.
78. Ibid., p. 138.
79. See Robert Bone's assessment of Cleo in *The Negro Novel in America*, p. 279.
80. West, *The Living Is Easy*, p. 346.

8.

The Mulatto as Race Leader

The two solutions to the marginal status that have been examined thus far involve assimilationist attitudes and behavior on the part of the mixed blood. Of central importance in the decision to pass or to secure a place in the mulatto upper class is the individual's attitude toward race. Ambivalence toward himself and other blacks, especially full-blooded Negroes, or hatred for self and for the lower caste, are the most commonly held attitudes of permanent, complete passers and the mulatto bourgeoisie. However, it is possible, of course, for light-skinned members of the lower caste to identify with that group. Indeed, due to the likelihood of the mixed blood's having had a superior education, he may decide to devote himself to attempting to raise the status of his black brothers.

To help blacks achieve a sense of their own pride and dignity and a belief in their ability to gain some measure of control over their own lives has been a major goal of black political movements in the nineteenth and twentieth centuries. Some black leaders have argued that the means of achieving these goals involve accommodation to whites and adoption of white bourgeois values (Booker T. Washington). Others have urged a political program based upon the attaining of full citizenship rights (W. E. B. Du Bois). Finally, various types of black nationalist philosophies have been espoused (Marcus Garvey and others) Whichever one of these three general political paths is followed, a basic part of the program must be the indoctrination of the black masses with a sense of racial pride and self-esteem. For without this sense of one's worth, no individual or group can achieve genuine liberation. So long as one carries the burden of self-hatred, so long as the oppressed individual has internalized the oppressor's concept of him, genuine freedom is impossible.

Since, as we have seen, the mixed blood has even greater reason to identify with the dominant caste than does his full-blooded brother, his identification with the lower caste must be developed and nurtured. "By losing himself in a cause larger than himself," Everett Stonequist explains, "the marginal nationalist overrides, if he does not solve, his own personal conflicts." [1] Stonequist theorizes that a primary cause of the mulatto's emergence as a leader of his race is "the disparity between his aspirations and his status"; this disparity will "make him the kind of marginal man who integrates his personality through reacting back to the Negro group and working to raise its status." [2] Once again we see the fusion of the personal and the political, the psychological and the social, in the attitudes and behavior of the American mulatto as presented both in sociological studies and, as we shall see, in the American novel. The following passage, taken from Edward Reuter's *The Mulatto in the United States,* best describes the gradual identification of the mulatto with the black group. Identification with the dominant group—called by Reuter "the superior group"—is assumed to have been the mixed blood's initial response to his marginal status:

> The mulatto feels himself in alliance with the black group and in the cooperation of common activities there arises a sympathetic understanding and appreciation which fuses the mulatto, in sentiments and attitudes, with the larger whole. He is identified with the black group, feels the mute longing of the common folk, feels himself a part of it, is moulded by it,

and comes, little by little, to realize himself as a factor in the common life and purpose of the group. He ceases to be, in thought and feeling, a stranger among his people; he learns to appreciate them, ceases to be ashamed of his relationship to them, ceases to resent being classed with them. Their problems become his problems; their life, his life. The mulatto thus ceases to be a problem within a problem; he becomes a functioning unit in the social life of an evolving people.[3]

Once the mulatto has decided to live his life within the black caste, then he must strive for and achieve some sense of contentment in that role—otherwise, he may end up like Joe Christmas, a man who can find no peace within human society. The key to happiness within the lower caste is the successful identification with that group. When Rhoda Aldgate discovers her Negro "blood," she thinks: "I can endure them [blacks] if I can love them, and I shall love them if I try to help them." [4] Her prescription for herself is precisely the same as that given by Reuter and Stonequist. She feels that she will solve her personal problem by working to raise the status of this still alien people. Her ultimate decision, however, is to continue in her role as a white woman.

The Slave: or Memoirs of Archy Moore (1836), on the other hand, provides a fictional example of the spiritual progression of the mixed blood, a journey through hatred and contempt to love and compassion. Archy's history is a familiar one: he was born in Virginia on a plantation owned by his father, Col. Charles Moore. Archy's mother is a beautiful, almost-white slave girl. Color distinctions were important to the slaves, as we have seen, and Archy's statements provide ample proof of this: "like most of the lighter complexioned slaves, I felt a sort of contempt for my duskier brothers in misfortune. I kept myself as much as possible, at a distance from them, and scorned to associate with men a little darker than myself. So ready are slaves to imbibe all the ridiculous prejudices of their oppressors, and themselves to add new links to the chains, which deprive them of their liberty!" [5] He and his mother increased their own unhappiness, Archy says, by trying to regard themselves as members of "a superior race." And in spite of the fact that he had learned that "a slave, whether white or black, is still a slave; and that the master, heedless of his victim's complexion, handles the whip with perfect impartiality;—still, like my poor mother, *I thought myself of a superior caste.* " [6] In other words, Archy and his mother were trying desperately to make themselves into a buffer group, a cultural intermediary between the whites and the "full-blooded" blacks. Archy says that he and his mother maintained their illusion in spite of the ill will to which their folly had exposed them. He and his mother persist in alienating themselves from the other slaves.

Archy is sold to various masters and has positions of great importance on the plantations where he is enslaved. Although Archy says that it was only through experience that he came to change his attitude about color and status, we can guess that his increased contact with other house and field slaves had an influence on him: "I had long since renounced that silly prejudice and foolish pride, which at an earlier period, had kept me aloof from my fellow servants, and had justly earned me, their hatred and dislike. Experience had made me wiser, and I no longer took sides with our oppressors by joining them in the false notion of their own natural superstructure of American slavery." [7] Here Archy indicates his understanding of racism: both oppression by the dominant caste and the self-inflicted oppression of self-contempt and self-hatred work together to maim and brutalize the black man. Once Archy has abandoned his "silly prejudice and foolish pride," he can "cease to be a problem within a problem." The hardships of the black caste can become his own—to fight and rectify. And, in fact, Archy does join with another slave, a full-blooded black man, and commits acts of sabotage against the system that oppresses them.

Neil Kingsblood, another mulatto who has to solve the dilemma of his identity, vacillates at first between acceptance and rejection of the lower caste. In the end, however, he becomes a "race man"; he gains so much respect for blacks and has so much empathy for their—his—struggle that he says he would prefer to be a Negro even if it turned out that he really was white. Harry Leroy and his sister Iola, in Frances E. W. Harper's *Iola Leroy,* both horrified to learn of their Negro origins, become teachers and leaders of their race during the late nineteenth century. Indeed, the major theme of

Mrs. Harper's novel is the necessity of mulatto identification with blacks.

Mrs. Harper, Pauline Hopkins and Sutton E. Griggs, as well as others, depict the mulatto as a leader of his race. While many mulattoes no doubt maintained their intraracial prejudices and upper-class status, it is also true that mulattoes "became the political leaders of the freedmen during Reconstruction, as well as their teachers, professional and business people." [8] Indeed, as Horace Mann Bond makes clear, the relationship between Negro educators and Negro political leadership was integral: "The Negro school-teacher was held in such veneration by his patrons that it was inevitable that he should become, with the local pastor, the voice of political leadership. The doctrine of political expression was no less a part of the American ideal newly acquired by the freedmen than that of education; they were two inseparable handmaidens which have accompanied each other in all parts of the country and with reference to all racial and social groups." [9] Thus, Harry Leroy the teacher is also Harry Leroy the race leader. And while he undoubtedly sought to inculcate Anglo-Saxon values and modes of conduct, he (and Harper herself) believe that this was the way to promote black pride. In Charles Chesnutt's *The House Behind the Cedars,* Rena Walden's decision to become a teacher in a Negro school (after she has been exposed as a passer) signifies that she is attempting to switch her allegiance to the black group. But she knows that she must first overcome her own negative attitudes toward full-blooded blacks: "Her early training had not directed her thoughts to the darker people with whose fate her own was bound up so closely, but rather away from them. She had been taught to despise them because they were not so white as she was, and had been slaves while she was free." [10]

In Elizabeth Coker's 1950 novel, *Daughter of Strangers,* Charlotte Le Jeune—the young mulatto girl who had fought desperately against identification with her mother's race—decides after years of struggle to try to identify with the black caste. Her mistress tells Charlotte: "You have had advantages beyond any Negro I know of, and when freedom comes for the slaves you must be ready for power. You must shape your life with that in view, and be ready to grasp it when it comes your way. You must be willing to join your race and like it." [11]

But Charlotte is always praying for "a middle way, a place where the two roads of me can cross and come together." [12] Hagar, a fiercely dignified old slave woman, says of the eighteen-year-old Charlotte that "She de kind kin take Denmark Vesey place w'en freedom come effen her don' lose herself befor' han'." [13] And to the all-but-white girl, she explains: "Yunnuh got two meanings to you' life and yunnuh got to accept dat fack. Yunnuh gotter to be a link 'tween de black an' de white." [14] Leon Cavillo, an educated free-man-of-color, also tells Charlotte that "if people like you and me will act as guideposts, we can help channel the Congo so that it will enrich this land as fruitfully as the more peaceful-flowing rivers." [15] Once Charlotte decides to try to live as a member of the black caste, to consider herself one with it, she is rewarded with a powerful response: "And at day's end the Normandy Negroes watched and waited for the light-skinned woman who was running their plantation like a white woman, yet who was one of them. They nodded and waved to her as she passed. . . . We might be like her someday, they began to think, or our children might. . . . freedom will come in our lifetime and we must be ready for it. She can show us the way now that she has come from her cocoon and walks among us as one of us." [16]

Elizabeth Coker's melodramatic novel is unusual in that it presents all of the standard tragic mulatto material and then makes a reversal and moves the heroine into the role of race leader. She is told that she can be an intermediary, a buffer, between the upper and lower castes by bringing her "Caucasian" skills to the Negro group. But only by accepting her status as a black woman can she be a true link between the two groups.

John Broderip, the protagonist of Rebecca Harding Davis's 1867 novel, *Waiting for the Verdict*, becomes a race leader *and* a martyr, thus combining the "race man" figure and the black hero as Christ type. Like Charlotte, his character can be construed as fitting the pattern of the tragic mulatto—up to a point. The brilliant mulatto surgeon dies at the end of the novel, but his is not a bitter, unfulfilled death. Both his brother and his best friend tell Broderip to be a Moses to his people, and Broderip decides to lead a company of black soldiers.

Broderip knows that he will never return from the war (his lungs are poor), and he prepares for his leavetaking by establishing his mansion as an orphanage and by giving away all his other possessions. He is going to certain death, but his is not a suicide but a Christlike sacrifice. He is at peace with himself and the world; he is not "destroying himself" in a fit of bitterness. Davis makes clear the nature of his last days by drawing the following parallel:

> [Broderip] turned to the man's face on the wall. A childless, wifeless, homeless man, of birth as poor, and skin as dark as his own, who had gone down into the dregs of the people, giving up a man's whole birthright to lead a great reform, to cleanse the souls of imbruted men and women. By that light the mulatto of these days read the story of Jesus of Nazareth. He often stood when darkness came, as he did now, before the coarse print, his forefinger on it, his eyes contracted on the face, asking it questions through the shadows of eighteen centuries; his eyes contracted, and wet sometimes, as no human being had ever seen them, asking, as of one who had borne it, "Was it an easy thing to be trodden under foot of every man without a cause? What was this for a man—*a man* to do in the world, to live wifeless and childless? Where was the recompense?" [17]

The Reverend Conrad says of Broderip that "it's through his negro blood that humanity's got hold of him." [18] Broderip tells one of his friends that he is dying a happy man because he is able to help his people. The last we hear of Broderip is that he had been extremely brave "right to the end." While Rebecca Harding Davis's portrait of a race leader is the romanticized view of an abolitionist, John Broderip must not be overlooked because he establishes his identity as a man through embracing the blacks and their cause.

The novels discussed thus far have not dealt with concrete racial ideologies. In *Daughter of Strangers,* Charlotte is told simply to be a leader of her people. Several novels have blacks as teachers. Even in a novel like *Iola Leroy,* which is polemical, the "lesson" of the novel being that many mulattoes do identify with the lower caste and that it is not the white blood found in blacks that accounts for the achievements of the race—even in this novel, there is almost no discussion of the prevailing racial philosophies of Mrs. Harper's period. To attain a better understanding of the novels which will be discussed shortly, however, it is necessary to review briefly the central ideas within the politically conscious black community.

Historically, black responses to American racism have fallen into one of three basic ideological frameworks: accommodationism (as expressed by Booker T. Washington and others.); the movement for full citizenship rights and cultural pluralism (expressed, for example, by W. E. B. Du Bois); and the separatist movement characterized by militant racial nationalism. The latter ideology is reflected in the migration and colonization movements, which were important at various times from the 1840s to the 1890s, the Garveyite movement of the second decade of the twentieth century, and the Black Muslims. Separatist ideology even led to the establishment of all-Negro utopian communities in the late nineteenth century. There was an attempt to create an all-Negro state in the Oklahoma Territory in the 1890s, according to August Meier, who points out that "The all-Negro communities reflected the idea of an *imperium in imperio* as contemporaries referred to it. ... They emphasized racial solidarity to solve the Negro's problems and envisaged a Utopian society where Negroes could live untouched by discrimination and undertake their own elevation without white assistance or interference." [19]

As Negroes came to perceive the hollowness of the white promise of racial harmony and advancement for the black man, many Negro leaders naturally turned to other solutions for the suffering and exploitation of their people. This was the situation prior to the Civil War and at the end of the nineteenth century. (The cultural nationalism of the 1920s is different from the separatist movements under discussion and arose under dissimilar conditions.) During Reconstruction, however, and throughout much of the twentieth century, a sense of cautious optimism—mingled with anger and despair—has characterized the black struggle for integration. Integration is not synonymous with accommodation or amalgamation, and the means of achieving integration has been the primary source of disagreement among many black political groups. Throughout his study, Meier emphasizes the importance of self-help, racial pride, and group solidarity as key ideas among *all* of the political groups of the nineteenth and twentieth centuries. The important point is that these general ideas could be applied in different ways by Booker T. Washington or Du Bois or the separatist groups of the nineties. Booker T. Washington used these principles as part of "an accommodating technique," while Du Bois stressed these same ideas in his fight for full citizenship rights.

Certain aspects of the intellectual milieu of the late nineteenth century had an important influence on American Negro thought. As Meier says, "The strongly economic, materialistic, laissez-faire, and Social Darwinist cast of late nineteenth-century American thought" [20] exerted a significant influence on the racial ideology of the black group:

> While Negroes never abandoned their emphasis upon the Christian and humanitarian and democratic elements in the American tradition, and though their outlook never became as secular as that of many of their fellow Americans, like the latter they more and more viewed wealth as the symbol of success, while political activity, from which they were largely debarred, sank into the background. What they did was to adopt the ideas of the gospel of wealth and Social Darwinism and apply them to their own racial situation. [The broad approach of the Reconstruction period changed to] a narrower emphasis upon wealth and the frugal virtues, the creation of an independent farming and business class, and racial solidarity in an impersonal economic and Social Darwinist competition for survival that would allegedly create (as even many Negros often said), an advanced and progressive race out of a childlike backward race.[21]

From this statement, it should be apparent that Booker T. Washington did not initiate the trend toward industrial and agricultural education or the establishment of a bourgeois Weltanschauung among blacks. Rather, he brought these tendencies to a climax. "The central theme in Washington's philosophy was that through thrift, industry, and Christian character Negroes would eventually attain their constitutional rights. To Washington it seemed only proper that Negroes would have to measure up to American, i.e., white standards of morality and material prosperity if they were to succeed in the Social Darwinist race of life." [22]

Two brief summaries of Washington's major ideas and attitudes will help distinguish between Washington's ideology and others of the same period. E. U. Essien-Udom, in his introduction to

Philosophy and Opinions of Marcus Garvey, sums up the "Atlanta Compromise" in the following manner: "Do not antagonize the white majority. Do not ask for the right to vote. Do not fight for civil liberties or against segregation. Go to school. Work hard. Save money. Buy property. Some day, the other things may come." [23] Meier, again: "He emphasized duties rather than rights; the Negro's faults rather than his grievances; his opportunities rather than his difficulties. He stressed economics above politics, industrial above liberal education, self-help above dependence on the national government. . . . he professed a deep love for the South and a profound faith in the goodness of the Southern whites—at least of the 'better class.' " [24]

Washington's philosophy appalled some blacks, especially the intelligentsia. Washington's foremost critic was W. E. B. Du Bois, who, with other dissenting blacks, formed the Niagara movement in 1905. This organization stressed political action and the attainment of full civil rights; it emphasized the inequality of economic opportunity and called for all types of education for black people. Rather than gradualism and conciliation, agitation for immediate and complete integration was advocated. In *The Souls of Black Folk,* Du Bois examined what he called "the triple paradox" of Washington's racial ideology.

> 1. He is striving nobly to make Negro artisans, business men and property-owners; but it is utterly impossible, under modern competitive methods for workingmen and property-owners to defend their rights and exist without the right of suffrage.
> 2. He insists on thrift and self-respect, but at the same time counsels a silent submission to civic inferiority such as is bound to sap the manhood of any race in the long run.
> 3. He advocates common-school and industrial training, and deprecates institutions of higher learning; but neither the Negro commonschools, nor Tuskegee itself, could remain open a day were it not for teachers trained in Negro colleges, or trained by their graduates.[25]

As Meier points out, "it was Du Bois who most explicitly revealed the impact of oppression and of the American creed in creating ambivalent loyalties toward race and nation in the minds of

American Negroes. [And] . . . above all he insisted that Negroes wanted to be both Negroes and American, maintaining their racial integrity while associating on the freest terms with all American citizens, participating in American culture in its broadest sense, and contributing to it in fullest freedom." [26]

In addition to Sutton Griggs, two other black authors wrote polemical novels which dealt with these problems of racial ideology during the early twentieth century. G. Langhorne Pryor's 1902 novel, *Neither Bond nor Free* and Pauline E. Hopkins's 1900 novel, *Contending Forces: A Romance Illustrative of Negro Life North and South,* are both vehicles for their authors' political views—Pryor's a plea for Washingtonian "conservatism," Hopkins's a dramatization of the ideology of W. E. B. Du Bois and the "radical" faction.

Pryor uses his novel not only to promote the conservative point of view but to attack the priorities of the radicals. Throughout the novel Washington's program of moral uplift, industrial education, cooperation with southern whites, and gradualism and conciliation—as opposed to political agitation—are stressed. In addition to the numerous passages of political debate to be found in the novel, Pryor uses his major characters to embody political principles. Merna Attaway, a lovely mulatto woman, is a race champion and a teacher. Her work is performed gratis and is "purely a labor of love and charity." [27] She is a staunch supporter of the bourgeois ethic as the means to Negro advancement. Her lover, Edward Strother, also mulatto, is a blacksmith, inventor, scholar, and Sunday school teacher. He, too, believes in the conservative ideology. Toussaint Ripley, another mulatto, the spokesman for the radical point of view, *leaves* schoolteaching to become a professional politician. Merna chastises Toussaint for his decision to leave teaching: "There is much work for the reformer to do along that line, but he must not avoid the work of the dungeon for the broad field of politics." [28] In a later political discussion, Merna declares that "Nothing, in my judgment, can be accomplished for our people by politics." [29] It is not political agitation and a liberal education but industrial education that can remedy the plight of the American Negro. In a key speech given later in the novel, Merna's lover, Edward Strother, forcefully argues in favor of the bourgeois ethic. "To be somebody we must be a producer, a money maker and a decent citizen. To be nobody you have only to be a consumer and a spendthrift." [30] Industrial education will teach the black man to be a "producer": "Look with me over this town and see our college and high school graduates lounging about and waiting for dreams to ripen into gold, or standing around with their hands in their pockets, while the hoe is resting in the field, and the foreign labor is filling the place we ought to occupy." He concludes with an appeal to the Social Darwinist principle of "survival of the fittest": "This country of ours is striding along to new activities and new glories. We must not be idlers in the way." [31]

All of the key ideas espoused by Booker T. Washington are to be found in Pryor's novel. Like *Iola Leroy* and *Contending Forces*, *Neither Bond nor Free* is dreadfully written: the style is stilted; the novel is "preachy"; the characters are totally unconvincing and lifeless. But these novels are documents of historical, if not literary, importance. In the writings of these black authors we gain some notion of how the ideas of Washington, Du Bois, and others were being received in the black community. Many of the novels present dialogues rather than one-sided polemics. Thus, while more attention is paid to presenting Washingtonian political principles in *Neither Bond nor Free*, Du Boisean attitudes are also given eloquent expression. At one point, Merna repeats the argument for "self-help" that played so large a part in conservative ideology: "We must equip ourselves with manhood, ability, character, industry and success is surely ours." Toussaint Ripley answers with one of Du Bois's arguments: "what we sadly need is equal industrial opportunity." But Merna is adamant (as well as sententious): "There must always be a man for an opportunity." [32] Toussaint is not allowed to rebut Merna at this point, but later in the novel he repeats Du Bois's salient attack on Washington's faith in the gospel of wealth as the answer to the black man's plight: "The astounding argument has been made in your hearing that the negro in order to succeed with the white people must surrender his manhood, trample his ballot in the dust, practice self-effacement until he can march blindfolded to the rear." [33]

At several points in the novel, Merna, Strother, or another conservative says that the black man is not yet fit to have the right of suffrage, that whites are still usually the best politicians in guarding the Negro's interests. Furthermore, that black people should seek to "court and deserve the friendship of the best white people in their neighborhood." [34] But Pryor allows Toussaint to attack a race leader named Oscar Richards because of Richards's conservative philosophy: "He is teaching our young men and young women to regard the white people as their superiors—telling them that they must find a place amid the humble pursuits of life as they are not fitted for the higher stations to which all white people aspire. . . . I am a race man. I mean to see to it that my race cultivates the true spirit of race pride, putting their own people before every other race. Look at the white man: he honors his race. Well, I want our people to look up and be true and fearless men." [35] But it is clear that Toussaint's ideas are not favored. As I have already pointed out, he leaves the teaching profession in order to become a politician, a decision of which Pryor is critical. Toussaint even loses Merna's approval as he becomes further embroiled in politics and liquor. His belief in racial pride is attacked as "un-Christian," and his advocacy of political agitation is denounced on the grounds that the American Negro is yet too ignorant to deserve the ballot. First, he must be a "producer" and a saver.

Contending Forces: A Romance Illustrative of Negro Life North and South has all of the faults of Pryor's novel plus an incredible and incredibly complicated plot. There is far less debate, but Hopkins's ideology is as distinctly Du Boisean as Pryor's is Washingtonian. Sappho, Hopkins's beautiful golden-haired "black" heroine, is opposed to industrial education exclusively. She insists that political rights are essential for any genuine advancement for blacks: "Temporizing will not benefit us; rather, it will leave us branded as cowards, not worthy of a freeman's respect—an alien people, without a country and without a home." [36] Another spokesman for the author argues that "Blacks must unite and not destroy each other's self-respect and just try to make a buck in the white man's world. *These are the contending forces that are dooming this race to despair!*" [37]

Although the politics of black conservatism wields increasingly less influence as the twentieth century progresses, one can still find expressions of it in both fact and fiction. In T. S. Stribling's 1922 novel, *Birthright,* Peter Siner, the Harvard-educated mulatto protagonist of the novel, returns to his native southern town and plans to teach school. He hopes eventually to develop an institute like Tuskegee and purchases a tract of land as his initial step toward achieving his goal.

Peter Siner genuinely wants to emulate Booker T. Washington. But several other fictional characters pretend to be race leaders when, in fact, they are concerned only with consolidating their own wealth and power. Ralph Ellison's Dr. Bledsoe *(Invisible Man)* is one such man. In J. Saunders Redding's 1950 novel, *Stranger and Alone,* both President Wimbush, head of Arcadia State College for Negroes, and Shelton Howden, Redding's unlikable protagonist, are considered "leaders of their race" by both blacks and whites. However, like Dr. Bledsoe, Wimbush and Howden are contemptuous of blacks and have spiritually isolated themselves from the black cause. Identification with blacks and a genuine concern for raising the status of a people they consider their own are prerequisites for the legitimate race leader. Therefore, the hatred for blacks and the self-hatred that Bledsoe, Wimbush, and Howden exhibit disqualify them for this role. Howden has always been the victim of an almost overwhelming inferiority complex, the result of his status as a "half-white bastard." He does not want to help blacks; he wants above all to succeed in the white man's world, on the white man's terms. His thoughts on the race question are astonishingly simple: "People who whined about the race question were simply rationalizing their own failures." [38] Shelton works against blacks. As supervisor of Negro schools in his state, he makes up a program which later forms the basis of the state's defense against the charge of maintaining a discriminatory salary level for black teachers. As a black "leader," Shelton has to belong to all of the more prestigious black organizations, but he really thinks that those who work for black advancement are either fools or dangerous radicals. Shelton eventually acts as a spy against his own group.

In *Alien Land,* Willard Savoy's 1949 novel, one of the two major protagonists is a mulatto race leader. Charles Roberts, a brilliant lawyer who returns to his race in order to work for the Negro cause, is a leader of the Freedom League, a Du Boisean organization devoted to working for political and social justice for the black man. The politics of Charles Roberts represents the philosophy of the NAACP and related groups, all of which were regarded at the time as militant but not radical—an assessment dependent, of course, upon the observer's politics. Until radical groups like the Black Panthers came to the forefront, the NAACP and CORE, with their emphasis on political and civil rights, represented the triumph in the twentieth century of the ideology of W. E. B. Du Bois over that of Booker T. Washington.

In the last quarter of the nineteenth century and in the first part of the twentieth century, however, there was an intense struggle between these conservative and radical viewpoints. Those involved in this struggle were, naturally, black educators, ministers (these two categories often overlapping), politicians, and intellectuals of all kinds—among them some of the novelists discussed here. The novels of Sutton Griggs—*Imperium in Imperio* (1899), *Overshadowed* (1901), *Unfettered* (1902), *The Hindered Hand* (1905), and *Pointing the Way* (1908)—best exemplify this ideological struggle.

Although Robert Bone argues that Griggs's books "are badly written and tractarian in the extreme," [39] an estimate with which Griggs's defender Hugh M. Gloster does not disagree in the least—they are invaluable historical documents. It is always difficult to determine how accurately a work of fiction corresponds with the social reality it is supposed to mirror—and Griggs's plots and many of his characters are fantastic, indeed unbelievable; but we do find sufficient corroborative evidence in the political literature of the period to view Griggs's novels as accurately reflecting the conflicts among the racial ideologies of his day. Furthermore, Griggs's novels had a large distribution among black readers, although his works were virtually unknown to white Americans of his time.

Griggs's novels continue to interest students of African-American thought and culture because as the prominent black critic, Addison Gayle, Jr., has remarked, "To read Griggs is to be propelled light-years into the future, bypassing the era of the Harlem Renaissance, the years of reaction by such writers as Baldwin and Ellison, to arrive, finally, in the modern era.... He is a novelist of ideas, and it is here that his strength lay. Look to him in 1889 and already the age of Marcus Garvey has arrived, the internecine warfare between Blacks of differing skin color becomes more intensified, the effects of class stratification and the headlong rush of men to negate their own cultural artifacts displayed in argumentative prose reminiscent of the nineteen fifties and beyond." [40]

Griggs's novels are difficult to understand, largely because of his convoluted plots, strange characterization, and the ideological contradictions in his works. Rather than presenting the philosophy of Booker T. Washington and then plainly rejecting it, or espousing the program of Du Bois and attacking the separatists, Griggs presents a confused and confusing picture of his own racial ideology. But it is precisely this ambivalence that makes Griggs an important novelist to study, for "his vacillation between one pole which is militant . . . and another pole which is . . . accommodationist faithfully reflects the political dilemma of the Negro intellectual prior to World War I." [28] Despite his importance, however, Sutton Griggs's novels have not been adequately analyzed.

In both *Imperium in Imperio* and *The Hindered Hand,* there are paired protagonists, one of whom represents the conservative viewpoint, the other some form of radical ideology. In each of the novels the paired characters are presented most positively, for Griggs wants his readers to attend carefully to both arguments. In fact, it seems likely that these paired figures represent the two (or more) aspects of Griggs's own thought on the race problem. Thus, we might view his novels as a kind of internal debate in fictional form.

The paired characters in *Imperium in Imperio* are Belton Piedmont and Bernard Belgrave. Belton, who is dark skinned, suffers every disadvantage because of his color. Bernard, the light-skinned son of a well-educated mulatto woman and one of America's leading statesmen, enjoys the many advantages that his virtually white color bestows. Belton's ideas, which are themselves radical in some ways, triumph. Bernard dies nobly in support of his violent beliefs. In *The Hindered Hand,* the pairing is similar. Ensal Ellwood, dark skinned and conservative, is pitted against Earl Bluefield, light skinned and radical. Here too the less extreme ideas of Ellwood triumph.

In *Imperium in Imperio,* Griggs had been antimulatto. One of his major characters in that novel, Viola Martin, an almost-white young woman who is loved by and loves Bernard, nevertheless commits suicide rather than marry him. In her suicide letter, she explains that she had read a scientific study which proved that the Negro race was being sapped of its vitality, in fact was being slowly exterminated, through miscegenation. So Viola decides to part—in every honorable way—mulattoes who wish to marry; she also works to persuade black women to shun white men.

In *Pointing the Way,* however, not only do the mulatto hero and heroine marry but they overcome many obstacles in working to reach their goal. Furthermore, Baug Peppers, the light-skinned hero of the novel, propounds a plan exactly the opposite of Viola's. He wants to prevent dark-skinned members of his race from marrying. Baug says that every means, short of miscegenation, must be employed in order to promote the lightening of the Negro group. Baug invokes the "process of natural selection."

Griggs's attitude toward the white race remains essentially unchanged throughout his novels. The emphasis upon the role to be played by the Anglo-Saxon with regard to black advancement may vary from one novel to the next, but Griggs's solutions are *never* separatist in nature. The closest he comes to advocating a separatist position is in *Imperium in Imperio,* but his final repudiation of separatism is essential to our understanding of his political philosophy. In both *Pointing the Way* and *Imperium in Imperio,* the achievements of the Anglo-Saxon race are applauded. This point is presented at least as powerfully in *Imperium in Imperio* as in Griggs's last novel, *Pointing the Way.* In both his first and his last novels, the conservative viewpoint is triumphant, although conservatism has different meanings in the two novels. Robert Bone is probably wrong to say that *Imperium in Imperio,* Griggs's first novel, represents the "militant and challenging" side of Griggs; that Griggs's militancy "has its source in a fanatical nationalism." [42] Addison· Gayle's assessment seems more convincing: Griggs "wavers between revolution as symbolized by Bluefield and passive action as symbolized in the person of Ensal. If forced to choose, there is little doubt, in this novel or the others, that his choice would have weighed heavily upon the side of men like Ensal and Piedmont, would have chosen conservatism over militancy. Yet he was too honest a man to sublimate his anger." [43]

Belton Piedmont, hero of Griggs's first novel, is a staunch

believer in the greatness of the Anglo-Saxon race. At his high school graduation he gives a speech entitled "The Contribution of the Anglo-Saxon to the Cause of Human Liberty." This idea is reiterated again at the end of the novel when Belton speaks before the *Imperium in Imperio*, urging the members of his race not to wage war against the United States. Belton says that although the black man was not paid in coin for all his years of toil, he was paid with that which outweighs money:

> He received instruction in the arts of civilization, a knowledge of the English language, and a conception of the one true God and his Christ.
>
> Allow me to note this great fact; that by enslavement in America the negro has come into possession of the great English language. He is thus made heir to all the richest thoughts on earth. Had he retained his mother tongue, it would perhaps have been centuries untold before the master-pieces of earth were given him. As it is we can enjoy the championship of Shakespeare, Milton, Bunyan. . . . Nor must we ever forget that it was the Anglo-Saxon who pointed us to the Lamb of God that takes away the sins of the world.[44]

Belton's white patron, a Mr. King, says that "the liberty-loving negro was the legitimate offspring, and not a bastard [of] the whites. . . . On the other hand, the negro should . . . recognize that the lofty conception of the dignity of man and the value and true character of liberty were taught him by the Anglo-Saxon." [45] King exerts an important influence on Belton, both by his ideas and by his generosity in sending Belton to college. Belton decides, as a result of his acquaintance with Mr. King, that he will never class all white men together, "whatever might be the provocation, and to never regard any class as totally depraved." [46]

The glory of the Anglo-Saxon is reiterated in both *The Hindered Hand* and *Pointing the Way*. In addition, the advocacy of a policy of cooperation between freedom-loving blacks and whites, a program that is suggested in *Imperium in Imperio*, is stated explicitly in Griggs's last two novels. In *The Hindered Hand*, as in *Imperium in Imperio* and *Pointing the Way*, an important white character represents the enlightened southern white man who is eager to promote a (slow) program of racial advancement for the Negro. This white character, Mr. Maul, makes a public speech against lynch law. He risks his political career (he is running for Congress) in order to rail against the proud Anglo-Saxon race that has "fallen so low that we are to ask that the Negro meekly lay down in our pathway, while we enjoy the pleasant sport of boring holes through his body?" [47] He concludes by asserting that he believes in white supremacy, but not in the way he sees it going on around him. At the end of the novel, Ensal asks Mr. Maul and all those like him (i.e., the better class of whites) to assert themselves to solve the Negro problem. The blacks, Ensal says, are going to organize the "Eclectic Party," a political organization that will work to dissipate party worship. "The great misfortune of the political situation," Griggs's hero concludes, "is that the Negroes and the better element of whites never pull together in one political harness." [48]

Baug Peppers, the mulatto hero of *Pointing the Way*, plays the familiar role of defending Anglo-Saxon honor. He says that he abhors the one-party system in the South because blacks and whites alike have been robbed of *"that unfettered ferment of the whole Anglo-Saxon spirit, that grand, free play of all the forces of your racial soul that has in reality been the source of the political greatness of your race."* [emphasis in original] [49] Like Maul's comment, Baug Pepper's argument is cleverly designed to provoke, to shame, the whites into cooperation—or at least into a policy of noninterference—with those blacks who are trying to raise their own status and that of their entire caste. Baug is arguing a test case on disenfranchisement clauses in state constitutions before the Supreme Court. In the name of Anglo-Saxon blood, Baug says:

> I repudiate the thought of asking a handicap for the colored man in its race with him. I bring to you the message the true white Southerner would have me deliver: "I want no laws of indulgence for me and mine. I spurn the thought of a lower test for Anglo-Saxon blood. If my son with a thousand years of civilization behind him cannot stand up in an equal fight with the great grandson of a heathen and a savage, if he must be

pampered and coddled with special laws, then I say with all my soul let him go to the wall." [50]

Baug's answer to the race problem is the same as Ensal's, Belton's, and Mr. King's: liberal whites must unite with responsible blacks to work for the betterment of the Negro race: "That man, white or black, who can construct a political yoke in which the Negroes and the best white people of the South may work together in harmony will deserve more than the presidency. He will deserve a place in the ranks of the immortals alongside the two other great Southerners, Thomas Jefferson, . . . and Abraham Lincoln." [51]

Baug's belief in race cooperation is echoed by two other central characters in the novel. Seth Molair, a white lawyer, says that his family had believed that slavery was wrong but felt that the South could better work out the problem alone. He says that political cooperation between the better elements of whites and blacks is what is needed in the South. Uncle Jack, an old Negro man and an extreme Uncle Tom type, is presented as a black folk hero who had been absolutely devoted to his master and mistress and had taken care of the family when the master fought for the Confederacy. Yet he wanted freedom and desires to see blacks advance. He says that the Negroes have always been able to recognize "real quality white folks" and have always wanted to work with them. He asks the heroine of *Pointing the Way* (in words that are later echoed by Baug Peppers): "do yer think de bes' white people will evah 'gree ter wuk 'long wid de cullud people in de same perlittercul yoke? Dat is de qusshun." [52]

Violence is rejected throughout Griggs's works, as is any action that could be construed as traitorous to the Republic. In *The Hindered Hand*, Griggs employs the character of Gus Martin in order to repudiate violent black nationalism. Like Earl Bluefield, the light-skinned radical protagonist of *The Hindered Hand*, whose ideas are pitted against those of dark-skinned, conservative Ensal Ellwood, Gus is presented sympathetically, but his ideas are rejected nonetheless. He is described as ordinarily being tractable, but his attitudes are changing. On one occasion, he "questioned the existence of God, and, begging pardon, asserted that the Gospel was the Negro's greatest curse, that it unmanned the race. As for the United States government, he said, 'The flag ain't any more to me than any other dirty rag.' " [53] Griggs describes Gus as a child of the new race philosophy which holds that each individual should resent the injustices put upon him and should kill the enemy. He is murdered while pursuing this policy.

In addition to the violent means Earl suggests for making white Americans aware of the Negro's plight and the conditions under which they live—a plan that is naturally rejected by Ensal—Griggs gives his conservative protagonist a further opportunity to demonstrate his loyalty to the United States government. A certain Mr. A. Hostility(!) comes to visit Ensal and explains that he is implacably opposed to the worldwide domination of the Anglo-Saxon race. He wants to enable the Slav peoples to have this power and asks Ensal to help him. Hostility has a jar filled with yellow fever germs, to which the Negro is immune, and wants Ensal to help him release them. Southern whites will die by the millions; Ensal is appalled.

In *Pointing the Way*, Baug Peppers says that he is "a patriot. I love the South. I would like to see the South take its old-time place in the councils of the nation." [54] Even in *Imperium in Imperio*, the novel in which the most radical ideas are considered, violence and treason are rejected. Bernard, leader of the Imperium in Imperio, suggests a plan (which everyone but Belton accepts) to seize Austin, Texas; destroy the United States Navy if necessary; and, having entered into secret negotiations with the enemies of the United States, demand the surrender of Texas and Louisiana. Belton says that Bernard's plan is treason: he loves the Union and the South and could die as his forefathers did, fighting for his country's honor. He says that "love of country is one of the deepest passions in the human bosom." [55]

Although these characters reject violence as a solution to the race problem, they do not remain silent on the subject of repression by the powers that be. In *The Hindered Hand*, Ensal Ellwood speaks out against repression, and says that it is unfortunately "the order of the day, and [since] the process of the survival of the fittest [is] operating . . . that man who best exemplifies the repressive faculty will survive in the political warfare." [56] Earl Bluefield also addresses himself to this issue and combines an attack on industrial education and conservative ideology at the same time that he attacks repression by white society: "How great an army of carpenters can hammer the spirit of repression out of those who hold that the eternal repression of the Negro is the nation's only safeguard?" [57]

Throughout Griggs's novels, he deplores the debasement of the Anglo-Saxon spirit through the repression of the black man. Baug Peppers says: "With your great men gone into hiding and your weaker spirits in the saddle, elected to office without regard to the colored people, they often, oh, often, actually turn the government into an engine of oppression." [58] Combining Social Darwinist concepts (note Ensal's statement above) with a belief in the power of American democracy, Griggs places the following words in the mouth of the president of the United States in *Pointing the Way:* "America is a great Darwinian field, dedicated by fate to the cause of genuine democracy, the rule of the united judgment of men. Here we are to have the wild, grand play of universally and absolutely unfettered forces, and out of the strenuous struggling the fittest are to survive, and the final man is to be evolved. I believe simply in giving the colored man the same chance in this great Darwinian field that other men are given, no more, no less." [59]

By the conclusion of *Imperium in Imperio,* Griggs rejects the revolutionary, separatist solution as an answer to white repression. As Robert Bone explains: "the symbolic drama which is being enacted is clear enough. Griggs's blind impulse toward retaliation and revenge is striving for mastery with a more moderate, and more realistic approach." [60] Because "the Negro finds himself an unprotected foreigner in his own home," [61] Belton explains to Bernard that the Imperium in Imperio was formed "in order to supply this needed protection. [Those involved] are determined to secure their full rights as American citizens, and take an oath to give their very blood for the cause." [62] To achieve this end there exists in the United States a separate government of 7,500,000 whose purpose is to secure political rights and freedom for enslaved blacks all over the world. The Imperium in Imperio has its own democratic unicameral body with one executive officer; its own courts, army, and treasury. After increased repression by whites, Bernard and the Imperium decide, as I have indicated, to wage war on the United States. Belton protests against this plan and says that blacks should spend four years trying to make the white man aware of the now increased abilities of the black man to carry out the responsibilities of full citizenship. Blacks must impress whites that "the Anglo-Saxon has a New Negro on his hands and must surrender what belongs to him." [63] If they fail by all other means to secure their rights, the Imperium in Imperio should emigrate to Texas where, with a majority of votes, they will secure possession of the state government. There they will remain to work out their destiny as a separate and distinct race in the United States. Neither Bernard's war nor Belton's separatist program is carried out because one of the members of the Imperium, Berl Trout, exposes the Imperium and their (Bernard's) plan. Belton, the great conservative, goes to his death in support of his beliefs.

Although Belton is labeled a "conservative" by the other members of the Imperium, he had led a student strike at his own all-Negro college. The object of the strike had been the right of Negro teachers to eat with their white counterparts. Griggs's authorial commentary on this evidence of black solidarity is important and revealing: "The cringing, fawning, sniffling, cowardly Negro which slavery left, had disappeared, and a new Negro, self-respecting, fearless, and determined in the assertion of his rights was at hand." [64] When Belton later becomes a teacher in Richmond, he organizes a joint stock company, starts a weekly journal, and conducts a job printing company. Here are practical applications of the Washingtonian principles of self-help and racial solidarity. The student strike suggests the use of racial solidarity to promote black power in a more radical political maneuver after the style of Du Bois.

Perhaps the philosophy that best represents the author's beliefs is contained in Belton's attack against Bernard's war plans. He says that the black man is now ready for full civil rights, but—in the true Washingtonian spirit—he says that blacks had been repugnant to whites because of "our grotesque dress, our broken language, our ignorant curiosity, and, on the part of many, our boorish manners." He stresses the black man's opportunities rather than the impediments to his advancement. Local courts are bad, but the Supreme Court can be relied upon. Mob law is a curse, but even here they should look to see if they share some of the responsibility. "Our race has furnished some brutes lower than the beasts of the field." [65] Then, however, the tone of the speech shifts from Washingtonian ideology to Du Boisean thought. Belton says that the black man must work to get back the ballot. He must exert all his efforts in this direction.

Belton's speech represents, in fact, a useful summary of Griggs's racial ideology. Like Belton, Ensal Ellwood repudiates violence. Earl's plan for making white America aware of the condition of the black man is to take five hundred men, charge the United States government building, and issue a proclamation setting forth the grievances of the race when they are asked to surrender. Ensal wants to write a lengthy description of the intolerable conditions under which the black man lives and get one into every American home and see that it is translated into the languages of the world. As I have already pointed out, in both *The Hindered Hand* and *Pointing the Way,* the necessity for political freedom for blacks is stressed as strongly as it is in *Imperium in Imperio.* The means to achieve that freedom are somewhat different, although we must remember that separatism is disavowed in *Imperium in Imperio.* Griggs rejects emigration, specifically in *Overshadowed, Imperium in Imperio,* and *The Hindered Hand,* and tacitly in all of his novels. In *Overshadowed,* a gloomy, pessimistic novel, the philosophy of Booker T. Washington is rejected as well as separatist ideology. This rejection of Washingtonian philosophy is not typical of Griggs's thought, as we have seen. In *Unfettered,* Dorlan Warthell, the black politician and protagonist of the novel, plans to use the Negro vote to force the United States to grant political independence to the Philippines. One of the Imperium's stated functions is to fight the worldwide oppression of blacks (in *Imperium in Imperio*). In an appended essay to *Unfettered* called "Dorlan's Plan: Sequel to *Unfettered:* A Dissertation on the Race Problem," Griggs presents his own racial program, which represents the union of conservative and radical philosophy seen throughout his novels. If anything, the emphasis in this essay is on conservative ideology, which in the final analysis is where Griggs seems to stand—in spite of discussion of "oppression" and the vote. The following review of "Dorlan's Plan," from *Negro Voices in American Fiction,* presents, in my opinion, an incisive summary of Griggs's political philosophy:

> This essay, a serious approach to the problem of racial adjustment in the United States, points out that the major task is to institute merit and not color as the standard of preferment. . . . the race is urged to "meet and combat the timorous conservatism that has hitherto impeded our progress." The Negro is advised not to rely wholly upon the Republican Party. Listed as necessary in the task of preparing the race for a better future are character development, worthy home life, public school education for the masses, technological schools for industrial workers, and universities for the training of "men capable of interpreting and influencing world movements, men able to adjust the race to any new conditions that may arise." Land ownership and a back-to-the-farm movement are recommended. Good government and simple justice, not race supremacy and partisan patronage, are defined as desirable goals of political action. Cultivation of the friendship of the Southern white man as well as of the citizens of other sections of the country and of other nations is also emphasized as a *sine qua non* of enlightened racial policy.[66]

The mulatto character who chooses to identify with the black group has already overcome (at least in part) the sense of superiority that his light skin may at times afford him. Caucasian skin coloring and facial features often erect a barrier between the mulatto and the black group which only some are able to overcome (Charlotte Le Jeune in *Daughter of Strangers,* Iola and Harry Leroy in *Iola Leroy,* and Archy Moore in *The Slave: or Memoirs of Archy Moore,* among others). Since many of the mulatto characters in the American novel have been reared as white or in other ways have been given opportunities denied to most darker-skinned Negroes, they are in a position to transform their identification with the lower caste into positive political, social, and economic action directed at raising the status of the entire black group. Thus, many mulatto race leaders become educators (Charlotte Le Jeune in *Daughters of Strangers,* Iola and Harry Leroy in *Iola Leroy,* Merna Attaway and Edward Strother in *Neither Bond nor Free);* politicians (Charles Roberts in *Alien Land;* Toussaint Ripley in *Neither Bond nor Free;* Belton Piedmont and Bernard Belgrave in *Imperium in Imperio;* Ensal Ellwood, Earl Bluefield, and Viola Martin in *The Hindered Hand);* or artistic leaders (Lissa in *Mamba's Daughters*).

While the mulatto race leader is "done with apologies" for being himself and has a self-conscious pride in being black, he does not necessarily have a permanent solution to the race problem. Again and again, black and white novelists elevate the mulatto into a race leader in order to articulate a dialogue concerning the future of the Negro race in America; the best means to achieve full political, economic, and social rights for black people; separatism versus assimilation and the role of whites in the struggle for black liberation. Thus, in their choice of this kind of character, American novelists have seized upon the most effective means of fictionalizing the psychological, social, and political dimensions of being black in white America.

NOTES

1. Everett V. Stonequist, *The Marginal Man: A Study in Personality Conflict* (1937; rpt. New York: Russell & Russell, 1961), p. 174.
2. Stonequist, "Race Mixture and the Mulatto," in *Race Relations and the Race Problem: A Definition and an Analysis,* ed. Edgar T. Thompson (Durham, N.C.: Duke University Press, 1939), p. 254.
3. Edward Reuter, *The Mulatto in the United States* (1936; rpt. New York: Negro Universities Press, 1961), pp. 362-63.
4. William Dean Howells, *An Imperative Duty* (New York: Harper & Brothers, 1892), p. 95.
5. Richard Hildreth, *The Slave: or Memoirs of Archy Moore* (1836; rpt. Upper Saddle River, N.J.: Gregg Press, 1968), pp. 16-17.
6. Ibid., pp. 191, 41.
7. Ibid., pp. 61-62.
8. Gunnar Myrdal, *An American Dilemma: The Negro Problem and Modern Democracy* (New York: Harper & Brothers, 1944), p. 697.
9. Horace Mann Bond, *The Education of the Negro in the American Social Order* (New York: Prentice-Hall, 1934), pp. 31-32.
10. Charles Chesnutt, *The House Behind the Cedars* (Cambridge, Mass.: The Riverside Press, 1900), p. 193.

11. Elizabeth Coker, *Daughter of Strangers* (New York: E. P. Dutton & Company, 1950), p. 100.
12. Ibid., p. 235.
13. Ibid., p. 157.
14. Ibid., p. 247.
15. Ibid., p. 298.
16. Ibid., p. 278.
17. Rebecca Harding Davis, *Waiting for the Verdict* (1867; rpt. Upper Saddle River, N.J.: Gregg Press, 1968), p. 325.
18. Ibid., pp. 326-27.
19. August Meier, *Negro Thought in America, 1880-1915: Racial Ideologies in the Age of Booker T. Washington* (Ann Arbor: University of Michigan Press, 1963), p. 271.
20. Ibid., p. 24.
21. Ibid.
22. Ibid., p. 103.
23. E. U. Essien-Udom, ed., Introduction, *Philosophy and Opinions of Marcus Garvey or Africa for the Africans,* 2d ed. (London: Frank Cass & Co., 1967), pp. xiv-xv.
24. Meier, *Negro Thought in America, 1880-1915,* p. 116.
25. W. E. B. Du Bois, *The Souls of Black Folk: Essays and Sketches,* 2d ed. (Chicago: A. C. McClurg & Company, 1903), p. 47.
26. Meier, *Negro Thought in America, 1880-1915,* pp. 190, 204-5.
27. G. Langhorne Pryor, *Neither Bond nor Free* (New York: J. B. Ogilvie Company, 1902), p. 175.
28. Ibid., p. 31.
29. Ibid., p. 79.
30. Ibid., pp. 194-95.
31. Ibid., pp. 196-97.
32. Ibid., p. 80.
33. Ibid., p. 198.
34. Ibid., p. 136.
35. Ibid., pp. 153-55.
36. Pauline Hopkins, *Contending Forces: A Romance Illustrative of Negro Life North and South* (Boston: The Colored Co-operative Publishing Company, 1900), p. 125.
37. Ibid., p. 256.
38. J. Saunders Redding, *Stranger and Alone* (New York: Harcourt, Brace & Company, 1950), p. 100.
39. Robert A. Bone, *The Negro Novel in America,* rev. ed. (New Haven, Conn.: Yale University Press, 1968), p. 32.
40. Addison Gayle, Jr., *The Way of the New World: The Black Novel in America* (Garden City, N.Y.: Anchor Press, 1975), p. 60.
41. Bone, *The Negro Novel in America,* p. 34.
42. Ibid.
43. Gayle, *The Way of the New World,* p. 69.

44. Sutton E. Griggs, *Imperium in Imperio* (1899; rpt. New York: Arno Press and the New York Times, 1969), pp. 231-32.
45. Ibid., p. 47.
46. Ibid.
47. Sutton E. Griggs, *The Hindered Hand: or The Reign of the Repressionist*, 3d rev. ed. (Nashville, Tenn.: Orion Publishing Company, 1905), p. 174.
48. Ibid., p. 286.
49. Sutton E. Griggs, *Pointing the Way* (Nashville, Tenn.: Orion Publishing Company, 1908), p. 117.
50. Ibid., p. 228.
51. Ibid., p. 122.
52. Ibid., p. 99.
53. Griggs, *The Hindered Hand*, p. 37.
54. Ibid., pp. 118-19.
55. Griggs, *Imperium in Imperio*, p. 252.
56. Griggs, *The Hindered Hand*, pp. 152-53.
57. Ibid., p. 254.
58. Griggs, *Pointing the Way*, p. 120.
59. Ibid., pp. 191-92.
60. Bone, *The Negro Novel in America*, p. 33.
61. Griggs, *Imperium in Imperio*, pp. 182-83.
62. Ibid.
63. Ibid., p. 245.
64. Ibid., pp. 62-63.
65. Ibid., p. 242.
66. Hugh M. Gloster, *Negro Voices in American Fiction* (Chapel Hill: University of North Carolina, 1948), pp. 61-62.

9.

The Mulatto As Existential Man

In any historical era, certain individuals are not able to fit into the cultural mainstream of their society. In our own time, this problem is attested to by the prevalent use of such concepts as "alienation," "fragmentation," and "anomie." In fact, what best distinguishes the technological civilization of the twentieth century is its increased numbers of disaffected members. Thus, many who traditionally would be expected to accept the mores of their culture—the affluent young, for example—instead reject them with scorn, cynicism, indifference, or despair. If many middle-' and upper-class white Americans cannot find an acceptable identity, how then can black Americans, operating within a white racist context, be expected to find a satisfying role to play in an increasingly dehumanized and dehumanizing culture? This question returns us to the issues posed at the beginning of this study: How is the mixed-blood individual to forge an identity and satisfying social role within a two-caste society?

Much of this study has been an exploration of the solutions—or at least the adjustments—that the American mulatto has made to his oftentimes unsatisfactory status, as presented through the medium of fiction. The preceding chapter emphasized those fictional mulattoes whose situation moved them to positive action or to active rebellion, rather than to a state of passive victimization. In this kind of novel the mulatto emerges as race leader. Nowhere is this sense of mission better expressed than in W. E. B. Du Bois's account of his own response to marginality: "As time flew I felt not so much disowned and rejected as rather drawn up into higher spaces and made part of a mightier mission. At times I almost pitied my pale companions, who were not of the Lord's anointed and who saw in their dreams no splendid quests of golden fleeces." [1] Characters in the novels of Sutton Griggs, Frances E. W. Harper, and Pauline Hopkins, among others, often express this sense of mission.

On the other hand, we have seen the thrust toward assimilationism in the novels of passing and in the fiction of the mulatto bourgeoisie. Both passing and the desire for acquisition have usually been regarded by blacks as forms of escapism and of denial of self. Fear (of white society and of their own unrecognized anger) and self-hatred (in response to their ambivalent or hostile feelings toward the black group) are the constant companions of these fictional mulattoes who attempt to deny their heritage—or so their plight is presented in many black-authored novels. The price of assimilation into the dominant white group is too often the identity of the individual. For he cannot deny his own history and hope to achieve inner peace and relief from the *Angst* which may be hidden even from himself. The novels of Nella Larsen and Walter White, and *The Autobiography of an Ex-Coloured Man, Comedy, American Style,* and *The Living Is Easy,* among novels by blacks, all reflect this point of view. Among white-authored novels, *Waiting for the Verdict, Daughter of Strangers,* and *Band of Angels* also fictionalize these ideas. Jessie Fauset's work at times reflects a yearning for white middle-class "respectability" and all that that implies, as do *The Garies and Their Friends, Alien Land,* Charles Chesnutt's works, and many of the novels which focus on the tragic mulatto heroine *(Gulf Stream* presents this classic stereotype). The difference between those discussed immediately prior is that these latter novelists do not attack, but rather condone, the aspirations of their mulatto bourgeois characters in their passing or their aping of white life-styles.

This chapter will explore the fictional history of the mulatto who cannot adjust to his marginality either through escapism (by passing or by adapting the values of the dominant group) or through identification with the oppressed group—the character whose cultural conflicts have been "severe enough to demoralize the individual, throwing him into continual restlessness, and initiating a process of disorganization which ends in dissipation, crime, suicide or psychosis." [2]

In *Cane,* Jean Toomer tells the story of Ralph Kabnis, a northern-born mulatto who has gone south as a teacher. He is restless and is dissatisfied with his life in many ways—all of which relate to his marginality. Throughout the story, Kabnis yearns for connection; for communion with those around him; with the land; with his own past and the collective past of his race; and finally, with himself. Toomer's story is a powerfully wrought study of this man's loneliness, isolation, and marginality.

Kabnis has attempted to shield his anguish, even from himself, behind a cynical facade. Yet he is thoroughly aware of his unfulfilled spiritual and psychological needs. At the very opening of the story, he says to himself: "Ralph Kabnis is a dream." He explains his insubstantiality in terms of his inability to find the key to unlock himself: "If I, the dream (not what is weak and afraid in me) could become the face of the South. How my lips would sing for it, my song being the lips of its soul." But he cuts short his lyrical meditation: he cannot believe in that mystical life-giving quality that part of him so desperately seeks. So the cynical Kabnis, the "dream" answers the "face of the South": "Soul. Soul hell. There ain't no such thing. What in hell was that?" [3] Yet the Georgia landscape will give him no peace. He is tortured by its beauty and asks for "an ugly world" in which he can maintain the identity of the sophisticated northern observer. Thus, paradoxically, it seems, he says: "Dear Jesus, do not chain me to myself and set these hills and valleys, heaving with folksongs, so close to me that I cannot reach them." [4]

While Kabnis cannot get in touch with the life around him, neither can he find refuge in the past. Like the present, it is alien to him. Like James Baldwin, he can seem to find no creations that contain his history. With Baldwin, Ralph Kabnis could say, "I might search in vain for any reflection of myself. I was an interloper; this was not my heritage." [5] The fact that Baldwin's reference is to the great art of Western civilization, to its culture, and that Kabnis is trying to find his heritage in the "primitive" soul of the South, simply emphasizes the marginality of both figures. Kabnis knows he is unfitted for the jungle, and he does yearn to accept his double heritage. Ralph Kabnis is a product of a divided and guilty America which would rather not claim him as her own. Kabnis says: "The whole world is a conspiracy to sin, especially in America, and against me. I'm th' victim of their sin. I'm what sin is." [6] In this last statement, Kabnis shows that he has been unable to escape the unwarranted guilt that America imposes upon those who cannot measure up to its ideology of success.

In the story, there is an old black man who does nothing but sit in the corner of a basement. Yet Lewis (who seems to be Toomer's *raisoneur*) says of him: "He is symbol, flesh and spirit of the past," to which Kabnis replies: "he ain't my past. My ancestors were Southern bluebloods—" Lewis takes up the argument: "And black." Kabnis: "Ain't much difference between blue an black." Lewis: "Enough to draw a denial from you. Can't hold them, can you? Master; slave. Soil; and the overarching heavens. Dusk; dawn. They fight and bastardize you." [7]

There is no release and rebirth for Kabnis. In fact, by the end of the piece, he seems even more alienated and isolated from those around him than he was at its beginning. None of the other characters has been able to relieve his despair, and the fact that Kabnis himself tries unsuccessfully to escape his marginality makes the conclusion of the story especially pessimistic. Each of the other characters has a definite sense of his own identity. There is Hanby, the suave, Bledsoe-like president of the school at which Kabnis has been a teacher. And Professor Layman, "tall, heavy, loose-jointed Georgia Negro, by turns teacher and preacher," [8] understands that where he comes from a "nigger's a nigger." He knows how to accommodate to the system, yet does not appear to be overly unctuous. Fred Halsey, a blacksmith, is, as Lewis says, "an artist in his own way." Lewis is "what a stronger Kabnis might have been." [9] He seems to understand himself and the other characters in the story. He is respectful toward Father John, and it is he who calls the old man a symbol of the past. While Lewis is at ease with Father John, Kabnis cannot get beyond his scorn for—and fear of—this reminder of his past. When Kabnis enters the workshop which is the setting of most of the action, he dons a robe that is like a costume. Somehow it seems to represent his communion, even if only tentative, with the others in the workshop. But at the story's end, Kabnis takes off the robe and glances at Carrie (Fred's sister) and Father John, who are wreathed in the sunlight coming through the window. Kabnis, alone, outside their holy union, departs.

The message of Nella Larsen's *Quicksand* (1928) is contained in the epigraph to the novel, a quotation from Langston Hughes:

> My old man died in a fine big house,
> My ma died in a shack.
> I wonder where I'm gonna die,
> Being neither white nor black? [10]

Nella Larsen recounts the odyssey of the marginal figure in search of her identity. The heroine of the novel, Helga Crane, lives virtually every kind of life available to a black woman of her era. In this respect, she is much like James Weldon Johnson's Ex-Coloured Man, and like him, she ultimately throws away all of her possibilities for a meaningful, fulfilling life. By the time she dimly comprehends her self-hatred, the ever-present sense of alienation from others and of marginality that have plagued her all of her life, it is too late to change her "fate." She has at last run out of chances.

Born to a white woman, a Swedish immigrant, and a Negro man who left her mother when Helga was still a young child, the beautiful mulatto girl was raised in the hostile environment of her white stepfather's home. Only her mother's brother Peter seemed to take an interest in Helga, and when she was fifteen (upon the death of her mother), he sent Helga to a school for Negro girls. At first she was ecstatically happy, for she was finally "among her own." But after a time, she realized that even here she was a marginal figure, alone because she had no place to which, or people to whom, she belonged: "There had been always a feeling of strangeness, of outsideness, and one of holding her breath for fear that it wouldn't last. It hadn't. It had dwindled gradually into eclipse of painful isolation." [11]

Perhaps worst of all is Helga's self-hatred, her internalization of the low esteem with which white society regards her. If Helga's feelings were limited to those of hatred toward the Negro group, she would have probably adjusted well at Naxos (a school where she taught briefly), which epitomized the values and aspirations of the black bourgeoisie. However, she also rejects the values of the black bourgeoisie and identifies strongly with certain aspects of black life.

Life among the Harlem intelligentsia affords Helga no sustained happiness either. Again she experiences the familiar pattern: excitement and enthusiasm about her new mode of life and an initial feeling of "belonging"; and then a gradually increasing sense of alienation from her situation, as this feeling of well-being gives way to the familiar sense of marginality. The novel is filled with images of suffocation. At first Harlem had thrilled Helga, but after a time she feels as if she is drowning in a sea of darkness: "It was as if she were shut up, boxed up, with hundreds of her race, closed up with that something in the racial character which had always been, to her, inexplicable, alien. Why, she demanded in fierce rebellion, should she be yoked to these despised black folk?" [12]

Given $5,000 by her uncle Peter, she uses the money to go to Copenhagen to live with a wealthy white aunt and uncle. She is happy for quite some time in this environment, and her sense of belonging returns (even though she realizes that she is being exploited as an exquisite oddity). But once again disillusionment and unhappiness begin to haunt Helga. She comes to realize that just as she had once felt suffocated by an all-black world, here she is drowning in an all-white one and yearns to be with black people. When she returns to Harlem, she feels contentment in being surrounded by thousands of black faces: "These were her people. Nothing, she had come to understand now, could ever change that. Strange that she had never really valued this kinship until distance had shown her its worth. How absurd she had been to think that another country, other people, could liberate her from the ties which bound her forever to these terrible, these fascinating, these lovable, dark hordes. Ties that were of the spirit." [13]

Helga Crane is the classical marginal figure: her divided loyalty and ambivalent attitude explain "the fluctuating and contradictory opinions and actions of the marginal person." [14] And Helga's continuous restlessness is a major factor in understanding her personality. Her life is one continual process of experimentation, each effort being directed toward finding a status that will bring with it peace, but not stagnation. But Helga can never find this "still point." When she returns to America, it is with the realization "of the division of her life into two parts in two lands, into physical freedom in Europe and spiritual freedom in America." [15]

There is one man in the novel in whom Helga is interested, but her love is not consummated. Larsen does hint at several points that Helga might have found the peace and happiness she sought through marriage to this black race leader. When Helga loses him forever, she falls into despair. Once more she seeks respite by trying to immerse herself in a new way of life. She stumbles into a storefront church where she meets and immediately marries the Reverend Mr. Pleasant Green. She is so anxious to lose herself in the larger cause of helping poor blacks in Alabama (Reverend Green's home state) that she manages to convince herself that she has at last found her destiny. But once again the feeling of restlessness, discontent, and finally, suffocation engulf Helga. Her belief in God fails her; she sees her husband for what he is—a self-righteous, unctuous, ignorant backwoods preacher. The squalor and indignity of the life she has endured for three years become unbearable. Within the first twenty months of her marriage, Helga gives birth to three children, male twins and a girl. After the birth of a fourth child Helga has a breakdown. No longer sustained by God, man, or self, she vows to leave. But she has no money, no strength, and no clear resolution to leave her children. And even as she dreams of cities and clothes and books, we see that she is trapped forever. Larsen ends her novel on this note: "And hardly had she left her bed and become able to walk again without pain, hardly had the children returned home again from the homes of the neighbors, when she began to have her fifth child." [16] What can possibly await Helga Crane? Madness or suicide or both—at best a life of anguish and despair.

Helga Crane's inability to identify fully with either the white or the nonwhite castes; her love-hate feelings toward blacks and toward herself; and her restlessness and unhappiness are described well by Larsen. What is not clear is whether Helga Crane is trying to destroy herself; her behavior seems to be directed more toward finding a solution to her cultural and personal dilemma. This is not always the case with the marginal figure. Sometimes his inability to adjust to his role is so great that his actions are directed consciously or unconsciously toward self-destruction. His restlessness becomes pathological; he is unable to commit himself to anyone or anything; his destructive drives may be turned outward as well as inward; the furious rage which obsesses him can only be extinguished through death.

Two examples of this particular type of marginal man are Charles Etienne Saint-Valery Bon and Joe Christmas—both creations of William Faulkner, the novelist who has dealt with the marginal man in American fiction with greater skill than any other author. Charles Etienne Saint-Valery Bon appears in Faulkner's 1936 novel *Absalom, Absalom!* In Chapter 3, the character of Charles Bon, the mulatto son of Thomas Sutpen, was discussed. While Bon understood full well his marginal position in southern society, his obsession was to gain recognition from his father, through which he could establish a place within a familial and societal structure. In this attempt, he was unsuccessful. His son, Charles Etienne Saint-Valery Bon, born of a morganatic marriage between Bon and a *femme de coleur* of New Orleans, is irrevocably alienated from both white and black society. He is a martyr, created out of both the collective insanity of his society and his own furious despair. He fought with Negroes during crap games; he married a "coal black and apelike woman" whom he flung in the face of his white aunt, who had partially reared him, and "in the faces of all and any who would retaliate; the negro stevedores and deckhands on steamboats or in city honkey-tonks who thought he was a white man and believed it only the more strongly when he denied it; the white men who, when he said he was a negro, believed that he lied in order to save his skin, or worse: from sheer besotment of sexual perversion." [17] In every way, Charles Etienne Saint-Valery Bon tried to die. And by the age of twenty-five he is dead—struck down by disease; but even in death he cannot control his fate.

In many ways, the history of Joe Christmas, in *Light in August*

(1932), is a repetition of Bon's. He, too, has as his literary ancestor the tragic mulatto character of nineteenth-century fiction. But rather than being the victim of his "blood," Joe is the victim of the social definitions of "white" and "black." Indeed, neither Joe nor anyone else ever knows for certain whether he even has any Negro blood. Left on the steps of an orphanage on Christmas Eve, the boy spends his first five years under the watchful eyes of Doc Hines, his fanatical Negrophobic grandfather. Through Doc, the boy comes to think that he is different; because of Joe's "foreign" looks, the children begin to call him "nigger." From the orphanage, Joe passes into the hands of the Calvinist fanatic McEachern, who adopts the boy. After a fight in which Joe thinks he has killed McEachern, the young man runs away. He remains in his travels what he was at the orphanage and at his adoptive parents' home: rootless, alone, alienated from those around him and from himself, unable to find peace. Peace comes only with the death he suffers for the murder of yet another fanatic, a woman named Joanna Burden, an outcast from southern society because of her Yankee connections and her work on behalf of the Negro.

In *Cane,* Ralph Kabnis referred to himself as a "dream." Robert Bone likens him to a scarecrow: "Consumed with self-hatred and cut off from any organic connection with the past, he resembles nothing so much as a scarecrow: 'Kabnis, a promise of soil-soaked beauty; uprooted, thinning out. Suspended a few feet above the soil whose touch would resurrect him.' " [18] While Faulkner's view of the problem of the mulatto is more complex than Toomer's, both authors recognize that a human being who has been denied his sense of connectedness to self, family, and culture can have no genuine selfhood, no core, no center from which to confront himself or the world. Thus, Joe Christmas is described throughout the novel as being a "shadow." He lives his life "in shadow" and is never really "seen" by anyone, himself included. Each character in the novel "dresses" the scarecrow that is Joe Christmas—even to the naming of the unknown baby left on the orphanage steps—in the beliefs, myths, and obsessions that haunt the mind of the South.

In the orphanage, the children live on the fringes of their society, on the margin of acceptability. Yet even here, Joe Christmas is somehow different. Framed in "the quiet and empty corridor, . . .

he was like a shadow, small even for his five years, sober and quiet as a shadow." [19] Joe is often seen framed against a long, receding horizon, a figure utterly alone, always a stranger wherever he goes: "Nothing can look quite as lonely as a big man going along an empty street. Yet though he was not large, not tall, he contrived somehow to look more lonely than a lone telephone pole in the middle of a desert. In the wide, empty, shadow-brooded street he looked like a phantom, a spirit, strayed out of its own world, and lost." [17] And the very first time Faulkner introduces Joe Christmas, he says: "there was something definitely rootless about him, as though no town nor city was his, no street, no walls, no square of earth his home." [18] Passages like these and numerous others—as well as Faulkner's careful detailing of Joe's inability to find affection and nurturing from any of the relationships in which he is involved throughout his life—have led Alfred Kazin to comment that "Joe Christmas is the most solitary character in American fiction, the most extreme phase conceivable of American loneliness. He is never seen full face, but always as a silhouette, a dark shadow haunting others, a shadow upon the road he constantly runs." [22]

Joe Christmas bears his insufferable loneliness and isolation because, in Faulkner's own explanation of his character:

> Joe Christmas . . . didn't know what he was. He knew that he would never know what he was, and his only salvation in order to live with himself was to repudiate mankind, to live outside the human race. And he tried to do that but nobody would let him, the human race itself wouldn't let him. And I don't think he was bad, I think he was tragic. And his tragedy was that he didn't know what he was and would never know, and that to me is the most tragic condition that an individual can have—to not know who he was.[23]

To emphasize Joe's absolute estrangement from society, Faulkner never shows us Joe's inner feelings. Joe "thought that it was loneliness which he was trying to escape and not himself." [24] But Faulkner makes it clear that Joe is trying to run from himself even as—paradoxically—he tries to find himself. He is, as Faulkner says, "doomed with motion, driven by the courage of flagged and spurred despair." [25]

The paradox of Joe's flight can best be understood by recognizing Joe Christmas as a "marginal man." Joe lives within the framework of the dehumanizing caste system of the Deep South. What Joe is running *from* is the societally imposed definition of self. Since his culture recognizes only two categories of human beings—whites and nonwhites—the mixed-blood individual is thrust into one group or the other. If he rejects the imposition of definition from outside himself and attempts instead to create his own self-definition, he finds himself cut off, alienated from the rest of human society. For mankind is afraid of the chaos that lies outside the boundaries of the definitions it has imposed upon itself—afraid even though these definitions do not allow him to define himself as human. These codes, Richard Chase says, "have become compulsive patterns which man clings to in fear and trembling while the pattern emasculates him." [26] In a sense, then, we are all self-crucified. We are our own victims even as we victimize others. Hightower understands this *"crucifixion of themselves and one another"* [*emphasis in original*]. As he explains to Byron Bunch, "to pity him [Joe Christmas] would be to admit self-doubt and to hope for and need pity themselves." [27] It is Hightower's understanding of the ways in which we destroy ourselves and others that leads him to utter the words that can stand as an epitaph for Joe Christmas and all those who live in Jefferson: "Poor man. Poor mankind." [28] Olga Vickery summarizes this complex theme most aptly when she writes that all three major characters in the novel—Joe Christmas, Reverend Hightower, and Joanna Burden—"have all been self-created martyrs to an idea. . . . Society, no less deluded, attacks and sacrifices them in the name of the same ideas. Their personal histories, like the history of [the town of] Jefferson, consist of a perpetual denial of life for the sake of empty rituals, each of which enshrines some abstraction." [29]

The "idea" to which Joe has been sacrificed is, of course, "Race"—with its attendant beliefs, myths, and social facts—what I have called "racist ideology." In *Faulkner and the Negro*, Charles Nilon asserts that through the character of Joe Christmas, "Faulkner investigates the social responses of an individual and the people around him to the connotative meanings of 'Negro.' " [30] In fact, both the whites and Joe know how to respond to the "Negro." What they are not certain of is how to respond to the mixed blood like Joe Christmas. Since he calls into question the very caste system upon which life in the South is based, the whites in Jefferson are able to respond only with fury to Joe's very existence. Pity for him would be unthinkable. And since Joe accepts society's definitions, at least in part, he too responds with fury both to himself and to his environment: "The conflict within Joe Christmas is like the conflict between white and Negro people in the South, embodying within a single individual the problem of a region. Joe is a metaphorical expression of the South's dilemma. Thus, he is neither black nor white, but two opposing concepts, each seeking existence, if not dominance, in the same area." [31]

One of the central passages in the novel helps explain the duality of Joe Christmas's existence. When Joanna Burden tells Joe about the curses upon both the black and white races, she speaks of two separate curses. As John M. Bradbury puts it, "Joe carries a double burden; he is at once the black cross which the white man in his long guilt must bear and face every day of his life, and the enduring victim of white exploitation, suffering finally spread as on a cross and emasculated for his own guilt and for the sins of the white race." [32] In other words, in the terms employed in this study, Joe Christmas is a marginal man.

At the end of the novel, Faulkner uses the lawyer, Gavin Stevens, to present the familiar racist interpretation of Joe Christmas's final acts:

> But his blood would not be quiet, let him save it. It would not be either one or the other and let his body save itself. Because the black blood drove him first to the negro cabin. And then the white blood drove him out of there, as it was the black blood which snatched up the pistol and the white blood which would not let him fire it. And it was the white blood which sent him to the minister. ... It was the black blood which swept him by his own desire beyond the aid of any man, swept him up into that ecstasy out of a black jungle where life has already ceased. [33]

But it is doubtful that Faulkner is speaking through Gavin Stevens, that Stevens's invocation of "blood" is Faulkner's own. Rather, the emphasis of the novel is on the social, psychological, and existentialist dimensions of marginality. To the idea of "Negro" the people of Jefferson sacrifice Joe Christmas and their own humanity: "Poor man. Poor mankind."

Only in the last hours before death does Joe Christmas escape from the soul-constricting definitions of "white" and "Negro." The countrymen of Jefferson squat on their haunches and tell how after the murder, Joe came walking into Mottstown in broad daylight: "He never acted like either a nigger or a white man. That was it. That was what made the folks so mad." [34] During the rest of Joe Christmas's short life, however, he had chosen to accept—or had been forced to accept—his culture's definitions of "white" and "Negro."

From the beginning, Joe Christmas knew that he was "different," that somehow he was sinful, guilty of some unknown offense. And as he grows up in the orphanage, the still small child learns that the name for his difference is "nigger." To Doc Hines, the dietitian, and the other children at the orphanage, this magic word provides sufficient excuse for exclusion of, and even cruelty toward, the boy. Thus, at a very young age begins Joe's fundamental uncertainty about his selfhood and his place in society. The solution to Joe's lack of self-acceptance could have come through compassion, understanding, and love. But when he confides to Bobbie, the waitress whom he loves when he is a young man, that he thinks he is part "nigger," she and her companions beat and rob him. Never again is he courageous enough to risk rejection. After his traumatic disillusionment, Joe is unwilling to throw himself upon the mercy of society. Whether or not he victimizes himself as he attempts to avoid society's victimization is up to the individual reader of *Light in August* to decide.

When he arises after his loss of innocence (the beating by Bobbie's friends), he enters the "street," the path he seems doomed to follow until his death. The street runs for thousands of miles over the United States; the street runs in time for fifteen years. During these years, Joe Christmas is "in turn laborer, miner, prospector, gambling tout; he enlisted in the army, served four months and deserted and was never caught." [35] Always Joe is "doomed with motion, driven by the courage of flagged and spurred despair." [36] He uses the "fact" of his Negro blood as a weapon against society and himself. He beds with white women, and when he has no money, he tells them he is a black man. In so doing, he is both using white society's own value system to his advantage and declaring himself a slave to that very code. In other words, when Joe says that he is a Negro, he is seeking revenge and is asking to be punished—just as he has always been punished. The punishment he receives is rejection. Joe presents himself as a pariah to these prostitutes and, in turn, is exempted from paying, as other customers do. But he does pay a price, the price he always pays: rejection.

During part of the time he travels the street, Joe lives in much the same way as does Charles Etienne Saint-Valery Bon. At times he lives as a white man; at other times as a black man. His inner fury drives him to inflict and receive punishment:

> He stayed sick for two years. Sometimes he would remember how he had once tricked or teased white men into calling him a negro in order to fight them, to beat them or be beaten; how he fought the negro who called him white. [Then] . . . He lived with negroes, shunning white people. He ate with them, slept with them, belligerent, unpredictable, uncommunicative. He now lived as man and wife with a woman who resembled an ebony carving. At night he would lie in bed beside her, sleepless, beginning to breathe deep and hard. He would do it deliberately, feeling, even watching, his white chest arch deeper and deeper within his ribcage, trying to breathe into himself the dark odor, the dark and inscrutable thinking and being of negroes, with each suspiration trying to expel from himself the white blood and the white thinking and being. And all the while his nostrils at the odor which he was trying to make his own would whiten and tauten, his whole being writhe and strain with physical outrage and spiritual denial.[37]

Like so many of the other mulatto characters discussed in this study, Joe Christmas cannot find a place within either caste because he is neither wholly one nor the other. Unlike most of them, however, Joe Christmas is never able to identify himself with the white or with the black group. There is no adjustment for Joe, no peace but that of death.

In never knowing who he is, Joe Christmas is both the

traditional marginal man and modern existentialist man as well. These two aspects of Faulkner's character merge in the questions: What is the self? How are its dimensions determined—through the individual's exertion of "free will" or through the power of forces entirely external to him? Derived from the stereotypical tragic mulatto character, who is most certainly Joe Christmas's literary ancestor, Faulkner's protagonist is a figure of enormous complexity. Through him, Faulkner raises questions about the very nature of modern man and his relationship to society: How do we define ourselves? In what ways does our culture deny us our humanity by refusing us the possibility of achieving it?

Some critics have protested that Joe Christmas is not a tragic hero, that Faulkner has (merely) written a case history about societally induced deviant behavior. Richard Chase takes this view, arguing that Joe Christmas is neither villain nor Christ figure:

> He suffers, he is a divided man, he is marginal and bereaved; he is "outraged." He asks merely to live, to share the human experience, and to be an individual. . . . He has in other words some power of giving his doomed life meaning by insisting as long as he can on his right to be human. . . . But the main difference between Joe Christmas and Oedipus (or any other tragic hero in the full classic sense) is that Christmas really *is* a victim; he never has a chance, and a chance, or at least the illusion of a chance, a tragic hero must have. . . . There is no mystery, no disastrous choice, no noble action, no tragic recognition. Instead there are heredity, environment, neurotic causation, social maladjustment.[38]

The opposite approach is taken by John L. Longley, Jr., in his essay, "Joe Christmas: The Hero in the Modern World." He contends that Faulkner takes pains to make Joe's freedom absolute. Joe is *not* the helpless victim of his previous conditioning: "Surely it is obvious that the wellspring of all his actions is his refusal to surrender to that conditioning. . . . All his life, people attempt to force him to be what they insist he must be." [39] Surely we see Joe Christmas's struggle against societally imposed definitions of himself. He *will* be Joe Christmas—note his rejection of any other name—even if that divided self is ultimately destroyed in the attempt. We have already seen the way in which he is both rebel and victim in his relationships with the white prostitutes. Joe exhibits the same duality in his relationship with his adopted father. As McEachern beats the boy during one of their many confrontations, Faulkner says: "It would have been hard to say which face was the more rapt, more calm, more convinced." [40] In spite of Joe's refusal to take McEachern's name, he is his father's son. And in Joe's hatred and fury toward both himself and society—white and black—there is evidence of the cultural sickness that has afflicted such dissimilar figures as Doc Hines and Joanna Burden.

Like so many other mulatto characters, Joe is tormented by his ambivalence toward himself and his culture. Although he does continually struggle against the dehumanizing forces of the cultural stereotypes within which he is supposed to define himself, he often contributes to that very dehumanizing process, as evidenced in his attitude toward women and in his failure to establish any deep or lasting relationships. He becomes, *"in part,* an ally of his world against himself." [41] Thus, as David L. Minter says, "At virtually every point [Joe] is both active and passive, both agent and victim." [42] Alfred Kazin makes the point that Joe Christmas illustrates "man's endless complicity in his own history," [43] that is, Joe is both agent and victim. Faulkner expresses this duality several times. When Joe decides to run away from the McEachern farm, Faulkner says of him: "He felt like an eagle: hard, sufficient, potent, remorseless, strong. But that passed, though he did not then know that, like the eagle, his own flesh as all space was still a cage." [44]

Throughout the novel, Faulkner employs the image of the unending street as a symbol of Joe's fate. Usually the street image is connected with the concept of determinism. However, at one point Faulkner says that "the savage and lonely street [was one] which he had chosen of his own will." [45] And before his death, Joe realizes fully the nature of the street that he has been traveling for thirty years: "It had made a circle and he is still inside of it. Though during the last seven days he has had no paved street, yet he has travelled further than in all the thirty years before. And yet he is still inside the circle. 'And yet I have been further in these seven days than in all the thirty years,' he thinks. 'But I have never got outside that circle. I have never broken out of the ring of what I have already done and cannot ever undo,' he thinks quietly." [46]

These passages taken together best illustrate Faulkner's view of the question of free will versus determinism. Joe Christmas did choose his fate in one sense: he *chose* not to allow Mrs. McEachern to love him, for example. But he made this choice as a result of what had occurred to him in the orphanage. Because of what had already happened to Joe Christmas, he could not allow himself to trust this woman. So the appearance of choice is an appearance only. Like all of us, Joe Christmas thinks he is free (at least until he realizes that his past acts and choices determine all present and future "choices" and actions). He makes choices, as we all do, while at the same time, the choices he makes are already determined by what he has been and done.

Joe Christmas's tragedy is that he tries to escape both himself and his culture. He does not understand that he is still a .part of society, if only by virtue of attempts at withdrawal and denial. Thus he is doomed to travel down the street of his life; he is doomed to perpetual motion. There are only two ways to transcend this motion, to find the peace that Joe says he has always wanted. Lena Grove is the only character who is simply not subject to society's rules and definitions. "Life"—and its natural rhythms— is her Master. Because she gives herself up totally to Life, she has "an inward-lighted quality of tranquil and calm unreason and detachment." [47]

The other means by which to achieve peace is discovered by one of the other outsiders in the novel, the Reverend Gail Hightower. At last he understands that "only through choice and commitment can man realize that he is, . . . that existence (free action) precedes essence (the nature of self). The [last] step is the discovery of one's common humanity, the responsibility of freedom." [48] Joe Christmas never understands, except perhaps just before his death, that "The world is like an enormous spider web and if you touch it, however lightly, at any point, the vibration ripples to the remotest perimeter and the drowsy spider feels the tingle and is drowsy no more and springs out to fling the gossamer coils about you who have touched the web and then inject the black, numbing poison under your hide. It does not matter whether or not you meant to brush the web of things." [49] This is Joe Christmas's ultimate tragedy: he is never able to establish a sufficient sense of connectedness with other human beings in his culture, which, in turn, would have enabled him to accept responsibility toward them. All his life, Alfred Kazin says, Joe Christmas "is an abstraction seeking to become a human being." [50] Through his acceptance of responsibility, Joe Christmas could have ceased to be an abstraction and instead could have become a "man."

Through his final act of suffering, Joe Christmas becomes an image of all suffering Mankind. And at the moment of his ritual "crucifixion," he achieves peace at last: "For a long moment he looked up at them with peaceful and unfathomable and unbearable eyes. . . . The man seemed to rise soaring into their memories forever and ever. They are not to lose it. . . . It will be there, musing, quiet, steadfast, not fading and not particularly threatful, but of itself alone serene, of itself alone triumphant." [51]

But the central social issue examined in *Light in August* remains unanswered and, indeed, unanswerable: the question Joe Christmas asks Joanna Burden could not be answered by Faulkner in 1932, nor can it be answered by us in 1978: "Just when do men that have different blood in them stop hating one another?" [52] Nor was Faulkner able to provide a positive response to Erik Erikson's question: "What historical actuality can the American Negro count on and what wider identity will permit him to be self-certain as a Negro (or a descendant of Negroes) *and* be integrated as an American?" [53]

In *Light in August*, Faulkner has brilliantly documented the reciprocal relationship between the individual maladjustment of the mulatto and the sickness of his culture in general. It is the stereotypes, myths, fears, delusions, and actual past history of the culture that help to determine the behavior of the individuals living within that society. And Faulkner and many of the other novelists discussed in this study present a bleak picture of the ways in which our particular American reality has fostered social, political, and economic inequality between the races and almost overwhelming obstacles to a healthy adjustment for full- and mixed-blood American blacks.

NOTES

1. W. E. B. Du Bois, *Darkwater: Voices from Within the Veil* (1920; rpt. New York: AMS Press, 1969), pp. 11-12.

2. Everett Stonequist, *The Marginal Man: A Study in Personality and Culture Conflict* (1937; rpt. New York: Russell & Russell, 1961), pp. 159-160. See John Dollard's *Caste and Class in a Southern Town* wherein he cites a study from 1914 in which light-skinned Negro women institutionalized for psychosis insisted that they were the only white patients among the "niggers." Sometimes these women claimed to be the mothers of white nurses and physicians. (Reported in Mary O'Malley, "Psychoses in the Colored Race," *American Journal of Insanity* [1914], vol. 71, p. 325, in John Dollard, *Caste and Class in a Southern Town* [New Haven, Conn.: Yale University Press, 1937], p. 71.) This phenomenon had not changed by 1964, when Kenneth Clark reported that general studies of a thousand Negro psychiatric patients revealed psychoses involving a denial of their skin color and racial ancestry. (Reported in Kenneth B. Clark, *Prejudice and Your Child,* 2d ed. enl. [Boston: Beacon Press, 1963], p. 45.)

3. Jean Toomer, *Cane* (1923; rpt. New York: Harper & Row, 1969), p. 158.

4. Ibid., p. 161.

5. James Baldwin, *Notes of a Native Son* (Boston: Beacon Press, 1955), p. 4.

6. Toomer, *Cane,* p. 236.

7. Ibid., p. 218.

8. Ibid., p. 169.

9. Ibid., p. 189.

10. Nella Larsen, *Quicksand* (New York: Knopf, 1928), n.p.

11. Ibid., p. 52.

12. Ibid., pp. 120-21.

13. Ibid., p. 213.

14. Stonequist, *The Marginal Man,* p. 147.

15. Larsen, *Quicksand,* p. 215

16. Ibid., p. 302.

17. William Faulkner, *Absalom, Absalom!* (New York: Random House, 1936), pp. 206-7.

18. Robert A. Bone, *The Negro Novel in America,* rev. ed. (New Haven, Conn.: Yale University Press, 1968), p. 87.

19. Faulkner, *Light in August* (New York: Random House, 1932), p. 211.

20. Ibid., p. 106.

21. Ibid., p. 27.

22. Alfred Kazin, "The Stillness of *Light in August,*" *William Faulkner: Three Decades of Criticism,* ed. Frederick J. Hoffman and Olga W. Vickery (East Lansing: Michigan State University, 1960), p. 253.

23. *Faulkner in the University,* ed. Frederick L. Gwynn and Joseph L. Blotner (Charlottesville: The University Press of Virginia, 1959), p. 118 rpt. in David L. Minter, ed., *Twentieth Century Interpretations of Light in August* (Englewood Cliffs, N.J.: Prentice-Hall, 1969), p. 95.
24. Faulkner, *Light in August,* p. 213.
25. Ibid.
26. Richard Chase, "The Stone and the Crucifixion: Faulkner's *Light in August,*" the *Kenyon Review,* 10 (Autumn 1948), 543, in Charles Nilon, *Faulkner and the Negro,* University of Colorado Studies, Series in Language and Literature, no. 8 (Boulder: University of Colorado Press, 1962), p. 74.
27. Faulkner, *Light in August,* pp. 347-48.
28. Ibid., p. 93.
29. Olga Vickery, "The Shadow and the Mirror: *Light in August,*" *Twentieth Century Interpretations,* p. 26.
30. Charles Nilon, *Faulkner and the Negro,* University of Colorado Studies, Series in Language and Literature, no. 8 (Boulder: University of Colorado Press, 1962), p. 73.
31. Ibid., pp. 76-77.
32. John M. Bradbury, *Renaissance in the South* (Chapel Hill: University of North Carolina Press, 1963), p. 56.
33. Faulkner, *Light in August,* p. 424.
34. Ibid., p. 331.
35. Ibid., p. 211.
36. Ibid., p. 213.
37. Ibid., p. 212.
38. Chase, "Faulkner's *Light in August,*" *Twentieth Century Interpretations,* pp. 19-20.
39. John L. Longley, Jr., in *Three Decades of Criticism,* pp. 269-70.
40. Faulkner, *Light in August,* p. 140.
41. David L. Minter, Introduction, *Twentieth Century Interpretations,* p. 10.
42. Ibid., p. 8.
43. Kazin, "The Stillness of *Light in August,*" *Three Decades of Criticism,* p. 259.
44. Faulkner, *Light in August,* pp. 150-51.
45. Ibid., pp. 243-44.
46. Ibid., p. 321.
47. Ibid., p. 15.
48. Robert M. Slabey, "Joe Christmas, Faulkner's Marginal Man," *Phylon,* 21 (1960), 273.
49. Robert Penn Warren, *All the King's Men* (New York: Random House, 1953), p. 200.
50. Kazin, "The Stillness of *Light in August,*" *Twentieth Century Interpretations,* p. 252.
51. Faulkner, *Light in August,* p. 440.
52. Ibid., p. 236.
53. Erik Erikson, *Identity Youth and Crisis* (New York: W. W. Norton, 1968), p. 314.

Postscript

Recent Mulatto Fiction

The mulatto character also plays a significant role in three contemporary novels by distinguished black authors: Ernest J. Gaines's 1971 novel, *The Autobiography of Miss Jane Pittman;* John A. Williams's 1976 novel, *The Junior Bachelor Society;* and John Oliver Killens's 1971 novel, *The Cotillion or One Good Bull Is Half the Herd.*

Of the three, Gaines's novel reveals most clearly the continued utilization of historically significant material: white father-black son, white brother-black brother, and white man-mulatto woman relationships played against the backdrop of turn-of-the-century southern society. It is a tale which has been told many times before—by Twain and Faulkner, and by Pickens and Hughes, to name but a few who have fictionalized the devastating effects of racist ideology. Like so many of the other authors, both black and white, who have dealt with the mulatto character, Gaines indicts the "Code of the South" for diminishing the humanity of those who live within its confines.

One section of the *Autobiography,* which takes place during the late nineteenth century, deals with half brothers named Timmy, who is black, and Tee Bob, who is white. Like several other mulatto sons of aristocratic white fathers (Harry Gordon in Harriet Beecher Stowe's *Dred* and Bert Lewis in "Father and Son" by Langston Hughes), Timmy is very much his father's son, both physically and spiritually. Jane tells us that he is built just like his father, Robert Samson; they are both tall and skinny and have the same hooked nose. Tee Bob, on the other hand, is small and delicate. Jane says that Timmy is more like his father than Tee Bob would ever be: "When he was nothing but a child Timmy like to ride and hunt just like Robert always did. . . . Looking at Timmy, you looking at nobody but Robert Samson himself. Them shoulders up, them elbows in, riding there just like Robert. That straw hat cocked a little over his eyes, just like Robert for all the world." [1] The white father and his mulatto son are like each other in temperament, as well. Jane says that Timmy has "all of Robert's mischief ways. You stayed on your guard 'round either one of them. Robert didn't care what he did to white or black. Timmy didn't care what he did to men or women long as they was black." [2] While everyone, including Miss Amma Dean, Robert Samson's wife, knows that Timmy is Robert's son, Robert neither denies Timmy nor gives the boy extra love; Timmy receives few special privileges. To Robert, Timmy is a "black bastard," no more and no less, as is demonstrated later in the story.

When Tee Bob grows big enough to ride, Robert goes to the quarters and tells his son's mother that he wants Timmy to ride with Tee Bob. Verda's answer, as quoted by Jane, recalls the archetypal patterns in mulatto fiction discussed in Chapter 3: " 'Tee Bob's butler?' Verda said. 'His brother's butler?' " [3] Despite the difference in status, however, the brothers are very close. Although Tee Bob goes to school and Timmy looks after horses, the two boys (at this time, Timmy is twelve or thirteen and Tee Bob is six) ride together and talk and share.

This situation abides until an incident occurs that forces Timmy to leave the plantation. A white man who is jealous of Timmy, both because he is a Samson and a black man who he feels receives treatment too good for him, knocks Timmy down because he is "uppity." When Amma Dean tells Robert of the incident, she tells her husband that the white man ought to be put in jail. Robert tells her that this cannot be done. He says, according to Jane, that

" 'you pinned medals on a white man when he beat a nigger for drawing back his hand.' 'Even a half nigger?' Miss Amma Dean said. 'There ain't no such thing as a half nigger,' Robert said." [4] A few days later Robert gives Timmy some money and sends him away. He refuses to allow Timmy to say goodbye to his brother.

Tee Bob is a sensitive boy who never really understands or accepts the Code of the South. He can live with Timmy's riding behind him but not with Timmy's enforced departure. Jane says that everyone tried to explain the unwritten and generally unspoken rules of behavior to Tee Bob, but the boy never did learn them. His resistance against the dehumanizing system of racism is so great, in fact, that "He killed himself before he learned how he was supposed to live in this world." [5]

Tee Bob's suicide comes about because of his love for a beautiful mulatto schoolteacher named Mary Agnes LeFabre. She is descended from a long line of New Orleans Creoles. Her grandmother, almost white herself, had been one of the mulatto beauties who attended the quadroon balls about which George Washington Cable and others have written. As often happened, the grandmother formed a lifelong union with a white man named LeFabre, who gave his name to the children of the union and left them money, property, and even slaves.

The family later moves to a mulatto community at Creole Place (the brief portrayal of the community is reminiscent of the community presented in Lyle Saxon's 1937 novel, *Children of Strangers*). These people do their own farming; attend their own Catholic church presided over by a priest from the community; administer their own school, presided over by a teacher from the community; give their own dances and parties, attended only by their own group.

When Mary Agnes leaves Creole Place to teach school, her people tell her that she can never return to the community. But the young woman is determined to leave. Like Faulkner's Ike McCaslin (in *The Bear*), Mary Agnes LeFabre is compelled to try to atone for the past: "for the rest of her life, Mary Agnes was trying to make up for this: for what her own people had done her own people. Trying to make up for the past—and that you cannot do." [6]

Mary Agnes is a beautiful young woman, and Tee Bob falls in love with her as soon as he meets her. Mary Agnes can see how the young man feels about her, but she tells Jane that she is not afraid of Tee Bob because "he is more human being than he is white 〮man." [7] She is right, of course, and he looks at her with a love, Jane says, "that's way deep inside of . . . [him]. I have not seen too many men, of any color, look at women that way. . . . I saw in his face he was ready to go against his family, this whole world, for Mary Agnes." [8]

Neither his friends and family nor Mary Agnes herself, however, will allow Tee Bob to live his life outside the boundaries imposed by the caste system. When Tee Bob tells his best friend, Jimmy Caya, of his love for Mary Agnes, Jimmy Caya is brutally frank about the options open to Tee Bob: "If you want her you go to that house and take her. If you want her at that school, make them children go out in the yard and wait. Take her in that ditch if you can't wait to get her home. But she's there for that and nothing else." [9]

The night that Tee Bob is to announce his engagement, his desperation reaches its peak. He begs Mary Agnes to marry him; she refuses. In the confusion, Mary Agnes is knocked unconscious. Because Tee Bob cannot abide by the code of his society, he kills himself. Gaines employs a *raisoneur* (reminiscent of some of Faulkner's characters) to explain that "We all killed him. We tried to make him follow a set of rules our people gived us long ago. But these rules just ain't old enough, Jane. . . . Way, way back, men like Robert [Tee Bob] could love women like Mary Agnes. But somewhere along the way somebody wrote a new set of rules condemning all that. . . . Tee Bob couldn't obey. That's why we got rid of him. All of us. Me, you, the girl—all of us." [10]

Throughout the story, we have been told that Mary Agnes understands the rules in a way that Tee Bob cannot. But when she hit her head, Raynard speculates, something happened to her:

> "The past and the present got all mixed up. That stiff proudness left. Making up for the past left. She *was* the past now. She was grandma now, and he [Tee Bob] was that Creole gentleman. . . . It showed in the way she laid down there on the floor. Helpless; waiting. . . . when he saw it he ran away from there. Because now he thought maybe the white man was God. . . . Maybe the white man did have power that

he, himself, didn't know before now. . . . Then he was home. . . . Now he tried to forget what he had seen on the floor back there. But nothing in that library was go'n let him forget. Too many books on slavery in that room; too many books on history in there. . . . seeing her on the floor like that just hurried it up," he said.

"He was bound to kill himself anyhow?" [Jane asks]

"One day. He had to. For our sins."

"Poor Tee Bob."

"No. Poor us," Jules Raynard said.[11]

John A. Williams's 1976 novel, *The Junior Bachelor Society*, is a novel about a reunion of a group of middle-aged men who, as "underprivileged" adolescents, belonged to a social club they called the "junior bachelor society." Williams devotes a chapter to every member of the club—each of whom is a viable and convincing fictional character in his own right but who also represents a particular type of black man and illustrates one aspect of black experience. He brings them together for their reunion, builds suspense because of the murder of a policeman by one of the members of the Society, and then depicts the way the members achieve a resolution of the situation. Through their united struggle to help their childhood friend, a man who is now a pimp, the members assert their black manhood. Williams's use of the Junior Bachelor Society as a metaphor for black unity—drawn powerfully but not crudely—is very much reflective of contemporary black pride.

One of the members of the Society is a mulatto whose experiences with his own marginality, with passing and with the black bourgeoisie are reminiscent of other fictional mulattoes—as is his ultimate acceptance of the black experience. Clarence Henderson teaches English and Black Studies at one of the better universities in California, but he grew up in the same impoverished circumstances as the other members of the Society. There was one significant difference, however, between Clarence and the other boys—he was light enough to pass for white and was often mistaken for a white man. When the Junior Bachelor Society essentially became the high school basketball team, he was always thought to be the only white boy on the team whenever they went out of town. The fans away from home always rooted for him because they thought he was white; and the girls, he thought, "must've believed he was superbad to be good enough to play with a team full of spades." [12]

As a young man, Clarence does not understand all of the consequences of his color. Sometimes, of course, his Caucasian features and white skin coloring bring Clarence clearly identified benefits. He can become the "Walker-Through-Walls," his childhood fantasy figure, when he sits "in bars and restaurants where blacks could not go, . . . [picked] up women they feared to glance at." [13] Williams says that because of his ability to "walk through the walls of color, Henderson had learned much of both races' strengths, weaknesses, cunning." [14]

Long after adolescence has passed, Clarence grapples with other, more ambiguous, benefits of his mixed-blood heritage. As a young man, he is sought after by young black women. But it is his color, his physical traits—his approximation of the Caucasian male—that provides the attraction:

> They'd all wanted to give it to him then, touch his skin, play with his hair, and he, not knowing then what it was all about, believed at first it was *him*, the thing he was *inside*, that they wished to be close to. If only they'd shunned him, spat upon him, or meant it when they'd called him names. But no. The way they were opened his eyes, revealed his ability to walk through walls, and he saw them now, the younger women on his campus, in his class, on his travels, heard them in their rages, heard even better the plaintive echoes, like the distant sound of iron bells, and cursed their mutual history. He had been so easy.[15]

By the time Clarence is graduated from high school, he knows that he has to work "to make himself black," which he does by going to college in the South, where "he had been afraid to attempt to pass for white. In a way the treatment had worked. He was able to battle the ebb and flow of attraction, knowing that his base, his psyche was black, all of it, and that in that blackness lay his reason for existence." [16] Appropriately, at this point, Clarence is drawn to Jean Toomer and his works: "His papers had been on

Toomer, who else? Doing them for his master's and doctorate had been like examining himself, year after year, experience by experience." [17] But Toomer and Henderson achieve significantly different resolutions to their identity crises: Toomer turned his back on blacks and lived for years as a white man. "But he, Henderson, had . . . come nearly full circle. That emptiness which must have stretched before Toomer was not there for him. He had the Junior Bachelor Society." [18]

Both passing and the life-style of the black bourgeoisie are also fictionalized in Williams's novel. Henderson spends his eight weeks in boot camp as a white sailor, where he lives in fear that he will be exposed as a black man. He is not happy when he tells his new master-at-arms that he is black and not white. During this time, Clarence dates white WAVES. When it comes to marriage, however, unlike two of the other members of the Society who married white women, Clarence marries black—fair, but black; black, but also very bourgeois. Clarence and his wife sometimes pass for white, basically regarding it as an entertaining adventure.

Williams's portrait of Clarence Henderson is not melodramatic. Henderson is neither the race hero, the "sellout," nor the tormented victim so often found in mulatto fiction. He does face an identity crisis, and he does resolve it successfully. He retains his affiliation with the black group; he is a teacher of both Black Studies and English, and he does have a commitment to his profession. He is bitterly disappointed by the lack of interest in Black Studies evidenced by his black students. However, his concern does not interfere with his shrewd assessment that the Black Studies fad has almost run its course: "with a nimbleness he had used in sports, he sidestepped all efforts to place and confine him in Black Studies rather than English departments." [19]

Much of Clarence Henderson's history is different from that of his fellow Junior Bachelor Society members, and the differences are the direct results of Clarence's mixed racial makeup. But he and the other members of the Society share a sense of communion and of brotherhood that is part of each of their black selves. From pimp to college professor, from concert singer to factory worker, each of the members of the Junior Bachelor Society carries a sense of black pride and black unity.

Black pride and black unity are also very much the pivotal issues in John Oliver Killens's *The Cotillion or One Good Bull Is Half the Herd* (1971)—a novel which satirizes the black bourgeoisie in much the same way as Dorothy West's *The Living Is Easy* (1948). But Killens's book is more a paean to *all* black people—if not to what and who they are *right now,* then to what and who they can become when they truly achieve liberation. Killens is a significant black voice of the 1960s and 1970s. According to Addison Gayle, Jr., he is "the spiritual father of the new novelists. It is his direction—more so than that of Ellison—that the young writers have followed. He is the first of the modern period to begin anew, with conscious determination, the quest for new definitions, to attempt to give new meanings to old cultural artifacts." [20]

The black world about which Killens writes reflects both the old and the new attitudes of black people; he portrays those who still cling to the "white aesthetic" and those who joyfully embrace the "black aesthetic." It is the struggle between these two forces, as embodied by the major characters in the novel, and the triumph of the black aesthetic, that form the core of the novel.

There is nothing subtle about Killens's portrayal of the two groups. On one side are (mother of the heroine) Daphne Doreen Braithwàite Lovejoy, a "Caribbean lady" born of a Scottish father and a black field worker, whose primary joys in life are her Caucasian ancestry and her pretensions to a bourgeois life-style; and the "Femmes Fatales," the elite of black society in Brooklyn who hold a Cotillion every year for the daughters of "Frazier's Black Bourgeoisie and Hare's Anglo-Saxons." [21] On the other side are the heroine's father, Matthew Lovejoy, a man who "had taken up the banner of his blackness and carried it unfurled all the way from Garvey to Malcolm;" [22] and lover of the heroine and hero of the novel, Ben Ali Lamumba, a young black poet—a man proud to be black, an artist in the service of his people. Caught in the middle of this dialectic is Yoruba Evelyn Lovejoy, young, beautiful, and black, predisposed to accept her father's black pride as her own but unable to reject completely her mother's (Anglo) bourgeois expectations—until the climax of the novel, that is, when Yoruba experiences a true "coming out."

Daphne is drawn with such heavy-handed satirical strokes that Killens has Ben Ali Lamumba, his *raisoneur,* tell us that "Miss Daphne is a caricature of her own dear bourgeois self." [23] Daphne fancies herself an aristocrat, practically a queen, because of her Scottish father and her own regal bearing. Her slender upturned nose, her thin mouth, and proud bluish green eyes, she thinks, give her prerogatives that other mortals do not possess. She denies the beauty of her black heritage as powerfully as she affirms the majesty of her white ancestry. Daphne constantly belittles her husband because of his dark skin, lower-class ways, and black pride. Her fondest dreams are realized when the Femmes Fatales invite Yoruba to participate in the Cotillion.

The members of this exclusive women's club live in the kinds of homes Daphne admires and Killens brutally satirizes. He says that there is too much furniture everywhere, and there is a mess of pennants and banners from Yale and Harvard as well as from fraternities and sororities. But worst of all is that everything is sterile and lifeless—in fact, in one home, even the toilet seats are covered with plastic. There is one member of the group who deviates from the acceptable mode of behavior established by the other Femmes Fatales; however, she is so wealthy that she cannot be excluded from the club. It is she, Beverly Brap-bap, who, according to Killens, interprets the stilted English of the Femmes Fatales into Afro-Americanese. When one Miss Prissy says that her family lived and belonged to the first families "and all that rot," Mrs. Brap-bap interprets and says, "First Black families to work in the white folks' houses. Cooks, maids, chauffeurs. Redcaps, Pullman porters. Waiting tables at Gage and Tollner's was a status symbol." [24] Prissy also tells of the wonderful parties of old. Mrs. Brap-bap once again intervenes:

> They out-whited the rich white folks. From Friday through Sunday evening they partied. [Then she explains what the cousin clubs were.] . . . there were the "domestic cousins" who slept in and did all the housework. And lastly but not leastly, there were the "slave cousins" who helped with the housework, then went out to work every day and helped to pay the bills, and stayed upstairs when company came. It was all messed up. Sometimes, even the first families couldn't get it straight. Sometimes the "cousins" were actually servants with no other relationship. Sometimes the servants were actually

cousins helping them to hang onto the house. It could really get confusing. If they were really cousins, they were palmed off as servants. If they were really servants they were palmed off as cousins.[25]

Yoruba's father Matthew, Daphne's black and beautiful husband, has only contempt for the Femmes Fatales and their bourgeois pretensions and denial of their race and heritage. He calls them the "Fems Fat Tails, when he didn't call them straight-out Asses," [26] and he is outraged at the thought of his daughter's participation in the Cotillion sponsored by them. They are just as horrified by Matthew as he is by them: he is not only a redcap *and* a man of dark skin coloring, but he is proud of his blackness as well.

So the battle over Yoruba's participation in the Cotillion wages fiercely in the Lovejoy household. Yoruba, of course, is caught between her mother's and her father's value systems. There is a difference even in the manner in which her parents address their daughter: Matthew calls her Yoruba; Daphne always addresses the girl as Eve-lyn. While Yoruba is not very light skinned, her mother approves of the girl's high cheekbones, slender upturned nose, and long, beautiful black hair. Like Dorothy West's Cleo Judson (*The Living Is Easy*, 1948) and Chester Himes's Lillian Taylor (*The Third Generation*, 1953), Daphne Lovejoy "worked hard down through the years to mold her little girl into a thing of beauty and a joy eternal." Like Cleo‑ and Lillian, Daphne tried to impose, to will, Caucasian features on her child: "she used to make the girl pull her lips in and keep them in when she was a baby, so they grow thin like hers, and . . . she used to put clothespins on the baby's nostrils just to pinch them into a thin and slender shape. . . . she used to keep her away from the beaches and off the streets out of the sunlight, and never let the girl drink coffee, which would make her Blacker than she already was." [27]

While Yoruba feels considerable pride in her blackness and is often very impatient with her mother's adoration and imitation of "cultured" whites, she is actually very much attracted to both her mother's and her father's points of view: "How do you tell your mother you don't want to be a lady? That you rather be a good

Black Woman?" Yoruba thinks to herself early in the novel. But Killens immediately lets us know that "The truth of the matter [was], there was this great ambivalence in the girl; forever did the battle rage inside of her between her mother and her father, between ladyship and womanhood. The confrontation between black and white. Against her will did she feel a kind of triumph that she had been selected [to "come out" at the Cotillion]. She, Yoruba Evelyn, was to be a debutante. What was wrong with feeling good about it? Sometimes she felt like shouting: 'Will the real Yoruba Evelyn step forward please. And assert yourself?" [28]

Yoruba's conflict is a reflection of the dialectic at work within the black community as a whole. The Femmes Fatales live within the parameters of the white aesthetic. Killens satirizes them beautifully when he places these words in the mouth of one of the Femmes Fatales: "You young ladies have been thoroughly investigated, and you all have passed with flying colors. Flying colors. Your records are pure and white and spotless. There are no black marks in your record. Nothing black at all. Nothing black at all. You are all virgins and you must remain white and spotless and virginal until the Grand Cotillion is over." [29]

The member of the club who speaks these lines, Mrs. Patterson, abides by the white aesthetic in other ways as well. The following conversation, while handled in a humorous, satirical style, reflects some of the central preoccupations of mulatto fiction:

> Mrs. Patterson tells the group that her father was an octoroon. Charlene, one of the girls in the Cotillion, says, "What's an octoroon? He's a Negro, isn't he?"
>
> Mrs. Patterson sighed like it was her last breath on this happy earth. "My heavens! No! An octoroon is the offspring of a white person and a quadroon."
>
> "All right," Charlene said. "What's a quadroon? I know he's got to be a Negro."
>
> "A quadroon is decidedly not a Negro."
>
> Mrs. Brap-bap gave out with her favorite all-encompassing comment: "Shee-it!"
>
> "A quadroon is the offspring of a mulatto and a white. Mulatto and a white."

"Okay," Charlene said. "Now please, ma'am, tell us what a mulatto is."

Miss Prissy was completely breathless now. Uphill all the way like she was pumping on an English bike. And yet she mustered strength from some unknown source. She whispered, "A mulatto is the offspring of one who's white and the other who is Black."

"In other words," Mrs. Brap-bap said, "an octoroon is a Negro, a quadroon is a Negro, a mulatto is a Negro, a Negro is a Negro is a Negro, and after all your shucking and jiving, your founding father wasn't nothing but a spook whose mother got messed over by a white man."

"Well, anyhow, he had white blood. He had white blood. His blood was whiter than it was Black. And I have whiter blood than anybody in the Femmes Fatales!" [30]

Yoruba, on the other hand, often moves among people who wear their blackness as a badge of purity and righteousness. She

had been to Black happenings where the brothers and the sisters of the darkest complexions did violent putdowns on those unfortunates of the lighter hues, all in the spirit of Black unity. She had even caught herself at evil moments, bugging her own mother because her mother's color had suddenly become unstylish, as if her mother had ordered her pigmentation COD from Macy's. "You ought to get out in the sun more often, Mother. You don't want to be mistaken for a hunkie, when the real stuff hits the air-conditioner." Instantly Yoruba would realize what she was doing to her mother, a vicious thing, and feel guilty about doing it. But in the social sphere in which Yoruba circulated, it was the blacker the berries the rarer and more exquisite the wines (cats were brewing black champagne), and your light skin was a natural drag. Everything was topsy-turvy compared with what it used to be. The world was turning upside down, the bottom to the top, and erupting like Mount Etna.

Some in-a-hurry free-wheeling freely enterprising cats of Harlem, in the spirit of Black power, had opened up a

> Boutique-Afrique selling Afro wigs, . . . blackening powders
> and blackening creams made primarily from minstrel
> lampblack.[31]

The dialectical opposition between the white and black aesthetics is embodied in the traditional and nontraditional, radical ways
in which the Cotillion is viewed by the major characters in the
novel. It is Daphne's great triumph; it represents the closest
approximation of whiteness she can achieve. For Matt, the
Cotillion is an act of selling out to whitey. He is angry not only
because he hates to see black people imitate whites but also
because all of the money ends up in whitey's hands again—and the
money spent on clothes, dancing lessons, and the rental of the
Waldorf is considerable. Ben Ali despises the Cotillion because his
own people are "helping Whitey to cull off all the Black cream of
the crop and churn them into little white toothless harmless
bourgeois in black-face. . . . We are never going to be liberated as
long as we mimic the white boy's juju and his cultural symbols.
The Grand Cotillion is just another way of conking your head
instead of wearing it natural." [32]

However important the anger of Ben Ali and Matt, Killens
realizes that it is only by going beyond anger—toward love and
acceptance—that black unity can be achieved. While neither man
changes his evaluation of Daphne, the black bourgeoisie, or the
Cotillion, Ben Ali Lamumba—the new black artist—comes to a new
perception of these people and their aspirations and his relationship to them. When he tells a surprised Yoruba that he *will*
accompany her to the Cotillion, he makes the following speech. It
contains the heart of Killens's message to his black brothers and
sisters:

> After a while I said to myself, why the hell not? Can it do me
> any harm? Am I so damn delicate that I'm scared that in
> rubbing elbows with my Black bourgeois brothers and sisters
> more of them will rub off on me than of me rub off on them?
> If I'm that insecure, my Black Consciousness must be pretty
> thin and superficial. I mean, they're part of the Black-and-
> Beautiful thing as much as anybody else. Every father's child

of us has been brainwashed with the whitewash. All of us is trying to make that journey home.

... Your mother is not the enemy. She just truly ain't the enemy. If she is, then we are in a real big hurt. Cause your mother is where a whole heap of the Black and beautiful people of the Black Nation are at.[33]

As Killens moves his characters closer to the denouement, which naturally takes place the night of the long-awaited Cotillion, he prepares them for the event in two important ways. Daphne, Yoruba, and Ben Ali have the opportunity to work at a white cotillion; Ben Ali wants Daphne to witness at first hand the decadence of upper-class white society. His plans work beautifully. The event, which begins with elegance, ends as a drunken, dope-ridden orgy. The experience is the revelation Ben Ali hoped it would be. Daphne finally realizes, "all my life I live a lie. Kuh-dah! Worshiping the memory of my father, a white man who look upon me as one of his pickanninies. I got to hold onto something: I got to hold onto something, I keep thinking, even if it ain't real. I know now I been a vain, foolish woman all my life, but I always love my family, you and Matthew, and I going to always love you. . . . I'm so happy we go out to that Long Island fete. It was for true the last illusion. I ain't never really loved white people. I was just too re-spectful of them, 'cause they got all the power." [34]

Daphne even begins to call her daughter Yoruba rather than Eve-lyn. And Yoruba herself makes the final change that symbol-izes her journey home. She finally exchanges her "long, black, shiny velvet cascades of curly stuff spilling down beneath her shoulders" [35] for an Afro over which she "had vacillated, equivo-cated, rationalized, hemmed and hawed, and gone through other varied and sundry changes." [36] When Yoruba sees her hair, her private Cotillion begins: "there was a burst of sudden revelation, and she thought, Now I know the truer deeper meaning of Cotillion. Coming out! Yes! Coming out! I am a debutante coming out of my old self into a new society! She felt cotillionized for real. It was her grand debut into the maturation of her Blackness. The true Rites of Cotillion had begun for her. Metamorphosis!" [37]

Although Daphne has made tremendous strides on her "journey

home," she tells Yoruba and Ben Ali that she is not yet ready to shun the Cotillion completely. After the white cotillion, she tells Yoruba that black people can carry off their cotillion with more style and dignity. She says that it can be black and beautiful. She does not know, however, that Ben Ali plans to transform the Cotillion into and black-and-beautiful event that no one will ever forget. His plans include nothing less than the subversion of the white aesthetic and the glorification of the black aesthetic. He and Yoruba decide to wear African robes to the Cotillion. He explains his strategy to her: " 'Look,' he said, 'these colored cotillions are aimed against our race pride—against our sense of Black identity, against nationhood and unity. But we can make this thing tonight into its very opposite—and aim the guns the other way.' " [38]

When the Femmes Fatales realize what is about to happen, they are scandalized and there is much excitement as members of the two factions clash. Mrs. Brap-bap is naturally in support of the African dress and the naturals sported by Yoruba and two of the other girls. She says, "It'll be a different kind of cotillion and it'll make history. We'll make good hair bad hair and bad hair good hair." [39] When Yoruba's name is called, she walks nervously, but with dignity, to the stage. Some gasp, some faint, some applaud. As Killens tells us, when Yoruba debuted, "it was like the living end— of something. It was supreme cotillion." [40] Ben Ali jumps to his feet and says, "Black brothers and sisters, come out of the cotton patches! ... Follow us to liberation! Be done with false illusions!" [41] The final victory of the novel comes when Daphne, standing "for an endless moment ... torn between the old and the new, between illusion and reality," [42] turns her back upon the beckoning Miss Prissy and goes off to join her family. Daphne is able to complete her journey home because of the love of and faith in all black people demonstrated by Ben Ali Lamumba, the new black artist. Killens, according to Addison Gayle, Jr., is "more than any novelist in black literary history, ... the novelist of love." [43] And *The Cotillion* is a novel that clearly expresses Killens's love of his people and faith in their power.

A study of the mulatto character teaches us a great deal about the history of white and black America: our social structure; our sexual mores, myths, and stereotypes; the dynamics of the white and the black aesthetics; and the ways in which we have failed to make the American dream a reality for all of our citizens. It also teaches us something of the ways in which literature does and does not reflect reality.

In writing about the mulatto character, some American authors have reflected the racist ideologies of our culture while others have attacked them. The literature of the mulatto has been of widely varying quality. Hopefully, the increased sophistication of the presentation of the fictional mulatto—the movement away from simplistic biological explanations of behavior to penetrating analyses of the sociological, psychological, historical and existentialist dimensions of marginality—implies some progress in our cultural attitudes. Yet many of the issues raised in mulatto fiction remain unresolved. And the reason is clear. On the day when black Americans of all shades really believe in their beauty, in their values, and in their worth—when to be a mixed blood in this country will no longer create a conflict of crisis proportions—on that day, the mulatto character, as traditionally portrayed, should disappear from the American novel.

NOTES

1. Ernest J. Gaines, *The Autobiography of Miss Jane Pittman* (New York: Dial Press, 1971), pp. 136-37, 139.
2. Ibid., pp. 136-37.
3. Ibid., p. 137.
4. Ibid., p. 144.
5. Ibid., pp. 144-45.
6. Ibid., p. 156.
7. Ibid., p. 167.
8. Ibid., p. 171.
9. Ibid.
10. Ibid., p. 192.
11. Ibid., pp. 192-93.
12. John A. Williams, *The Junior Bachelor Society* (Garden City, N.Y.: Doubleday & Company, 1976), p. 55.
13. Ibid., p. 56.
14. Ibid., p. 57.
15. Ibid., p. 209.
16. Ibid., p. 159.
17. Ibid.

18. Ibid.
19. Ibid., p. 57.
20. Addison Gayle, Jr., *The Way of the New World: The Black Novel in America* (Garden City, N.Y.: Anchor Press, 1975), p. 261.
21. John Oliver Killens, *The Cotillion or One Good Bull Is Half the Herd* (New York: Trident Press, 1971), p. 76. Killens wants to make certain that we do not miss the sociological implications here.
22. Ibid., p. 39.
23. Ibid., p. 199.
24. Ibid., p. 141.
25. Ibid., pp. 142-43.
26. Ibid., p. 51.
27. Ibid., p. 53.
28. Ibid., p. 55.
29. Ibid., p. 85.
30. Ibid., pp. 141-42.
31. Ibid., pp. 75-76. Killens's satire is reminiscent of that in George Schuyler's *Black No More: Being an Account of the Strange and Wonderful Workings of Science in the Land of the Free, A.D. 1933-40* (New York: The Macaulay Company, 1931).
32. Ibid., p. 152.
33. Ibid., p. 199.
34. Ibid., p. 219.
35. Ibid., p. 223.
36. Ibid.
37. Ibid., pp. 226-27.
38. Ibid., p. 249.
39. Ibid., p. 254.
40. Ibid.
41. Ibid., p. 255.
42. Ibid.
43. Gayle, *The Way of the New World*, pp. 261-62.

Selected Bibliography

FICTION

Allee, Marjorie Hill. *The Great Tradition.* Boston and New York: Houghton Mifflin, 1937.

Anderson, Barbara. *Southbound.* New York: Farrar, Strauss, 1949.

Ashby, William. *Redder Blood.* New York: The Cosmopolitan Press, 1915.

Barnes, Geoffrey. *Dark Lustre.* New York: Alfred H. King, Inc., 1932.

Basso, Hamilton. *The View From Pompey's Head.* Garden City, N.Y.: Doubleday, 1954.

Bennett, John. *Madame Margot: A Grotesque Legend of Old Charleston.* New York: The Century Company, 1921.

Brown, William Wells. *Clotelle: A Tale of the Southern States.* 1855; rpt. Philadelphia: Albert Saifer, 1955.

Cable, George Washington. *The Grandissimes: A Story of Creole Life.* New York: Charles Scribner's Sons, 1898.

————. *Old Creole Days.* New York: Charles Scribner's Sons, 1919.

Caldwell, Erskine. *Place Called Esterville.* New York: Duell, Sloan and Pearce, 1949.

Caspary, Vera. *The White Girl.* New York: J. H. Sears & Company, Inc., 1929.

Cather, Willa. *Sapphira and the Slave Girl.* New York: Alfred A. Knopf, 1940.

Chesnutt, Charles W. *The House Behind the Cedars.* Cambridge, Mass.: The Riverside Press, 1900.

————. *The Marrow of Tradition.* Boston and New York: Houghton Mifflin Company, 1901.

————. *The Wife of His Youth and Other Stories of the Color Line.* 1899; rpt. Ridgewood, N.J.: The Gregg Press, 1967.

Chopin, Kate. *The Complete Works of Kate Chopin,* ed. Per Seyersted. Baton Rouge: Louisiana State University Press, 1970.

Coker, Elizabeth Boatwright. *Daughters of Strangers.* New York: E. P. Dutton & Company, Inc., 1950.

Coleman, Lonnie. *Clara.* New York: E. P. Dutton & Company, Inc., 1952.

Cooper, James Fenimore. *The Last of the Mohicans.* 1826; rpt. New York and London: G. P. Putnam's Sons, 1912.

Davis, Norah. *The Northerner.* New York: The Century Company, 1905.

Davis, Rebecca Harding. *Waiting for the Verdict.* 1867; rpt. Upper Saddle River, N.J.: The Gregg Press, 1968.

Denslow, Van Burean. *Owned and Disowned: or The Chattel Child.* New York: H. Dayton, 1857.

Dickerman, Hallie F. *Stephen Kent.* New York: The Hartney Press, 1935.

Dickinson, Anna E. *What Answer?* Boston: Ticknor and Fields, 1868.

Dixon, Thomas. *The Clansman: An Historical Romance of the Ku Klux Klan.* New York: Doubleday, Page & Company, 1905.

————. *The Leopard's Spots: A Romance of the White Man's Burden— 1865-1900.* New York: Doubleday, Page & Company, 1903.

Downing, Henry F. *The American Cavalryman: A Liberian Romance.* New York: The Neale Publishing Company, 1917.

Dreer, Herman. *The Immediate Jewel of His Soul.* St. Louis, Mo.: St. Louis Argus, 1919.

Durham, Robert Lee. *The Call of the South*. Boston: L. C. Page & Company, 1908.

Ellison, Ralph. *The Invisible Man*. New York: Random House, 1952.

Faulkner, William. *Absalom, Absalom!* New York: Random House, 1936.

——. *Intruder in the Dust*. New York: Random House, 1948.

——. "The Fire and the Hearth." *Go Down, Moses*. New York: Random House, 1942.

——. *Light in August*. New York: Random House, 1932.

Fauset, Jessie Redmon. *The Chinaberry Tree*. New York: Stokes, 1931.

——. *Comedy, American Style*. New York: Stokes, 1933.

——. *Plum Bun*. London: Elkin Mathews & Marrot Limited, 1928.

——. *There Is Confusion*. London: Chapman & Hall, 1924.

Feibleman, Peter S. *A Place Without Twilight*. Cleveland and New York: The World Publishing Company, 1957.

Fisher, Rudolph. *The Walls of Jericho*. 1928; rpt. New York: Arno Press and the New York Times, 1969.

Flannagan, Roy. *Amber Satyr*. Garden City, N.Y.: Doubleday, 1932.

Forrest, Leon. *The Bloodsworth Orphans*. New York: Random House, 1976.

Gaines, Ernest J. *The Autobiography of Miss Jane Pittman*. New York: The Dial Press, 1971.

Gaither, Frances. *Double Muscadine*. New York: Macmillan Company, 1949.

Gilbert, Mercedes. *Aunt Sara's Wooden God*. Boston: The Christopher Publishing Company, 1938.

Gilmore, F. Grant. *The Problem: A Military Novel*. Rochester, N.Y.: Press of Henry Conolly Company, 1915.

Grant, J. W. *Out of the Darkness: or Diabolism and Destiny*. Nashville, Tenn.: National Baptist Publishing Board, 1909.

Grau, Shirley Ann. *The Keepers of the House*. New York: Alfred A. Knopf, 1964.

Griggs, Sutton E. *The Hindered Hand: or The Reign of the Repressionist*. 3d rev. ed. Nashville, Tenn.: Orion Publishing Company, 1905.

——. *Imperium in Imperio*. 1899; rpt. New York: Arno Press and the New York Times, 1969.

——. *The Overshadowed*. Nashville, Tenn.: Orion Publishing Company, 1901.

———. *Pointing the Way.* Nashville, Tenn.: Orion Publishing Company, 1908.

Harper, Frances E. W. *Iola Leroy: or Shadows Uplifted.* 3d ed. Boston: James H. Earle, 1892.

Heyward, DuBose. *Mamba's Daughters.* Garden City, N.Y.: Doubleday, Doran & Company, 1929.

Hildreth, Richard. *The Slave: or Memoirs of Archy Moore.* 1836; rpt. Upper Saddle River, N.J.: The Gregg Press, 1968.

Hill, John H. *Princess Malah.* Washington, D.C.: The Associated Publishers, 1933.

Himes, Chester. *If He Hollers Let Him Go.* New York: New American Library, 1945.

———. *The Third Generation.* 1954; rpt. Chatham, N.J.: Chatham Bookseller, 1973.

Hopkins, Pauline E. *Contending Forces: A Romance Illustrative of Negro Life North and South.* Boston: The Colored Co-operative Publishing Company, 1900.

Hosmer, H. L. *Adela, the Octoroon.* Columbus: Follett & Foster, 1860.

Howells, William Dean. *An Imperative Duty.* New York: Harper & Brothers, 1892.

Hughes, Langston. *Something in Common and Other Stories.* 1933; rpt. Knopf; New York: Hill and Wang, 1963.

———. *The Ways of White Folks.* 1933; rpt. New York: Alfred A. Knopf, 1962.

Hurst, Fannie. *Imitation of Life.* New York and London: Harper & Brothers, 1933.

Hurston, Zora Neale. *Jonah's Gourd Vine.* 1934; rpt. Philadelphia: J. P. Lippincott Company, 1971.

———. *Their Eyes Were Watching God.* Philadelphia and London: J. B. Lippincott Company, 1937.

Ingraham, Joseph Holt. *The Quadroone; or St. Michael's Day.* New York: Harper & Brothers, 1841.

Johnson, Barbara Ferry. *Delta Blood.* New York: Avon, 1977.

Johnson, James Weldon. *The Autobiography of an Ex-Coloured Man.* 1912; rpt. New York: Knopf, 1970.

Jones, Joshua Henry. *By Sanction of Law.* Boston: B. J. Brimmer, 1924.

Jones, J. McHenry. *Hearts of Gold.* Wheeling, W. Va.: Daily Intelligences Job Press, 1896.

Joseph, Donald. *Straw in the Wind.* New York: Macmillan, 1946.

King, Grace. *Balcony Stories.* 1892; rpt. Ridgewood, N.J.: The Gregg Press, 1968.

Killens, John Oliver. *The Cotillion or One Good Bull Is Half the Herd.* New York: Trident Press, 1971.

Kimbrough, Edward. *Night Fire.* New York: Rinehart & Company, 1946.

Larsen, Nella. *Passing.* New York: Knopf, 1929.

———. *Quicksand.* New York: Knopf, 1928.

Lee, George Washington. *River George.* New York: The Macaulay Company, 1937.

Lee, John M. *Counterclockwise.* New York: Wendell Malliet and Company, 1940.

Lewis, Sinclair. *Kingsblood Royal.* New York: Random House, 1947.

McKay, Claude. *Gingertown.* 1932; rpt. New York: Books for Libraries Press, 1972.

Meade, Julian R. *The Back Door.* New York and Toronto: Longmans, Green & Company, 1938.

Micheaux, Oscar. *The Conquest.* Lincoln, Neb.: Woodruff Press, 1913.

———. *The Forged Note.* Lincoln: Western Book Supply, 1915.

———. *The Homesteader.* Lincoln: Western Book Supply, 1917.

———. *The Masquerade.* New York: Book Supply Company, 1947.

Millen, Gilmore. *Sweet Man.* New York: Viking Press, 1930.

Miller, Arthur. *Death of a Salesman. Arthur Miller's Collected Plays.* New York: Viking Press, 1961.

Norris, Frank. *The Octopus: A Story of California.* New York: Doubleday, Page & Company, 1904.

Nunez, Henry Nemours. *Chien Negre.* New York: Doubleday, 1938.

Onstott, Kyle. *Mandingo.* New York: Fawcett World Library, 1957.

Page, Thomas Nelson. *Red Rock: A Chronicle of Reconstruction.* New York: Charles Scribner's Sons, 1909.

Peterkin, Julia. *Black April.* Indianapolis: Bobbs-Merrill Company, 1927.

———. *Bright Skin.* Indianapolis: Bobbs-Merrill Company, 1932.

Pickens, William. *The Vengeance of the Gods and Three Other Stories of*

Real American Color Line Life. Philadelphia: A.M.E. Book Concern, 1922.

Pike, Mary. *Caste: A Story of Republican Equality.* Boston: Phillips & Samson, 1856.

Pope, Edith. *Colcorton.* New York: Charles Scribner's Sons, 1944.

Pryor, George Langhorne. *Neither Bond nor Free.* New York: J. B. Ogilvie Company, 1902.

Redding, J. Saunders. *Stranger and Alone.* New York: Harcourt, Brace, 1950.

Sanborn, Gertrude. *Veiled Aristocrats.* Washington, D.C.: The Associated Publishers, 1923.

Savoy, Willard. *Alien Land.* New York: E. P. Dutton & Company, 1949.

Saxon, Lyle. *Children of Strangers.* Boston: The Riverside Press, 1937.

Schuyler, George. *Black No More: Being an Account of the Strange and Wonderful Workings of Science in the Land of the Free, A.D. 1933-40.* New York: The Macaulay Company, 1931.

Scott, Evelyn. *Migrations.* New York: Albert & Charles Boni Publishers, 1927.

———. *The Wave.* New York: The Literary Guild of America, Inc., 1929.

Smith, Lillian. *Strange Fruit.* New York: Reynal & Hitchcock, 1944.

Smith, W. W. *The Yankee Slave Driver.* Publication information unavailable. 1860.

Snyder, Howard. *Earth Born: A Novel of the Plantation.* New York: The Century Company, 1929.

Spencer, Elizabeth. *The Voice at the Back Door.* New York: McGraw-Hill, 1956.

Stanley, Marie. *Gulf Stream.* New York: Coward-McCann, Inc., 1931.

Stein, Gertrude. *Melanctha: Each One as She May. Selected Writings of Gertrude Stein,* ed. Carl Van Vechten. New York: Random House, 1945.

Stowe, Harriet Beecher. *Dred. The Writings of Harriet Beecher Stowe.* 16 vols. Boston and New York: Houghton Mifflin & Company, 1906.

———. *Uncle Tom's Cabin or Life Among the Lowly.* 2 vols. 1852; rpt. New York: AMS Press, Inc., 1967.

Stribling, T. S. *Birthright.* New York: The Century Company, 1922.

———. *The Store.* New York: The Century Company, 1925.

Sumner, Mrs. Cid Rickette. *Quality.* Indianapolis and New York: Bobbs-Merrill Company, 1946.

Sutherland, Joan. *Challenge.* London and New York: Cassell & Company, Ltd., 1925.

Thomas, Will. *God Is for White Folks.* New York: Creative Age Press, 1947.

Thurman, Wallace. *The Blacker the Berry.* New York: Macaulay Company, 1929.

Tinker, Edward Laroque. *Toucoutou.* New York: Dodd, Mead & Company, 1928.

Toomer, Jean. *Cane.* 1923; rpt. New York: Harper & Row, 1969.

Tourgée, Albion. *Pactolus Prime.* 1890; rpt. Upper Saddle River, N.J.: The Gregg Press, 1968.

———. *A Royal Gentleman.* 1881; rpt. Ridgewood, N.J.: The Gregg Press, 1967.

Trowbridge, John Townsend. *Neighbor Jackwood.* Boston: Phillips & Sampson, 1857.

Turpin, Walter E. *O Canaan!* New York: Doubleday & Doran, 1939.

Twain, Mark. *The Adventures of Huckleberry Finn.* Harper & Brothers Edition. New York: P. F. Collier & Sons Company, 1912.

———. *The Chronicle of Young Satan. Mark Twain's Mysterious Stranger Manuscripts,* ed. William M. Gibson. Berkeley and Los Angeles: University of California Press, 1969.

———. *A Connecticut Yankee in King Arthur's Court.* Harper & Brothers Edition. New York: P. F. Collier & Sons Company, 1917.

———. *The Innocents Abroad.* Hartford, Conn.: American Publishing Company, 1869.

———. *The Prince and the Pauper: A Tale for Young People of All Ages.* Harper & Brothers Edition. New York: P. F. Collier & Sons Company, 1921.

———. *Pudd'nhead Wilson. Pudd'nhead Wilson and Those Extraordinary Twins.* Harper & Brothers Edition. New York: P. F. Collier & Sons Company, 1922.

———. *What Is Man? and Other Essays.* New York and London: Harper & Brothers, 1917.

Walker, Thomas H. B. *J. Johnson, or the Unknown Man: An Answer to Mr. Thomas Dixon's Sins of the Fathers.* De Land, Fla.: The E. O. Painter Printing Company, 1915.

Wall, Evans. *Love Fetish.* New York: The Macaulay Company, 1932.

———. *The No-Nation Girl.* New York and London: The Century Company, 1929.

Warren, Robert Penn. *All the Kings Men.* New York: Random House, 1953.

———. *Band of Angels.* New York: Random House, 1955.

Webb, Frank J. *The Garies and Their Friends.* 1857; rpt. New York: Arno Press and the New York Times, 1969.

West, Dorothy. *The Living Is Easy.* Boston: Houghton Mifflin, 1948.

Westheimer, David. *Summer on the Water.* New York: Macmillan, 1948.

White, Walter. *Flight.* New York: Knopf, 1926.

Williams, John A. *Captain Blackman.* Garden City, N.Y.: Doubleday, 1972.

———. *The Junior Bachelor Society.* Garden City, N.Y.: Doubleday & Company, 1976.

Yerby, Frank. *The Foxes of Harrow.* New York: The Dial Press, 1946.

———. *The Vixens.* New York: The Dial Press, 1947.

NONFICTION

Asselineau, Roger. *The Literary Reputation of Mark Twain from 1910 to 1950: A Critical Essay and a Bibliography.* Paris: Didier, 1954.

Baker, Ray Stannard. *Following the Color Line.* 1908; rpt. New York: Harper & Row, 1964.

———. *"The Tragedy of the Mulatto."* *American Magazine,* 65 (November-April 1907), 588-93.

Baldwin, James. *Notes of a Native Son.* Boston: Beacon Press, 1955.

Barton, Rebecca Chalmers. *Race Consciousness and the American Negro.* Copenhagen: Arnold Busck, 1934.

Benedict, Ruth. *Race: Science and Politics,* rev. ed. New York: Viking Press, 1945.

Bennett, Lerone, Jr. *Before the Mayflower: A History of the Negro in*

America, 1619-1964. Chicago: Johnson Publishing Company, 1964.

Berry, Brewton. *Almost.White.* New York: Macmillan, 1963.

Blankenship, Russell. *American Literature as an Expression of the National Mind.* New York: Holt & Company, 1931.

Boas, Franz. "Fallacies of Racial Inferiority." *Current History,* 25 (February 1927), 34-45.

Bohner, Charles H. *Robert Penn Warren.* New York: Twayne Publishers, 1964.

Bond, Horace Mann. *The Education of the Negro in the American Social Order.* New York: Prentice-Hall, 1934.

Bone, Robert A. *The Negro Novel in America,* rev. ed. New Haven, Conn.: Yale University Press, 1968.

Bradbury, John B. *Renaissance in the South.* Chapel Hill: University of North Carolina Press, 1963.

Braithwaite, William Stanley. "The Negro in American Literature." *Black Expression: Essays by and About Black Americans in the Creative Arts,* ed. Addison Gayle, Jr. New York: Weybright and Talley, 1969, pp. 169-82.

Brawley, Benjamin. *Early Negro American Writers.* 1935, rpt. Freeport, N.Y.: Books for Libraries Press, 1968.

Broom, Leonard and Norval Glenn. *Transformation of the American Negro.* New York: Harper & Row, 1965.

Brown, H. Rap. *Die Nigger Die!* New York: The Dial Press, Inc., 1969.

Brown, Sterling. "Alas the Poor Mulatto." *Opportunity,* 11 (1931), 91.

———. "Negro Character as Seen by White Authors." *Journal of Negro Education,* 2 (April 1933), 179-203.

———. *The Negro in American Fiction.* Washington, D.C.: The Associates in Negro Folk Education, 1937.

Bullock, Penelope. "The Mulatto in American Fiction." *Phylon,* 6 (First Quarter 1945), 78-82.

———. "The Treatment of the Mulatto in American Fiction from 1826 to 1902." Master's thesis, Atlanta University, 1944.

Butcher, Philip. *George W. Cable.* New York: Twayne Publishers, 1962.

Cable, George Washington. *The Negro Question,* ed. Arlin Turner. Garden City, N.Y.: Doubleday & Company, 1958.

Cady, Edwin H. *The Realist at War: The Mature Years, 1885-1920, of William Dean Howells.* Syracuse, N.Y.: Syracuse University Press, 1958.

Carroll, Charles. *The Negro a Beast: or In the Image of God.* St. Louis: American Book and Bible House, 1900.

Carter, Elmer A. "Crossing Over." *Opportunity,* 4, no. 48 (December 1926), 377.

Carter, Everett. *Howells and the Age of Realism.* Hamden, Conn.: Archon Books, 1966.

Chapman, Abraham. *The Negro in American Literature and a Bibliography of Literature by and About Negro Americans.* Stevens Point, Wisconsin, 1966.

Chesnutt, Charles Waddell. "Post-Bellum-Pre-Harlem." *The Crisis,* 38 (June 1931), 193-94.

Chesnutt, Helen M. *Charles Waddell Chesnutt: Pioneer of the Color Line.* Chapel Hill: University of North Carolina Press, 1952.

Clark, Kenneth B. *Dark Ghetto: Dilemmas of Social Power.* New York: Harper & Row, 1965.

———. *Prejudice and Your Child.* 2d ed. enl. Boston: Beacon Press, 1963.

Clarke, John Henrik, ed. *William Styron's Nat Turner: Ten Black Writers Respond.* Boston: Beacon Press, 1968.

Coles, Robert. *Children of Crisis: A Study of Courage and Fear.* Boston: Little, Brown, 1967.

Copeland, Lewis C. "The Negro as a Contrast Conception." *Race Relations and the Race Problem: A Definition and an Analysis,* ed. Edgar T. Thompson. Durham, N.C.: Duke University Press, 1939.

Cox, James Melville. *Mark Twain: The Fate of Humor.* Princeton, N.J.: Princeton University Press, 1966.

Crèvecoeur, Michael Guillaume St. Jean de. *Letters from an American Farmer.* 1782; rpt. Glouster, Mass.: Peter Smith, 1968.

Cruse, Harold. *The Crisis of the Negro Intellectual.* New York: William Morrow & Company, Inc., 1967.

Daniels, George, ed. *Darwinism Comes to America.* Waltham, Mass.: Blaisdell Publishing Company, 1968.

Darwin, Charles. *The Descent of Man, and Selection in Relation to Sex.* 2 vols. New York: D. Appleton and Company, 1871.

———. *On the Origin of Species.* Facsimile. New York: Atheneum, 1967

Davis, David Brion. *The Problem of Slavery in Western Culture*. Ithaca, N.Y.: Cornell University Press, 1966.

Daykin, Walter. "Negro Types in American White Fiction." *Sociology and Social Research*, 22 (1937), 45-52.

Dollard, John. *Caste and Class in a Southern Town*. New Haven, Conn.: Yale University Press, 1937.

Du Bois, W. E. Burghardt. *Darkwater: Voices from Within the Veil*. 1920; rpt. New York: AMS Press, 1969.

———. *The Souls of Black Folk*. Chicago: A. C. McClurg and Company, 1903.

Dunbar-Nelson, Alice. "People of Color in Louisiana, Part I." *Journal of Negro History*, 1, no. 4 (October 1916), 361-76.

———. "People of Color in Louisiana, Part II." *Journal of Negro History*, 2, no. 1 (January 1917), 51-78.

Eckley, Wilton E. "The Novels of T. S. Stribling: A Socio-Literary Study." Diss., Western Reserve University, 1965.

Edwards, G. Franklin. *The Negro Professional Class*. Glencoe, Ill.: The Free Press, 1959.

Ellison, Ralph. *Shadow and Act*. New York: Random House, 1953, 1964.

———. "Twentieth-Century Fiction and the Black Mask of Humanity." *Images of the Negro in American Literature*, ed. Seymour L. Gross and John Edward Hardy. Chicago and London: University of Chicago Press, 1966, pp. 120-37.

Embree, Edwin R. *Brown America*. New York: Viking Press, 1931.

Erikson, Erik. *Identity: Youth and Crisis*. New York: W. W. Norton, 1968.

Fiedler, Leslie. *Love and Death in the American Novel*, rev. ed. New York: Stein and Day, 1966.

Foner, Philip S. *Mark Twain, Social Critic*. New York: International Publishers, 1958.

Ford, Nick Aaron. *The Contemporary Negro Novel: A Study in Race Relations*. Boston: Meador Publishing Company, 1936.

Frazier, E. Franklin. *Black Bourgeoisie*. New York: The Free Press, 1969.

———. "Children in Black and Mulatto Families." *American Journal of Sociology*, 39, no. 1 (July 1933), 12-29.

———. *The Free Negro Family*. Nashville, Tenn: Fisk University Press, 1932.

————. *The Negro in the United States,* rev. ed. New York: Macmillan, 1957.

Fredrickson, George M. *The Black Image in the White Mind: The Debate on Afro-American Character and Destiny, 1817-1914.* New York, Evanston, San Francisco, London: Harper & Row, 1971.

Freimarck, John. *"Pudd'nhead Wilson:* A Tale of Blood and Brotherhood." *University Review,* 33-34 (October 1967-June 1968), 303-6.

Fryckstedt, Olga W. *In Quest of America: A Study of Howell's Early Development as a Novelist.* Cambridge, Mass.: Harvard University Press, 1958.

Garvey, Marcus. *Philosophy and Opinions of Marcus Garvey or Africa for the Africans,* ed. E. U. Essien-Udom. 2d ed. London: Frank Cass & Co. Ltd., 1967.

Gayle, Jr., Addison. *The Black Aesthetic.* New York: Doubleday & Company, Inc., 1972.

————, ed. *Black Expression: Essays by and About Black Americans in the Creative Arts.* New York: Weybright and Talley, 1969.

————. *The Way of the New World: The Black Novel in America.* Garden City, N.Y.: Anchor Press, 1975.

Geismer, Maxwell David. *Twain: An American Prophet.* Boston: Houghton Mifflin, 1970.

Genovese, Eugene D. *Roll, Jordan, Roll: The World the Slaves Made.* New York: Pantheon Books, 1974.

Gibson, William and Arms, George. *A Bibliography of William Dean Howells.* New York: New York Public Library, 1948.

Gilbert, Robert. "Attitudes Toward the Negro in Southern Social Studies and Novels, 1932-1952." Diss., Vanderbilt University, 1953.

Glicksberg, Charles I. "Bias, Fiction, and the Negro." *Phylon,* 12 (1952), 127-35.

Gloster, Hugh M. "American Negro Fiction from Charles W. Chesnutt to Richard Wright." Diss., New York University, 1942.

————. *Negro Voices in American Fiction.* Chapel Hill: University of North Carolina, 1948.

————. "Sutton E. Griggs, Novelist of the New Negro." *Phylon,* 4 (Fourth Quarter 1943), 335-45.

Gossett, Thomas F. *Race: The History of an Idea in America.* Dallas, Tex.: Southern Methodist University Press, 1963.

Green, Ely. *Ely: Too Black, Too White,* ed. Elizabeth N. and Arthur

Ben Chitty. Amherst: University of Massachusetts Press, 1970.

Greer, Scott. "Joe Christmas and the Social Self." *Mississippi Quarterly*, 11 (1958), 160-171.

Griffin, John Howard. *Black Like Me.* Boston: Houghton Mifflin, 1961.

Gross, Seymour L. "Introduction: Stereotype to Archetype: The Negro in American Literary Criticism." *Images of the Negro in American Literature*, ed. Seymour L. Gross and John Edward Hardy. Chicago and London: University of Chicago Press, 1966.

—— and John Edward Hardy, eds. *Images of the Negro in American Literature*, Chicago and London: University of Chicago Press, 1966.

Handlin, Oscar. "A Book That Changed American Life." *New York Times Book Review*, April 21, 1963.

Hare, Nathan. *The Black Anglo-Saxons.* New York: Marzani & Munsell, 1965.

Harris, Abraham L. *The Negro as Capitalist.* Philadelphia: American Academy of Political and Social Science, 1936.

Hatcher, Harlan. *Creating the Modern Novel.* New York: Farrar & Rinehart, Inc., 1935.

Hernton, Calvin C. *Sex and Racism in America.* Garden City, N.Y.: Doubleday & Company, 1965.

Herskovitz, Melville J. *The American Negro: A Study in Racial Crossing.* New York: Alfred A. Knopf, 1930.

Hoffman, Frederick J. *The Art of Southern Fiction.* Carbondale: Southern Illinois University Press, 1967.

—— and Olga W. Vickery, eds. *William Faulkner: Three Decades of Criticism.* East Lansing: Michigan State University, 1960.

Hoffman, Frederick L. *Race Traits and Tendencies of the American Negro.* New York: Publication of the American Economic Association, Nos. 1, 2, and 3, 1896.

Hofstadter, Richard. *Social Darwinism in American Thought*, rev. ed. Boston: Beacon Press, 1955.

Holman, C. Hugh. *Three Modes of Modern Southern Fiction.* Athens, Ga.: University of Georgia Press, 1966.

Howells, William Dean. *Criticism and Fiction*, ed. Clara Marburg Kirk and Rudolph Kirk. New York: New York University Press, 1959.

Huggins, Nat. *Harlem Renaissance.* New York: Oxford University Press, 1971.

Hughes, Carl Milton. *The Negro Novelist.* New York: The Citadel Press, 1953.

Jackson, Luther P. *Free Negro Labor and Property Holding in Virginia, 1830-1860.* New York: Appleton-Century-Crofts, 1942.

Johnson, Beulah V. "The Treatment of the Negro Woman as a Major Character in American Novels 1900-1950." Diss., New York University, 1955.

Jordan, Winthrop. *White Over Black: American Attitudes Toward the Negro, 1559-1812.* Chapel Hill: University of North Carolina Press, 1968.

Kardiner, Abram and Lionel Ovesey. *The Mark of Oppression: A Psychological Study of the American Negro.* Cleveland: World Publishing Company, 1951.

Karon, Bertram P. *The Negro Personality: A Rigorous Investigation into the Effects of Culture.* New York: Norton, 1951.

Kazin, Alfred. "The Stillness of *Light in August.*" *William Faulkner: Three Decades of Criticism,* ed. Frederick J. Hoffman and Olga W. Vickery. East Lansing: Michigan State University, 1960, pp. 247-64.

Kelley, William. "The Ivy League Negro." *Growing Up American,* ed. Peter Nagourney and Susan Steiner. Belmont, Calif.: Wadsworth Publishing Company, Inc., 1972.

Kirk, Clara Marburg and Rudolph Kirk. *William Dean Howells.* New York: Twayne Publishing Company, 1965.

Larsson, Cloyte Murdock, ed. *Marriage Across the Color Line.* Chicago: Johnson Publishing Company, 1965.

Lind, Ilse Dusoir. "The Design and Meaning of *Absalom, Absalom!*" *William Faulkner: Three Decades of Criticism,* ed. Frederick J. Hoffman and Olga W. Vickery. East Lansing: Michigan State University, 1960, pp. 278-304.

Littlejohn, David. *Black on White: A Critical Survey of Writing by American Negroes.* New York: Grossman Publishing, 1966.

Locke, Alain. "American Literary Tradition and the Negro." *Sociology and Social Research,* 22 (1937), 215-22.

———. *The New Negro: An Interpretation.* New York: Albert & Charles Boni, 1925.

Loggins, Vernon. *The Negro Author: His Development in America.* New York: Columbia University Press, 1931.

Longley, John Lewis, Jr. "Joe Christmas: The Hero in the Modern World," *William Faulkner: Three Decades of Criticism,* ed. Frederick J. Hoffman and Olga W. Vickery. East Lansing: Michigan State University, 1960, pp. 265-77.

————. "Miscegenation as Symbol: *Band of Angels.*" *Robert Penn Warren: A Collection of Critical Essays,* ed. John Lewis Longley. New York: New York University Press, 1965, pp. 141-62.

————, ed. *Robert Penn Warren: A Collection of Critical Essays.* New York: New York University Press, 1965.

Margolies, Edward. *Native Sons: A Critical Study of Twentieth-Century Negro American Authors.* Philadelphia: University of Pennsylvania Press, 1968.

Meier, August. *Negro Thought in America, 1880-1915: Racial Ideologies in the Age of Booker T. Washington.* Ann Arbor: University of Michigan Press, 1963.

Minter, David L., ed. *Twentieth Century Interpretations of Light in August.* Englewood Cliffs, N.J.: Prentice-Hall, Inc., 1969.

Montagu, Ashley. *Man's Most Dangerous Myth: The Fallacy of Race.* 4th ed. Cleveland: World Publishing Company, 1964.

Myrdal, Gunnar. *An American Dilemma: The Negro Problem and Modern Democracy.* New York: Harper & Brothers, 1944.

Nagourney, Peter and Susan Steiner, eds. *Growing Up American.* Belmont, Calif.: Wadsworth Publishing Company, Inc., 1972.

Nilon, Charles Hampton. *Faulkner and the Negro.* University of Colorado Studies, Series in Language and Literature, No. 8. Boulder: University of Colorado Press, 1962.

Nott, Josiah Clark. *Indigenous Races of the Earth: or New Chapters of Ethnological Inquiry.* 8 vols. Philadelphia: J. B. Lippincott & Company, 1857.

Odum, Howard. *Social and Mental Traits of the Negro.* New York: Columbia University Press, 1930.

Regan, Robert. *Unpromising Heroes: Mark Twain and His Characters.* Berkeley and Los Angeles: University of California Press, 1966.

Reuter, Edward Byron. "Amalgamation," *Encyclopaedia of the Social Sciences.* Vol. 2.

——. *The Mulatto in the United States.* 1936; rpt. New York: Negro Universities Press, 1961.

——. *Race Mixture: Studies in Intermarriage -and Miscegenation.* New York: McGraw-Hill, 1931.

Rosenblatt, Roger. *Black Fiction.* Cambridge, Mass., and London: Harvard University Press, 1974.

Rowlette, Robert. *Twain's Pudd'nhead Wilson: The Development and Design.* Bowling Green, Ohio: Bowling Green University Popular Press, 1971.

Rowlette, Robert O. "Mark Twain's *Pudd'nhead Wilson: Its Themes and Their Development.*" Diss., University of Kansas, 1967.

Rubin, Louis D. *George Washington Cable.* New York: Pegasus, 1969.

——. *The Faraway Country.* Seattle: University of Washington Press, 1963.

—— and Robert D. Jacobs. *Southern Renascence.* Baltimore, Md.: Johns Hopkins Press, 1953.

Sartre, Jean Paul. "Freedom and Responsibility." *Being and Nothingness. Hard Rains,* ed. Robert Disch and Barry N. Schwartz. Englewood Cliffs, N.J.: Prentice-Hall, 1969.

Schuyler, George S. "Who Is 'Negro'? Who Is 'White'?" *Common Ground,* 1 (Autumn 1940), 53-56.

Seyersted, Per. *Kate Chopin: A Critical Biography.* Baton Rouge: University of Louisiana Press, 1969.

Sketches of the Higher Classes of Colored Society in Philadelphia, by a Southerner. Philadelphia: Merrihew & Thompson, Printers, 1841.

Slabey, Robert M. "Joe Christmas: Faulkner's Marginal Man." *Phylon,* 21 (1960), 266-77.

Smith, Helena M. "Negro Characterization in the American Novel: A Historical Survey by White Authors." Diss., Pennsylvania State University, 1959.

Smith, Henry Nash. *Mark Twain: The Development of a Writer.* Cambridge, Mass.: Belknap Press, 1962.

Smith, Lillian. *Killers of the Dream.* New York: W. W. Norton, 1949.

Stampp, Kenneth M. *The Peculiar Institution: Slavery in the Ante-bellum South.* New York: Alfred A. Knopf, 1956.

Stanton, William. *The Leopard's Spots: Scientific Attitudes Toward Race in America.* Chicago: University of Chicago Press, 1960.

Steward, Gustavus Adolphus. "The Black Girl Passes." *Social Forces* (September 1927), 99-103.

Stoddard, Theodore Lothrop. *The Revolt Against Civilization*. New York: Charles Scribner's Sons, 1922.

Stonequist, Everett V. *The Marginal Man: A Study in Personality and Culture Conflict*. 1937; rpt. New York: Russell & Russell, Inc., 1961.

————. "Race Mixture and the Mulatto." *Race Relations and the Race Problem: A Definition and an Analysis,* ed. Edgar T. Thompson. Durham, N.C.: Duke University Press, 1939.

Tischler, Nancy M. *Black Masks: Negro Characters in Modern Southern Fiction*. University Park: Pennsylvania State University Press, 1969.

Turner, Arlin. *George Washington Cable*. Durham, N.C.: Duke University Press, 1956.

Warner, W. Lloyd and Allison Davis. "A Comparative Study of American Caste." *Race Relations and the Race Problem: A Definition and an Analysis,* ed. Edgar T. Thompson. Durham, N.C.: Duke University Press, 1939.

Woodson, Carter G. *The Education of the Negro Prior to 1861*. 1919, 2d ed.; New York: Arno Press, 1968.

Wormley, Margaret Just. "The Negro in Southern Fiction: 1920-1940." Diss., Boston University, 1947.

Wright, Richard. "The Literature of the Negro in the United States." *Black Expression: Essays by and About Black Americans in the Creative Arts,* ed. Addison Gayle, Jr. New York: Weybright and Talley, 1969, pp. 198-229.

Yellin, Jean Fagan. *The Intricate Knot: Black Figures in American Literature, 1776-1863*. New York: New York University Press, 1972.

Ziff, Larzer. *The American 1890s: Life and Times of a Lost Generation*. New York: Viking Press, 1966.

Zinn, Howard. *The Southern Mystique*. New York: Alfred A. Knopf, 1964.

Index

Absalom, Absalom!, 74, 82, 91-94, 225
Adela, the Octoroon, 57
Agassiz, Louis, 26
"Age of Discussion," 60
Alien Land, 78, 142, 143, 146, 149, 159, 203, 215, 219
American Dilemma, An, 7, 165. *See* "Book That Changed American Life, A"
"American dilemma," 6-7
American dream, 6-7, 162-163, 174
Ashby, William M., 62
"Atlanta Compromise," 199
Autobiography of an Ex-Coloured Man, The, 15, 62, 83, 150-159, 219
Autobiography of Miss Jane Pittman, The, 15, 80, 238-242
Bachman, John, 24, 25

Baker, Ray Stannard, 65
Baldwin, James, 204, 220, 221
Band of Angels, 79, 83, 101, 127-137, 151, 219
Barnes, Geoffrey, 63, 103
Bear, The, 240
"Beating That Boy," 7
"Becky," 68
Being and Nothingness, 139n
Bennett, John, 103
Birth of a Nation, 50n
Birthright, 31, 202
Black Aesthetic, The, 16n
Black aesthetic, 7, 16n, 250
"Black baby myth," 34, 143
Black Bourgeoisie, 177
Black bourgeoisie: education of, 166-168; elitist communities of, 6, 11, 107, 164, 168, 179; histor-

ical development of, 163-165; marginality of, 178; rejection of black group by, 6, 162-163, 174-178; requirements for membership in, 6, 164-170, 179; satire of in *The Cotillion,* 245-253; satire of in *If He Hollers Let Him Go,* 172-174; satire of in *The Living Is Easy,* 178-187; satire of in *The Walls of Jericho,* 65-66

Blacker the Berry, The, 165

Black Expression, 49n

Black Family in Slavery and Freedom, 1750-1925, The, 17n

Black Fiction, 161n

Black Like Me, 143

Black Muslims, 197

Black nationalism, 191, 197. *See also* Black Muslims; Black Panthers; Garvey, Marcus; Malcolm X; Muhammed, Elijah

Black No More: Being an Account of the Strange and Wonderful Workings of Science in the Land of the Free, A.D., 1933-40, 70, 254n

Black Panthers, 204

"Black Writer and His Role, The," 5

"Black Writer Vis-à-Vis His Country, The," 6

Blake; of the Huts of America, 58

"blood," 29, 30, 229

Bloodworth Orphans, The, 81

Blue-veined societies, 115n, 165

Boas, Franz, 29

Bohner, Charles H., 134, 138n

"Bona and Paul," 69. *See Cane*

Bond, Horace Mann, 194

Bone, Robert, 61, 162, 168, 169, 170, 171, 179, 204, 206

"Book That Changed American Life, A," 16n. *See American Dilemma, An*

Boy's Town, A, 110

Bradsbury, John M., 229

Brown, H. Rap, 3-4

Brown, Sterling, 62, 100, 150

Brown, William Wells, 15, 57, 83, 95n, 100

"Brute Negro" stereotype, 28, 59-60, 73-74, 81. *See also* Negro stereotypes (general)

Bullock, Penelope, 54, 55

Butcher, Philip, 107

By Sanction of Law, 62

Cabell, J. L., 25

Cable, George Washington, 104-109

Cady, Edwin H., 109-110

Caldwell, Erskine, 73-74

Call of the South, The 25, 32, 129

Call of the Wild, The, 31

Cane, 63, 68-70, 220-222, 226

Carroll, Charles, 28

Caspary, Vera, 63, 103

Caste, 57

Caste and Class in a Southern Town, 236n

Cather, Willa, 14, 71

Chase, Richard, 228, 232

Chesnutt, Charles, 15, 61, 62, 86, 103, 115n, 124, 145, 194, 219

Child, Lydia Maria, 57

Children of Strangers, 76

Chinaberry, Tree, The, 61, 83, 108, 170

Chopin, Kate, 102-103

Clansman: An Historical Romance of the Ku Klux Klan, The, 25

Clara, 74

Clark, Kenneth, 236n

Clotelle: A Tale of the Southern States,

15, 57-58, 61, 83, 95n, 97n, 100, 169

Coker, Elizabeth, 78, 104, 123, 124, 194-195

Colcorton, 124, 143, 145

Color Line: A Brief in Behalf of the Unborn, The, 28

Comedy, American Style, 142, 143, 159, 165, 170, 178, 219

Confessions of Nat Turner, The, 127

Connecticut Yankee in King Arthur's Court, A, 37, 38, 40

Conquest, The, 62

Contending Forces: A Romance Illustrative of Negro Life North and South, 60, 170, 200-202

Conway, Moncure Daniel, 26

Cooper, James Fenimore, 31, 53-54

CORE, 204

Cotillion or One Good Bull Is Half the Herd, The, 15, 80, 238, 245-253

Craft, Ellen, 57

Craft, William, 57

Crania Americana, 24

Crisis experience, 15, 119-137

Crisis of the Negro Intellectual, The, 189n

Cruse, Harold, 189n

Dark Lustre, 63, 103

Darwin, Charles, 26, 27

Darwinism, 26-27

Daughter of Strangers, 74, 78, 104, 123, 124, 194, 196, 214, 219

Davis, David Brian, 21

Davis, Rebecca Harding, 146-147, 195-196

Delaney, Martin Robinson, 58, 96n

Delta Blood, 81

Denslow, Van Buren, 57

Descent of Man, The, 27

"Desirée's Baby," 102-103

Dickerman, Hallie F., 70

"Dickty," 14, 65-67

Dixon, Thomas, 15, 25, 50n, 59, 61

Doctrine of the Unity of the Human Race Examined on the Principles of Science, The, 24

Dollard, John, 236n

Double Muscadine, 71

Douglass, Frederick, 123

Downing, Henry F., 61

Dred: A Tale of the Dismal Swamp, 34-35, 57, 83, 86, 239

Dreer, Herman, 62

Du Bois, W. E. B., 5-6, 60, 61, 191, 197-201, 204, 205, 219

Du Boisean philosophy, 5, 200-205, 212

Dumas, Alexander, 154

Durham, Robert Lee, 16, 32-34, 59, 61

Early Negro middle class school, 103. *See* "Talented Tenth, the"

Ebony, 165

Eckley, Wilton E., 49n

Ellison, Ralph, 7, 16n, 150, 172, 175, 180, 203, 204, 245

Engerman, Stanley L., 17n

Erikson, Erik, 235

Essien-Udom, E. U., 198

"Esther," 69. *See Cane*

"Exiles," 171

"Father and Son," 83-85, 239

Faulkner, William, 14, 31, 86-92, 104, 225-235, 238, 240, 241

Faulkner and the Negro, 228

Fauset, Jessie, 15, 61, 64-65, 142-143, 159, 170-171, 178, 219

Feibleman, Peter, 79

"Fern," 68-69. *See Cane*

Fiedler, Leslie, 53, 129

"Fire and the Hearth, The," 87-91

Fisher, Rudolph, 65-68, 76, 149
Flight, 15, 123, 144, 146, 149, 159
Fogel, Robert W., 17n
Forrest, Leon, 81
Forster, E. M., 132
Foxes of Harrow, The, 71-72
Frazier, Franklin, 17n, 163, 167, 176-177, 245
Fredrickson, George M., 23, 25, 26, 27, 28, 56, 58
"Freedom and Responsibility," 138n
Free Negroes, 11-12, 203-204. *See also Gens de coleur*
Freimarck, John, 47
Freud, Sigmund, 178
Fuller, Hoyt, 16n
Gaines, Ernest J., 15, 80, 238, 241
Gaither, Frances, 71
Garies and Their Friends, The, 61, 74, 83, 102, 142, 143, 145, 149, 159, 170, 219
Garrison, William Lloyd, 56
Garvey, Marcus, 165, 191, 204, 245
Gayle, Jr., Addison, 6, 7, 16n, 17n, 49n, 58, 68, 76, 96n, 160n, 174, 188n, 204, 206, 245, 252
Genovese, Eugene D., 9, 10, 12, 17n, 19, 163
Gens de coleur, 107, 108. *See also* Free Negroes
Gerald, Carolyn F., 5, 16n
Gilmore, F. Grant, 61
Gloster, Hugh, 150, 204
God Is for White Folks, 143, 146
Go Down, Moses, 87-89. *See also* "Fire and the Hearth, The"
Gossett, Thomas, 23
Grandissimes, The, 105-109
Grau, Shirley Ann, 80, 144
Griffin, John, 143
Griffith, D. W., 50n

Griggs, Sutton, 25, 60, 62, 144, 165, 194, 200, 204-214, 219
Gulf Stream, 63, 103-104, 219
Gutman, Herbert, 17n
"Gutman Report, The," 17n
Handlin, Oscar, 16n
Hare, Nathan, 163, 171, 245
Harlem Renaissance, 189n
Harlem Renaissance, 15, 61-70, 76, 165, 177, 189n, 204
Harper, Frances E. W., 60, 61, 193-194, 196, 219
Haven, Gilbert, 26
Hegemonic function of law, 20
Hernton, Calvin C., 62, 73
Herrenvolk democracy, 18-19
Heyward, DuBose, 166, 168, 175, 189n
Hildreth, Richard, 15, 50n
Himes, Chester, 76, 77-78, 172-174, 247
Hindered Hand: or, The Reign of the Repressionist, The, 60, 144, 204, 205, 207, 209-210, 213, 215
"His Own Country," 49n
Hoffman, Frederick L., 28
Homesteader, The, 62
Hopkins, Pauline, 60, 170, 200, 202, 219
Hosmer, H. L., 57
House Behind the Cedars, The, 61, 74, 103, 124, 144, 145-146, 149, 152, 194
Howard's End, 132
Howe, Dr. Samuel Gridley, 26
Howells, William Dean, 104, 109-115, 125
Huggins, Nathan, 189n
Hughes, Langston, 76, 83-86, 140, 222, 238, 239
Hurst, Fannie, 123, 142

Hurston, Zora Neale, 75-76
Hybrid degeneration, 15, 16, 17n
If He Hollers Let Him Go, 76, 172-174
Imitation of Life, 123, 142, 143, 159
Immediate Jewel of His Soul, The, 62
Imperative Duty, An, 104, 109-115, 125
Imperium in Imperio: A Study of the Negro Race Problem, 58, 60, 204-208, 210, 211-213, 215
Innocents Abroad, The, 38
Intermarriage, 23-24, 26, 62, 165. *See also* Miscegenation
Intricate Knot, The, 95n
Intruder in the Dust, 82, 87-91
Invisible Man, 203
Iola Leroy, 60, 61, 83, 101, 123, 146, 193, 196, 201, 214-215
Jefferson, Thomas, 22-23, 48n, 209
"Joe Christmas: The Hero in the Modern World," 232
Johnson, Barbara Ferry, 81
Johnson, Beulah, 62
Johnson, James Weldon, 15, 62, 149, 150-151, 156-158
Jones, Joshua Henry, 62
Jordan, Winthrop, 9, 10, 11, 16n, 19, 20-21, 49n
Joyce, James, 132
Jung, C. J., 81, 178
Junior Bachelor Society, The, 15, 80, 238, 242-244
"Kabnis," 68. *See Cane*
Kardiner, Abram, 179
Karon, Bertram, 179
Kazin, Alfred, 227, 233, 235
Keepers of the House, The, 80, 85-86, 144-145
Kester, Paul, 49n
Killens, John Oliver, 6-7, 15, 17n, 80, 238, 245-252

Killers of the Dream, 82-83
Kingsblood Royal, 29-30, 79, 123-127, 159
"La Belle Zoraide," 65
Lamarck, Jean Baptiste, 32
Larsen, Nella, 15, 64, 65, 142, 143, 146, 159, 166-167, 171, 188n, 219, 222
Last of the Mohicans, The, 53-54
Le Conte, Joseph, 31-32
Leopard's Spots, The, 25, 74
Lewis, Sinclair, 14, 29-30, 79, 125, 127
Liberator, The, 56
Light in August, 74, 87, 104, 225-235
Lincoln, Abraham, 209
Lind, Ilse Dusoir, 91
Littlejohn, David, 70
Living Is Easy, The, 76, 178-187, 219, 245, 247
Locke, Alain, 53, 59
Lombroso, Cesare, 32
London, Jack, 31
Longley, Jr., John, 133, 232
L'Ouverture, Toussaint, 123
Love Fetish, 63, 103
McKay, Claude, 15, 25, 64, 76, 96n, 148-149, 159
McKeithan, Daniel Morley, 51n
"Madame Delphine," 105-106
Madame Margot, 103
Malcolm X, 245
Mamba's Daughters, 175, 189n, 215
Mandingo, 71
Marginality, 13-14, 100, 220. *See also* Black bourgeoisie; Marginal man; Mulatto; Mulatto character; Passer; Passing for white; Tragic mulatto stereotype.
Marginal Man, The, 5
Marginal man, 14, 122, 141. *See*

also Black bourgeoisie; Marginality; Mulatto; Mulatto character; Passer; Passing for white; Tragic mulatto stereotype

Margolies, Edward, 150, 157, 198

Marrow of Tradition, The, 61, 86

Maum Guinea, 56

Meier, August, 169, 197, 199

Melanctha: Each One as She May, 63-64

Millen, Gilmore, 64

Minter, David L., 233

Miscegenation: between black women and white men, 9; differing patterns of in two- and three-caste systems, 10-11; discouragement of, 23, 29; in *Absalom, Absalom!*, 93; in mulatto fiction, 73, 82. *See also* Intermarriage

"Miscegenation as Symbol: *Band of Angels*," 133

Mischeaux, Oscar, 61, 62

Monogenic-polygenic debate, 24-26

Morganatic marriage, 93, 225, 240

Morgan Manuscript of Mark Twain's Pudd'nhead Wilson, The, 51n

Morton, Dr. Samuel George, 24

Muhammed, Elijah, 165

Mulatto, 83

Mulatto: attitude of blacks toward, 14; biological definition of, 8; fictional treatment of, 11-13; historical use of the term, 9; in the West Indies, 10, 11; linguistic origin of the term, 9; percentage of in the United States in 1860, 11; position in American culture, 4, 8, 52-53; psychology of, 13-14, 52; racist definition of, 30; rejection of black culture, 6, 14; ster-

ility of, 19, 24, 25, 27. *See also* Marginality; Marginal man

Mulatto character: adjustments of, 218-220; as black bourgeois, 162-189; as buffer in *Daughter of Strangers*, 195; as buffer in *The Slave*, 193; as existential man, 218-237; as passer, 140-61; as race leader, 14, 78-79, 190-217; as tragic mulatto, 99-116; definition of, 13-14; depiction of by abolitionist authors, 14-15, 53-57, 74; depiction of by black authors, 15, 52-53, 57-58; depiction of by Negrophobe authors, 15, 53, 59-60, 61; depiction of in white-authored novels, 15, 52-53; 1865-1908, 58-61; identification with black group of, 191-192; in black- and white-authored mulatto fiction, 1932-1977, 70-81, 238-254; in black- and white-authored mulatto fiction, 1908-1924, 61-62; in Faulkner's novels, 74, 82, 87-94, 104, 225-235; in Harlem Renaissance fiction, 63, 64-70, 75-76, 83-85, 220-222, 226; in southern fiction, 53; in white-authored mulatto fiction, 1900-1930, 62-64; overview of, 94, 252-253; presentation of male vs. female, 74. *See also* "Brute Negro" stereotype; Negro stereotypes; Passer; Passing for white; Tragic mulatto stereotype

Mulatto fiction: archetypal themes in, 81-87, 239; existentialism in, 79-80, 122, 123-137; historical review of, 53-81; interdisciplinary study of, 8; literary quality of, 94; racist perspective in, 13

Mulatto in the United States, The, 191

Myrdal, Gunnar, 16n, 29, 141, 148, 165, 205
Mysterious Stranger, The, 39
NAACP, 204
"Near-White," 15, 25, 148-149
Negro a Beast, The, 28
Negro, A Menace to American Civilization, The, 28
Negro stereotypes (general): as character explanation, 81, 82; as justification for mistreatment, 29; exposure of in *Kingsblood Royal,* 30, 124-125; rejection of by blacks, 176. *See also* "Brute Negro" stereotype; Tragic mulatto stereotype
Negro Voices in American Fiction, 214
Neither Bond Nor Free, 60, 74, 169, 200, 215
Nilon, Charles, 89, 228
No-Nation Girl, The, 63, 103
Norris, Frank, 31-32
Notes on Virginia, 22-23
Nott, Dr. Josiah C., 25
"Novels of T. S. Stribling: A Socio-Literary Study, The," 49n
Octopus, The, 32
Old Creole Days, 105-106
Onstott, Kyle, 71
On the Origin of Species, 26, 27
Overshadowed, 204, 213
Ovesey, Lionel, 179
Owned and Disowned, 57
Pactolus Prime, 60
Page, Thomas Nelson, 59
Passer: as black Christ, 147; description of, 100, 141-142; fear of exposure by, 143-144, 148; healthy identity of, 149; rejection of loved one by, 144; relinquishment of by loved ones, 105-106, 144-145. *See also* Mulatto character; Passing for white; Tragic mulatto stereotype
Passing, 15, 142, 143, 146, 171, 216
Passing for white: as response to marginality, 14, 15, 219; at educational institutions, 142-143; by tragic mulatto character, 100; cultural reasons for, 142; definition of, 6, 162; in black-authored mulatto fiction, 1902-1924, 62; male vs. female experience of, 142, 148; overview of novel of, 158-159; professional reasons for, 143; reactions by blacks to, 145-146; reactions by whites to, 145-146. *See also* Mulatto character; Passer; Tragic mulatto stereotype
Phillips, Wendell, 153
Philosophy and Opinions of Marcus Garvey, 199
Pickens, William, 35-36, 238
Pike, Mary, 57
Placage, 72, 81
Place Called Esterville, 73-74
Place Without Twilight, A, 79-80
Plum Bun, 142, 143, 144, 146, 148-149, 159, 170
Pointing the Way, 60, 165, 204, 206-211, 213
Pope, Edith, 124, 143, 145
Prejudice and Your Child, 236n
Prince and the Pauper, The, 37
Pryor, G. Langhorne, 60, 169, 200-202
Pudd'nhead Wilson, 36, 37, 40-48, 86, 119
"Quadroons, The," 57
Quicksand, 15, 166, 167-168, 171, 188n, 222-224
Race Traits and Tendencies of the American Negro, 28

Racial atavism, 27, 28, 31, 50n, 71
"Racial disharmonies," theory of, 24, 28-29, 100
Racism, 3, 18, 23, 28, 197, 218-219. *See* Racist ideology
Racist ideology: and love, 149; and the tragic mulatto stereotype, 100; definition of, 1, 2; devastating effects of, 238; development of, 23-24; dominant forms of, 23-24; exploration of in "Father and Son," 83-85; exploration of in "The Fire and the Hearth," 88-90; exploration of in *Kingsblood Royal*, 29-30; in abolitionist novels, 13; in *Light in August*, 228; nineteenth-century manifestations of, 28, 31; relation to imperialism, 27; relation to Jim Crowism, 27; relation to Social Darwinism, 27-28. *See also* Mulatto; Negro stereotypes; Racism
Redder Blood, 62
Redding, J. Saunders, 76, 203
Red Rock: A Chronicle of Reconstruction, 59
Requiem for a Nun, 82
Reuter, Edward, 174, 191, 192
"Review of *An American Dilemma*," 7
Robert Penn Warren, 138n
Romantic racialism, 26, 56
Rosenblatt, Roger, 161n
Rowlette, Robert, 40, 51n
Running a Thousand Miles for Freedom, 57
Sapphira and the Slave Girl, 71
Sartre, Jean Paul, 130, 138-139n
Savoy, Willard, 78, 142, 143, 203
Saxon, Lyle, 76
Schuyler, George S., 70, 254n

Sex and Racism in America, 62, 73
Shufeldt, Robert W., 28
Slave: or Memoirs of Archy Moore, The, 57, 192, 214
Smith, Henry Nash, 44
Smith, Lillian, 82, 86
Smith, William B., 28
Smith, W. W., 100
Social Darwinism, 27, 198, 201, 211
Souls of Black Folk, The, 5-6, 199
Southerner, The, 74
Stanley, Marie, 63, 103
Stein, Gertrude, 14, 63-64
Stephen Kent, 70
Stonequist, Everett V., 5, 14, 120-122, 126, 191, 192
Store, The, 74
Stowe, Harriet Beecher, 15, 26, 34-35, 55-57, 58, 101
Stribling, T. S., 31, 49n, 202
Stranger and Alone, 76, 203
Styron, William, 127
Sumner, Mrs. Cid Rickette, 78
Sweet Man, 64
"Talented Tenth, the," 61, 171
Their Eyes Were Watching God, 75-76
There is Confusion, 61, 143, 152, 170
Third Generation, The, 77-78, 247
Thomas, Will, 143
Three-caste system, 9-10, 16n
Thurman, Wallace, 165
Time on the Cross, 17n
Tischler, Nancy, 53, 100
" 'Tite Poulette," 105
Toomer, Jean, 63, 68-70, 76, 220-221, 226, 243-244
Tourgée, Albion, 60
"Toussaint L'Ouverture," 153
Tragic mulatto stereotype: abolitionist authors' use of, 100-101; and racist ideology, 100; as Joe

Christmas's literary antecedent, 232; as passer, 102; black authors' use of, 63; description of, 99-100, 103-104; discussion of, 99-115; George Washington Cable's depiction of, 104-109; Howells's depiction of, 109-115; in novels by the Talented Tenth, 103; white authors' use of, 63, 100. *See also* Mulatto character

Treitschke, Heinrich, G., 167

Turner, Nat, 58

Twain, Mark, 14, 36-48, 51n, 109, 110, 121, 238

Two-caste system, 4, 9, 18

Ulysses, 132

Uncle Tom's Cabin, 55-56, 57, 96n, 101, 104, 108, 153

Unfettered, 204, 213-214

Up From Slavery, 7

Vandover and the Brute, 32

Van Vechten, Carl, 150

"Vengeance of the Gods, The," 35-36

Vickery, Olga, 228

Victor, Metta V., 56

Vixens, The, 73

Waiting for the Verdict, 147-148, 159, 195, 219

Wall, Evans, 63, 103

Walls of Jericho, The, 65-68, 149

Warren, Robert Penn, 14, 79, 81, 83, 104, 123, 127, 151

Washington, Booker T., 60, 123, 167, 168-169, 191, 197-199, 200, 201, 203, 204, 205

Washingtonian philosophy, 200, 202, 204, 205, 212

Way of the New World, The, 96n, 160n, 188n

Ways of White Folks, The, 83

Webb, Frank J., 61, 102, 145, 170

West, Dorothy, 76, 178-187, 245, 247

What Is Man?, 39, 44, 46

White, Walter, 15, 64, 123, 159, 171, 219

White aesthetic, the, 4-5, 16n

White Girl, The, 63. 103

White Over Black: American Attitudes Toward the Negro, 1550-1812, 16n, 49n

"Wife of Chino, The," 32

"Wife of His Youth, The," 115n

Williams, John A., 15, 80, 238, 242-244

Woodson, Carter G., 17n

Wright, Richard, 52

Yankee Slave Driver, The, 101

"Yard-nigger," 84

Yellin, Jean Fagan, 56, 57, 95n

Yerby, Frank, 71-73